D1148819

THE CRIMES OF
JOSEF FRITZL

THE CRIMES OF JOSEF FRITZL
UNCOVERING THE TRUTH

STEFANIE MARSH & BOJAN PANCEVSKI

HarperElement
An Imprint of HarperCollins*Publishers*
77–85 Fulham Palace Road,
Hammersmith, London W6 8JB

www.harpercollins.co.uk

and *HarperElement* are trademarks
of HarperCollins*Publishers* Ltd

First published by HarperElement 2009

1 3 5 7 9 10 8 6 4 2

A catalogue record of this book is
available from the British Library

ISBN 978-0-00-730055-6

Photographs: PA Photos (top left & right), REX Features (bottom left &
right), page 1; REX Features, Timmins / Stern / Picture Press, Inflight
GmbH, www.fotoflieger.at, pages 2&3; Getty Images, page 4; PA Photos
(bottom left), Getty Images (top & bottom right), page 5; PA Photos (top left,
bottom left & right), Getty Images (top right), page 6; Getty Images
(bottom), PA Photos (top), page 7; REX Features, page 8

Printed and bound in Great Britain by
Clays Ltd, St Ives plc

Mixed Sources
Product group from well-managed
forests and other controlled sources
www.fsc.org   Cert no. SW-COC-1806
© 1996 Forest Stewardship Council

CONTENTS

PART THREE

FOREWORD

It is difficult to write a book on a subject as complex as Josef Fritzl. And certainly there are many Austrians who would prefer such a book not to be published. In Austria there is little appetite to understand his crimes, and even less inclination to uncover the many factors that might have allowed for them to happen.

When the Fritzl case first came to light, in April 2008, Austria became the unwilling focus of massive media scrutiny. Not only were the gravity and range of his crimes against his children unparalleled in recent history, but they had emerged only two years after a strikingly similar case, also in Austria: 18-year-old Natascha Kampusch had, in 2006, escaped another purpose-built dungeon where she had been made to live since the age of ten by an electrical engineer who had abducted her. When the Kampusch case came to light it was regarded by most people as a unique case. But, suddenly, there was Josef Fritzl, and another cellar, and yet another story of prolonged incarceration and sexual abuse.

And although, in Amstetten, the police and social services have always declared themselves satisfied that the crimes of Josef Fritzl were unpreventable, his sentencing for life imprisonment, in March 2009, left many important questions unanswered regarding the role of the authorities. His trial lasted less than four days and neither the court, nor the Austrian media, showed itself to be inclined to get to the bottom of how it had been possible for Fritzl to have committed such terrible deeds for so long. There was no investigation into the role of the authorities; there has been not a single resignation and it was never determined whether there might have been any possible negligence on behalf of the officials that, over the years, had come to know the Fritzls. Experts from Scotland Yard expressed astonishment at the fact that many of Fritzl's family members were never questioned by police in detail or in a manner fit for cases of such complexity. The strong suspicion among many observers, was that this was a crime that could, many times, have been stopped in its tracks. The feeling was that justice had not been served. Meanwhile, not only the Amstetten authorities, but those high up in the Austrian government too, would continue to hold that they bore no responsibility for what happened for so many years to Elisabeth Fritzl and her children.

But there is another side of this story, one that has been equally neglected and one that we hope also to give justice to in this book. There can be few people who have read about the Fritzl case who haven't asked themselves how it was possible for Elisabeth Fritzl to have survived her twenty-four year incarceration. And, yet, she has emerged from a lifetime of unimaginable deprivation and terror, a heroic figure; a woman who, though her means were few and the fear in the cellar was great, protected her children against their father. Often, in so doing, she acted against her own interests. It was Elisabeth Fritzl who, over the years, did everything she could to ensure the safety of her children and strove to give them some semblance of comfort and normality in the cellar: it was she who educated them, it was she who would often persuade her father to bring down sufficient food to ensure their survival, and it was she who emerged from the cellar undiminished by the many years of imprisonment. Indeed, the most extraordinary aspect of this case is not the fact that Josef Fritzl was able to incarcerate his daughter for almost two and a half decades, it is Elisabeth Fritzl herself: we hope in this book to be able to shed some light on her astonishing courage and the incredible ability of the human spirit to overcome seemingly impossible conditions.

In the course of researching this book we have spoken to many people who knew Josef Fritzl personally, or were friends of the Fritzl family, as well as many of those who were directly involved in the case when it came to light: police, psychiatrists, doctors, and lawyers. Many of them expressed to us their wish that the intricate facts of the case be laid bare in a way that they will never be in Austria. Although we have endeavoured to name our sources where possible, several of the interviews we were granted by those involved in the case had to be conducted under conditions of anonymity. We are very grateful to those people who chose to speak out about this case, and to explain to us its intricacies, despite, in some instances, considerable pressure from above.

Finally, much has been written in the press about the effect on Josef Fritzl of his wartime childhood. And although Fritzl himself has sought to blame the evolution of his double life on the Nazi Austria of the late 1930s and early 1940s, it is not a claim that can be taken very seriously. What is undoubtable, however, is that, still now, Austria itself has yet to face its past, or analyse with any seriousness its impact on the present. As a result there continues to exist in Austria a culture of looking away, a squeamishness about examining in any depth the harsh truths about its society and a distaste for self-analysis. It is our view that Josef Fritzl's crimes were largely preventable, had the authorities been prepared to acknowledge the many clues laid before them over the years and that Elisabeth's fate in her father's cellar was not in fact inevitable, as has been suggested by at least one member of the Austrian government. We hope that this book, in addressing the circumstances of the Fritzl case, by examining his behaviour and descent into inhumanity, piece by piece, and by flagging the signs – both subtle and blatant – of his extreme cruelty, will in some way help to illustrate how important it is to look.

PROLOGUE

It was Dr Albert Reiter's habit to check on his patients for a couple of hours on a Saturday morning. So, by 7.15 a.m. on Saturday, 19 April 2008, he was already making the seven-minute drive to Amstetten Hospital. He'd had a coffee instead of breakfast at home, and now he lit up a cigarette.

At 7.30 a.m. he was in the lift up to the second floor: the Intensive Care unit of which he was the head.

As usual he stopped off in the staff room to discuss any problems that might have occurred among the patients overnight. There had been none and Reiter was soon making his way through the series of noiseless, code-accessed automatic doors, past the calm and well-administered horseshoe-shaped reception area – the department's nucleus – and to each of the unit's eight beds, distributed between two single and three double rooms. To help make the patients' experience as comfortable as possible, photographs of trees and flowing streams had been framed on the walls and a sign, hand-painted on a door panel by some of the nurses, read 'Waking-up Room' in cheerful rainbow colours. Reiter moved from bed to bed, each one flanked by its vast panel of elaborate, life-saving equipment on one side and by a large window on the other. On Reiter's instructions every bed space had been designed to have access to plenty of natural light from the south-facing windows that looked on to the hospital car park below. Beyond the car park Reiter saw that it was becoming a magnificent spring day.

It was getting on for 8.30 a.m. when a call came through from the hospital's accident and emergency room: paramedics had just brought in a critically ill young woman. Reiter sent down a junior doctor to look at the case. Five minutes later he joined him.

The girl was unconscious.

Laid out on a stretcher, she looked no more than 20 and was clearly terribly sick. Even Reiter's first glance told him that she was very close to death. Her name, Reiter was told, was Kerstin.

The emergency team had judged Kerstin's condition to be so grave they had immediately induced an artificial coma, a procedure which is narcotically generated and carried out only in extreme situations, such as when a patient experiences multiple organ failure. By decreasing brain activity, and therefore oxygen requirements and blood flow, it can reduce life-threatening swelling in the brain. Her lungs, kidney, and liver were failing. Reiter's first thought was that she might have been poisoned. He also suspected either an accidental drug overdose or a suicide attempt.

By sheer chance one of the paramedics in the ambulance carrying Kerstin happened to be Reiter's son. He now quickly summarized the events of the morning for his father. He told him that the girl had been picked up from a home in Ybbsstrasse in central Amstetten. The call had come in at around eight that morning from a man, the girl's grandfather: he had found the girl collapsed in front of his house; almost tripped over her, he'd said, going out to buy bread rolls. It had been a tremendous shock to the grandfather.

The sight of a teenage girl unconscious on a doorstep would have come as a shock to anyone first thing in the morning, but particularly to the old man, who'd never seen the girl before in his life. Apparently Kerstin had grown up away from home with her mother in some kind of sect; much more than that her grandfather didn't know. By the time the ambulance arrived, his son told Reiter, her grandfather had carried her into the house and laid her on a bed. Reiter's son had then helped lift her into an ambulance.

Reiter's son didn't know what to make of the girl's illness: there were so few clues that it was impossible to even hazard a diagnosis. The grandfather hadn't been able to tell him much and was probably too shocked to think straight anyway. One other thing had, however, occurred to Reiter's son. And he now passed this information on to his father. He'd had a funny feeling about the house in Ybbsstrasse. Something about the room Kerstin had been lying in. Apart from the bed, it contained no furniture. Nothing earth-shattering, he said, just a little strange. 'Write that down,' Albert Reiter told him. 'Make sure to write it all down.'

* * *

An hour and a half since she had been discovered on a doorstep in the Ybbsstrasse, forty-five minutes since she'd been put into an artificial coma in the hospital's emergency room, Kerstin was wheeled into Intensive Care. As you look up from the reception area, it is the room second from the left.

At 10.11 Dr Reiter got another call from downstairs. The girl's grandfather had arrived. A respectable type, a man in his early seventies, kindly, worried but trying not to show it – like any other anxious relative. To the point, sensibly but not expensively dressed: an ironed shirt tucked into high-waisted trousers, the laces of his practical thick-soled black boots neatly done up. His hair was combed back over a bald patch and his moustache was trimmed in the traditional style favoured among men of his generation in Austria. A father of seven and a respectable former engineer, Reiter learned.

The doctor led him into the unit and showed him Kerstin. The girl really was terribly ill, motionless, pale, and wired up to several drips. Reiter explained that, despite the hospital's best efforts, her condition was extremely fragile. 'The difficulty I have,' he said, 'is that we have no medical records – a doctor can only deduce so much from a patient's symptoms.' Without more information about the causes of her illness, he explained, he was battling with an invisible problem. At about 10.30 he did what he always did with his patients' relatives and invited Kerstin's grandfather to talk to him privately in his office.

Reiter's office was a ramshackle affair, a comforting place in which he liked to think that relatives felt more

comfortable talking. A blue sofa hugged the left corner
and a desk was wedged in on the right; the walls were
lined with bookshelves containing medical texts. Various
odds and ends had found their way into the room over
the years: a decorative, not fully operational water fountain; an espresso machine; a small wooden crucifix – left
over from his predecessor; a can of air freshener; an
ashtray or two; four or five stray bones plucked from a
synthetic skeleton; and assorted stacks of papers. In the
centre of the room were a coffee table and three chairs:
this is where Reiter now invited Josef Fritzl to take a seat.
What he wanted, he explained, was for Herr Fritzl to tell
him everything he knew: no detail could be too small to
mention.

Josef Fritzl repeated what he'd told paramedics:
Kerstin was his granddaughter but had grown up away
from home with her mother, whom he hadn't seen for
over twenty years, ever since she'd run away to live in a
sect. The first and only time he'd seen Kerstin had been
that morning when he discovered the girl on his
doorstep, passed out. He assumed she must have been
left there by her mother because over the years she had
abandoned various other children in the same way: three
babies in all, left on his doorstep throughout the nineties.
He and his wife, Rosemarie, had, with the agreement of
the council, taken in the children to raise as their own.

And the thing was, Fritzl explained, she always left a
note. She had done so again this morning. Fritzl now
produced from his pocket a folded-up sheet of plain letter
paper and laid it out on the table for Reiter to see. A girlish hand, it read:

Wednesday night: Kerstin had fits and took cough syrup and
   aspirin.
Thursday: Cough getting worse.
Friday: Fits getting worse. Kerstin is biting her lip and tongue.
   Please help her! Kerstin is so afraid of other people, she's
   never been in a hospital. Please ask my father for help,
   he's the only one she knows.
Kerstin, please hold on until we see each other again! We'll be
   there soon!

Cough medicine and aspirin. The only clues Reiter had. He called a nurse in to make a photocopy of the letter and asked Fritzl to continue with his story.

His daughter Elisabeth, always an unpredictable girl, said Fritzl, had disappeared in the mid-eighties when she was 18. It hadn't been the first time she had run away from home. She'd done so before when she was 16 and had, to his great embarrassment, eventually been picked up by the police in Vienna.

So when she disappeared for the second time, her father never believed it would be for ever. He told Reiter that he had alerted the police right away but that they had been worse than useless. It was the only moment in the interview in which Josef Fritzl became animated, the only time that his frustration got the better of him. They'd found no trace. Fritzl then spent several minutes complaining bitterly to Reiter about the failure of the authorities to track down his daughter. It was clearly a source of huge frustration and disappointment to him that, despite his best efforts, Elisabeth remained missing. He then added that Elisabeth had two other children in her care and, judging by the state of Kerstin, they were also at risk.

One thing was certain: wherever she was, she was not coping as every few years she'd have a baby and leave it on her father's doorstep with one of her desperate notes. How was it possible, Fritzl asked the doctor, not to find a girl in a small, well-behaved country like Austria?

It was a very sad and distressing story but Josef Fritzl was an excellent witness, Reiter found, conducting himself with great self-control during what must have been a very distressing moment. He laid out the facts with meticulous clarity and described his daughter vividly. Reiter pictured a troubled, confused, and possibly dangerous soul, who, having become entangled in a murky underground scene, had become a liability to her family. In his line of work he'd come across such cases before.

Would Kerstin die? Reiter anticipated the question before Fritzl had to ask it, and weighed up the chances of Kerstin's survival for her grandfather as tactfully as he could. Frankly, the odds were slim. Reiter asked Fritzl for his permission to alert the police about the note and he agreed.

The whole conversation took not more than thirty minutes. At around 11.30 they emerged from Reiter's office, the two men shook hands, and arranged to meet again at two o'clock that afternoon. Reiter telephoned the police and filed a report about the note that Fritzl had found on Kerstin's body; then he looked in on Kerstin before driving home. It was lunchtime but, not being in the habit of eating much before supper, he spent an hour or so mowing his lawn, trying to unscramble the riddle of Kerstin Fritzl's illness.

The case was a mystery and obviously revolved around one person: the mother. But there was little to go on. Poisoning? An overdose? Had Kerstin been trying to escape from the cult? Had her mother deliberately put her own daughter's life in danger as a result? Reiter's chief suspicion fell on Elisabeth. But nobody knew where she was: whether she was in the region or even in the country. She was a woman who had abandoned four children, perhaps an unstable person but also the only person capable of supplying the information necessary to save her daughter's life.

And then there were the stranger aspects of the case: a young woman lying unconscious in Ybbsstrasse – that's where Josef Fritzl lived with his wife Rosemarie, and their three fostered grand-children. It might have made sense if it had been one of those small, dead-end lanes that you come across in Austrian towns, somewhere higgledy-piggledy and hidden away. But Ybbsstrasse is neither a dead end, nor a lane, nor in any way hidden away out of sight. Ybbsstrasse, named after the river that runs alongside it, is a thoroughfare, the main artery out of town, busy with cars day and night. It is also a commercial area, lined with convenience food stores, a hairdresser, a travel agent, a supplier of building materials, a flower stall, a tattoo studio, two bars, and a bakery. The bakery, Bäckerei Pramreiter, is just three doors down from the house outside which Kerstin Fritzl was found passed out on a doorstep at eight in the morning. On Saturdays it opens at 7 a.m.

By the time Reiter had returned to hospital he had decided to persuade Josef Fritzl to make an appeal to his missing daughter through the media. He strongly felt that if Elisabeth Fritzl knew that her daughter's life was now in danger, she could not help but respond.

Fritzl agreed readily that involving the media was both the right decision and a matter of urgency. After signing a release form for this purpose, Fritzl looked in on Kerstin one last time and returned home, leaving Reiter to make the necessary arrangements.

Reiter felt a little out of his depth: it was a case that might require the involvement of the police. So he decided not to call the media directly but to telephone the State Prosecutor's office and was put through to Christiane Burkheiser. A short conversation ensued in which Reiter explained the situation and the Prosecutor reassured him that she would make the necessary arrangements.

At 5 p.m. on Saturday, 19 April, just over eight hours after Kerstin Fritzl had first been discovered abandoned and desperately ill on an Amstetten doorstep, the first appeal for the urgent return of her mother was broadcast on local radio.

Kerstin's condition showed no improvement by Sunday. And by Monday, 22 April the story of the abandoned girl who was being kept in an artificial coma had been reported several times in the local media but still there had been no sign of her mother. Nevertheless, national newspapers were beginning to latch onto the story and, as the week progressed and Kerstin's condition deteriorated, reports of the case multiplied and found their way onto television.

Meanwhile anxious relatives of Kerstin passed in and out of the room. Kerstin's mother, Elisabeth, was the fourth of seven children and now her brothers and sisters, their husbands and wives and children, descended on the hospital to do what they could. Josef Fritzl's wife, Rosemarie, visited – on the Tuesday – and talked briefly to the doctors about the practicalities of Kerstin's health-insurance status. She had been worried because, having grown up in a sect, the girl was essentially invisible to the authorities: she didn't have a birth certificate or a passport and wasn't insured. The doctors reassured her that, considering the parlous state of Kerstin's health, this was a matter which the hospital would deal with.

The next day, Wednesday, 23 April, Reiter had originally been scheduled to drive down to a medical conference near his home town in Carinthia but, with the snowballing media interest in Kerstin, his trip had to be repeatedly delayed. It was becoming a case of national interest.

On Thursday a reporter from Austria's national television channel, ORF, rang to let Reiter know that that it planned to broadcast a special feature on the story and asked if he would be interviewed. Hoping that such major coverage would finally encourage Kerstin's mother to emerge from wherever she'd been hiding for over twenty years, Reiter agreed to meet the journalist at the hospital on Friday morning. He finally left for Carinthia later that same day, satisfied that, wherever she was, Elisabeth Fritzl, or someone who knew Elisabeth Fritzl, was very likely to have heard the appeals. Whether or not she chose to respond was a different matter.

* * *

Albert Reiter is a doctor, a man used to seeing horrible things. It wouldn't be fair to say the Fritzl case was obsessing him – he had several other gravely ill patients and a seminar to chair – but Elisabeth Fritzl was very much on his mind as he drove southeast to Carinthia. Just as it had been a week ago, it was a beautiful spring day. The drive took four hours and Reiter's mood alternated between mild disappointment that there still had been no sign of Elisabeth, and happy anticipation of the conference ahead. The St Paul Emergency Medicine Conference is a highlight in many surgeon's calendar, and physicians from all over Austria look forward to this annual opportunity to catch up and exchange ideas. But by the time Reiter arrived, he only had time to attend a seminar or two. He went to bed early. At noon the next day he chaired a debate on the psychological impact of narcosis on intensive care patients and, having said his goodbyes, made tracks to leave.

It was Saturday, 26 April. A week had passed since Kerstin Fritzl had first been admitted to Amstetten Hospital. Reiter had just left the conference centre and was on his way back to the hotel when he got the call he had been waiting for all week. It was 4.30 p.m. 'Wonderful news,' said Josef Fritzl. 'She's back.'

Elisabeth had finally resurfaced and was now with her father in Amstetten. Reiter explained to Fritzl that it would take him several hours to get back from Carinthia but that he'd set off right away. He told Fritzl to meet him at the hospital with Elisabeth at 8.15 that evening and added that he'd call him on the way if there was heavy traffic. Fritzl agreed but there was one thing: his daughter had made it clear to him that the police were not to be contacted. Reiter said that he understood and rang off.

He drove a little faster than usual. He remembered how bitterly Josef Fritzl had expressed his disappointment at the incompetence of the police and felt proud that it was through his agency that Elisabeth had finally been persuaded to come forward. He was aware of what Elisabeth Fritzl had done to her children and possibly to the teenage girl in his unit, and knew too that it amounted to criminal neglect. He also wondered whether she'd brought with her to Amstetten the two other children still in her care. But what worried him most was the possibility that Elisabeth might attempt to visit her daughter and slip away again before he'd had the chance to speak to her. To prevent this from happening, he called Intensive Care and instructed the staff not to allow any visitors in to see Kerstin until he arrived.

Reiter then made a second phone call, a crucial one. He called Christiane Burkheiser, the State Prosecutor, and asked her to alert the police.

Reiter now sped along the motorway. An hour and a half from Amstetten he received one more call, from one of the Intensive Care staff. Reiter had been right. Elisabeth Fritzl and her father had arrived early to visit Kerstin but been sent home on Reiter's instructions.

At eight o'clock that Saturday evening Reiter arrived back in Amstetten and drove directly to the hospital. He took the lift up to Intensive Care, where he spent a few moments assessing Kerstin's deteriorating condition. At that moment he happened to glance out of the window. He saw an old black Mercedes pull up in the car park. Out stepped two figures: Josef Fritzl and a woman. Reiter prepared himself for one of the most difficult conversations of his medical career.

Everything about Elisabeth Fritzl seemed to confirm what her father had told Reiter. She was neatly dressed and still youthful in appearance: a few grey hairs but her pale skin was undamaged by the sun. She was clearly extremely fragile and spoke very little. She barely shook Reiter's hand. Wherever she'd been, in whatever cult, life had not been easy for her. Her father stood comfortingly at her side. Together they walked into Kerstin's room.

Her condition had worsened. But her mother was unable to shed much more light on what had happened in the days leading up to her daughter's hospitalization. There was something intensely guarded about Elisabeth, Reiter thought. She certainly seemed fond enough of her daughter; she just couldn't say anything. What was it? Shame? Fear that she would be investigated? The exchange ground to a halt after just a few minutes. Reiter felt confused and guilty. He now adamantly believed in Elisabeth Fritzl's guilt but he felt ashamed. He knew that, concealed in the reception area, the police were waiting for a signal from him to arrest her.

Reiter watched Elisabeth Fritzl whisper some encouraging words to her sleeping daughter. Then he watched her leave the unit with her father and sister. He gave the signal: a phone call. Downstairs three plainclothed policemen emerged from a corridor to arrest Elisabeth.

It had been an extremely long day: four hours of driving, this awful dilemma still unresolved, and the continuing mystery of Kerstin's deteriorating health. Reiter was exhausted. He went home, ate a quick supper, and, having briefly discussed the day with his wife, was asleep by 10.30.

At 2.30 a.m. he was woken up by the sound of knocking. In pyjamas and bathrobe he opened his front door to a young policeman: Dr Reiter was to call the head of police at St Pölten as a matter of urgency. He thanked the officer and dialled the number. He was put through to a chief inspector.

The phone call was brief and shocking. For an hour Elisabeth Fritzl had sat in St Pölten police station saying nothing. By 10.30 p.m. she had started to talk. By 11.15 p.m. nothing in Amstetten would ever be the same again.

PART ONE

PART ONE

CHAPTER ONE

BEGINNINGS

The Mostviertel is still a very beautiful part of Europe. Bounded by the Danube to the north and to the east by the Vienna woods, its tree-speckled meadows make up the rolling foothills of the Alps; a place where whitewashed, wooden-roofed houses cluster in pleasant little villages, cut through by streams with water pure enough to drink. It's a fairy-tale landscape: every village has its church, every roadside its Catholic shrine.

Important dates in the religious calendar that have been forgotten elsewhere in the country still mean something here. On Ascension Day long, solemn lines of local people process down the street: the women, some of them wearing *Dirndl*, the heavy-skirted folk costume of Austria. They are pious, down-to-earth people here, with a dialect that can sometimes be unintelligible even to other German-speakers. *Brot* (bread) is *Bracht*; *Milch* (milk) is *Mu*; an indecisive woman might find herself described as a *Suppnhehn*, a chicken fit only to be made into stock; a man in need of a haircut is a *Zodawaschl*.

And it is one of those places where everywhere you go you're reminded of the local talisman. For the Mostviertel, it's the pear: there isn't a shop, a market stall or a petrol station that doesn't sell pears, or foodstuffs made of pears, or pear-shaped key rings, or other souvenirs. Giant pears made of glazed papier-mâché or plastic squat by the sides of the main roads; they huddle in twos and threes in the middle of roundabouts. For the pear is the main ingredient of *Most*, the poor man's drink in central Europe long before beer. In the late eighteenth century, at the height of the Habsbury Empire's confidence, Emperor Joseph II, foreseeing *Most*'s commercial potential, decreed that he would award a silver medal to every person who planted 100 pear trees. Of course, the farmers of the region began planting them in every available corner and soon its low hills were transformed into a pretty but chaotic orchard, one of the world's densest: over a million fruit trees grew in its meadows. It was the Mostviertel's first economic boom. 'The *Most* built these houses,' its farmers boasted. And it was *Most* that built the little village of Amstetten.

For centuries Amstetten had been a mere speck on the map in the far west corner of the Mostviertel, where the River Ybbs snakes down from the Limestone Alps towards the Danube. For nearly a hundred years it thrived on the *Most* boom. The surrounding countryside was flat enough for the paper mills and steel plants that came with the industrial revolution to flourish here, but it was an accident of geography that was the making of the village. It so happened that Amstetten was located halfway between Vienna and Linz and close enough to the borders of both Germany and Italy for it to be an ideal railway junction, a stop-over where the main east–west and north–south lines crossed. In the late nineteenth century the village suddenly found itself growing into a town, and local farmers and paper and metal entrepreneurs began to settle there, erecting houses of sandstone and limestone quarried from the Alps. In the 1880s the long, anonymous dirt road that ran southwards from the main square earned itself a name: Ybbsstrasse, after the river. The Gattenbauers made their home here, as did the Aschenbrenners, the proud owners of the street's first grocery store. The ochre-painted house at 40 Ybbsstrasse was completed in 1892, a solid, symmetrical two-storey affair set around a courtyard, with a back garden, separate kitchen and scullery; room enough for a moderate-sized family of considerable means. Here lived a family named Fritzl.

The Fritzls had a daughter. Some time towards the end of the nineteenth-century, the owner of a mill in Ardagger, a hamlet several miles distant, made her an offer of marriage. Given his relative affluence – he lived in a cottage attached to his mill and was wealthy enough to employ several servants – it must have seemed a suitable match to her parents, and for a few months the marriage could have been said to be happy. But when the couple were unable to produce a child the miller's disappointment expressed itself in violence. He not only beat his wife but began a sexual relationship with a female servant which may or may not have been consensual.

When this servant became pregnant it must have seemed to the miller that he had magically stumbled across the solution to the problem of his marriage. Here was both the answer to the couple's childlessness and proof that it was not he but his wife who was at fault. Although he was well within his rights to demand a divorce – it was his prerogative in the eyes of the Catholic Church – he kept her in the house as his wife. Provided that she remain silent about the true parentage of the child and bring it up as if it were her own there would be no need for a separation.

So the child was born, the servant dismissed, and it was left to the miller's wife to raise it. Over time two more children were fathered by two more maids, both of whom were thrown out of the house once they had fulfilled their purpose. The miller had his family: two little girls and a boy born out of wedlock to three different women, brought up by a wife who had become little more than an accomplice in a lie. The youngest girl was born and baptized in Stift Ardagger, the eleventh-century church after which the hamlet is known, some time in the mid-1890s. Her name was Maria.

From Maria's account her father delighted in the deception he had practised. To the outside world Maria and her two siblings were brought up in a family that conformed in every way to the norms of conservative rural society. But behind the foot-thick stone walls of his house the miller constantly goaded his children with the truth about their origins. Maria would later remember how much he relished the disjunction between public appearances and their secret. She was never allowed to forget that she was illegitimate: it was her disgrace and the disgrace of the woman she thought of as her mother. As an *uneheliches Kind*, a bastard, she was a constant reminder of the inadequacy of the wife the miller had saddled himself with. The violent husband became a violent father, a terror to his unhallowed children. Maria spent her childhood and early adolescence longing to find the husband who could offer her a way out; she found him labouring on a nearby farm. According to her own account, she was in love, for the first and last time in her life.

And now there is a strange echo, one of those tragic twists that can define a life. A year of marriage passed, two years, three, but Maria's pregnancy never came. Her husband blamed her. 'You don't work properly,' he told her. 'You're not a woman.' A less complicated man than her father, he divorced her. Jobless, homeless and publicly humiliated, she returned to the cottage in Ardagger, only to find that life had become intolerable for her mother in the meantime: her husband's temper had grown so violent that she had begun to fear for her life. Roused by the return of her adoptive daughter, Anna now made an extraordinary decision. She had inherited the house in Ybbsstrasse in the late 1920s and had left it to stand empty: it was no place for an ageing woman on her own. But Maria's return was an opportunity for them both, and one day in 1932 the two women walked out. They walked the five miles from Ardagger to Amstetten, carrying only a few personal belongings (although no money, since they had none), and never came back. Amstetten was safety. And 40 Ybbsstrasse was all they had.

* * *

For Maria and her mother it was to be a period of bitter hardship, but times were hard for everyone. In 1933, just as Adolf Hitler's National Socialist Party was entering government in Germany, in Austria power was seized by the Front of the Fatherland, a conglomeration of the country's conservative and national parties, anti-Semitic, totalitarian, and besotted by Mussolini's achievements in Italy. After a civil insurrection in 1934 had been swiftly crushed, the Front dissolved Parliament and all other democratic institutions, banned rival political parties, and forced many Jews to resign from state-owned companies and the civil service. Opponents of the regime were sent to specially built prisons that were inspired in their design and purpose by the new complexes already being constructed in Germany. The first of these camps, Wöllersdorf, used for political prisoners, occupied an abandoned munitions factory thirty miles from Amstetten and was modelled on a camp that had been recently opened by the chief of the Munich police, Heinrich Himmler, just outside the Bavarian medieval town of Dachau.

Austria was torn apart by social discontent, hyperinflation, rampant xenophobia, and massive unemployment – a quarter of the population were jobless. Among them were Maria and her mother. But the collapsing economy did at least mean there were plenty of drifters requiring cheap accommodation, and although to Maria it seemed almost a crime to have to turn the family home into a doss-house, to put locks on the doors, and rent out her grandparents' rooms to strangers, the house was their only resource. To supplement the rent she was forced to leave Ybbsstrasse and seek employment in the kind of household that she felt her own should have been.

In 1934 Maria began a relationship, though never married, a man named Josef, about whom we know very little except that he was poor. Maria made no attempt to disguise her motive in seeking this union. She needed to correct the humiliation that had ruined her life and the life of her adoptive mother. She needed proof of her womanhood and she craved vengeance on the men who had brought her to this pass. To her astonishment, she quickly fell pregnant. The child, born in the house in Ybbsstrasse on 9 April 1935, was a boy. Although Maria had taken the name of her first husband and would be known throughout her life as Nenning, the baby bore his grandmother's maiden name.

Thus Josef Fritzl, an 'uneheliches kind' like his mother, entered the world.

As far as his mother was concerned, he had fulfilled his purpose on the day he was born. Maria had gloried in her pregnancy but was overburdened by the demands of motherhood: hugs and kisses were beyond her and when Josef cried or soiled his nappy or appealed to his mother for comfort, she would panic and slip into apathy, leaving the child screaming and filthy. Josef, Maria told his father as soon as the boy was born, was merely an 'alibi child', a vindication and nothing more. 'How could you have thought I loved you?' she taunted him.

So Josef Fritzl was born just a few years before the beginning of the Second World War, in a collapsing society, to a loveless mother who gave birth to him out of spite and a father who would gradually fade from his life.

He was born into a town of 990 houses and 9,300 souls; a town where jobs were so scarce that men were joining the army to fend off starvation. He was born on a street that was still a dust road, running north–south between the town hall and the River Ybbs, now heavily polluted with the waste of a pulp mill whose chimneys belched noxious yellowish fumes that could be smelled for miles. He was born in a town whose mayor, Hans Höller, was the chairman of the local anti-Semitic league; and where the local newspaper, the *Amstettner Anzeiger*, had been founded by a member of Austria's own pre-*Anschluss* Nationalist Socialist Party and staked out Jewish businesses in order to splash photographs of their customers across its pages: 'The farmer Franz Reiter from Neustadl has obviously not yet heard of Aryan shoemakers!'

Josef was not quite three years old when, on 12 March 1938, Hitler's troops rolled over the border from Germany into Austria, entering Amstetten the same day. This was the *Anschluss*, the annexation of Austria into Greater Germany. Three days later Hitler entered Vienna and was greeted by an ecstatic crowd of up to one million people, by some accounts. That same week the Nazis held a plebiscite and 99.7 per cent of Austrians voted to join the Third Reich. No fighting ever took place and Austria effectively ceased to exist as an independent nation. Outside Austria the *Anschluss* caused little concern among the world's leading powers. 'After all,' shrugged *The Times* in London, 'Scotland also joined England.' In May of that year the *Amstettner Anzeiger* was proud to report that 'the town swimming pool and sunbath declares that Jews are banned from entering.

Now we only have to get rid of the mosquitoes from our pool for it to become really ideal!'

Hans Höller was replaced by a new mayor, a pharmacist and passionate Nazi named Wolfgang Mitterdorfer, who immediately set about transforming the town. Mitterdorfer aspired to turn Amstetten into a *Führerstadt*, an honourable title by which the Nazis conferred special status on cities in the Third Reich. He announced plans to build a 'town fortress', a vast, rambling, neoclassical structure that would comprise a theatre, social housing, an event hall, and the headquarters of the Hitler Youth. In and around Ybbsstrasse new schools and 'body-training centres' were built, and for young children a puppet theatre where traditional fairy tales were interpreted along Nazi lines. Josef Fritzl was among the children invited to the first night, a reworking of the Brothers Grimm story 'The Devil's Golden Hair' featuring new characters: a Policeman, a Mayor, a Jew, a 'Churchill', and an Englishman.

By the summer of 1938 Mitterdorfer was able to declare that all twenty-eight of Amstetten's Jews had been expelled. The town was officially 'free of Jews'. War came a year later, when Josef Fritzl was four. Decades later he could still remember the terrible day when his father, conscripted into the Wehrmacht, had to leave for the Eastern Front, and how his mother's face had shown only relief.

As the tide of the Second World War started to turn against the Axis powers, the blessing of Amstetten's location became a curse. The main railways supplying both Germany and Italy intersected in the town, so it was in the cross-hairs of the Allied bombers. Mitterdorfer, always the keen planner, began to construct a vast network of underground bunkers in the hills surrounding the town. These bunkers were essentially long corridors tunnelled deep into the hillsides of the Mostviertel. Great molehills of rubble and sand, evidence of their hasty excavation, were heaped at their entrances and since urination and defecation were strictly banned under the bunkers' house rules, these served the evacuees as toilets. Inside, it was unheated and unventilated, dark, cold, and always stuffy; people fainted frequently. The only furnishings were a handful of benches donated by the Red Cross, while a smattering of electric lights saved the inhabitants from complete darkness. But when the first Allied bombs fell on Amstetten on 19 November 1944 the town was ready.

From that day on the sirens sounded almost continuously and the people of Amstetten found themselves spending days, not hours, in their shelters. Twelve thousand bombs would be dropped on the town over the next six months: more bombs than inhabitants. There were times when almost the entire population was hiding beneath the surface. The first in after the sirens began to wail might gain a precious seat; others either sat on the ground or never left the house without a chair which they would haul in with them, along with a suitcase containing their most important possessions: passports, jewellery, money, marriage certificates, ownership deeds, tinned food.

But Maria was a strange and solitary woman who had become obsessive about the house. She refused to leave it even during an air raid; ignored the sirens which would send the other inhabitants of 40 Ybbsstrasse scurrying underground. Josef would be swept along with the other lodgers and refugees living in the house to the safety of the bunkers while his mother sat grimly in her kitchen, prepared to face death in her home rather than emerge from a bunker to find it obliterated. Certainly she didn't have enough maternal feeling to accompany her son to the shelters, and that winter Josef spent many days separated from her, feeling alternately terrified and protected: scared of what might be happening to his mother above ground; secure in the bunker below. It wasn't the worst feeling of his childhood: for an 8-year-old boy, a bunker could be a secret world, a safe place his mother would never come to, a place of shelter, and a chance to play with children his age.

The house in Ybbsstrasse had been fully occupied throughout the war but now, as refugees poured into Austria from the north and east, landlords were required to provide shelter to whoever might need it. Number 40 was overflowing with people: families were living in the corridors and sleeping on the stairs at night. As starving hordes of Austrians and Germans fleeing the Russian advance overwhelmed the town, Maria was ordered to take in even more lodgers. It was too much for her: she refused and was reported to the authorities. Early one morning the security forces arrived at the house and ordered Maria to get into the back of a lorry, and while Josef wept at the doorway his mother was driven away to Mauthausen-Gusen, one of the worst of the Nazis' extermination camps.

Josef spent the final months of the war in an orphanage, from which he attempted to escape on at least one occasion, climbing aboard a train bound for Amstetten and hiding beneath a bench. When police discovered him they told the 10-year-old Josef that his mother was dead.

Thirty miles from Amstetten, the sparsely populated area outside Mauthausen, a pretty Austrian town tucked into a hairpin bend of the Danube, was the site of one of the Nazi's most ambitious projects. Prisoners from the concentration camp at Dachau had been sent to build an even larger facility where political prisoners could be held. Although it was controlled by the German state, Mauthausen, which had, by 1944, been twinned with the nearby German camp of Gusen, was conceived as a private company. This commercial enterprise was founded by DEST, a German mining company that was soon buying up land around the granite quarries which had originally served to pave the streets of Vienna. When war arrived and the number of political prisoners suddenly exploded, Mauthausen-Gusen's investors realized that it could be put to far more lucrative use as a labour camp whose inmates would work for free in the quarries or be hired out to local manufacturers and farmers. Soon Mauthausen-Gusen controlled over fifty satellite camps throughout Austria, two of which were just outside Amstetten. The prisoners held in these two camps cost very little to keep and were easy to transport there because of Amstetten's convenient position on the railway network. In addition, the labour force was unique in that the supply of workers was inexhaustible, and when a prisoner's productivity dropped at either of the camps, he or she would simply be transported to Mauthausen-Gusen and killed.

The place became a hugely profitable death camp, the Nazis' biggest. The only camp designated Grade III ('for the incorrigible political enemies of the Reich'), it was underpinned by the twin principles of *Vernichtung durch Arbeit* ('Extermination through work') and *Rückkehr Unerwünscht* ('Return undesirable'). It was the slave labourers of Mauthausen-Gusen who were responsible for the construction of Austria's largest steelworks, in Linz: the Reichswerke Hermann Goering. Many smaller businesses also profited. Steyr munitions, an Austrian arms company; Puch automobiles; and Österreichische Sauerwerks, the largest employer in Amstetten – all built their businesses with the slave labour of Mauthausen-Gusen. In 1943 life expectancy in the camp was six months; by the end of the war it was three.

In comparison with Mauthausen-Gusen, 'one could almost say those [other] camps were paradises', to quote a Jewish survivor. But the Nazis' definition of 'incorrigible political enemies of the Reich' extended far beyond Jews, and Maria found herself incarcerated with communists, socialists, a troop of Polish boy scouts, homosexuals, Romanies, Jehovah's Witnesses, anarchists, Spanish republicans who had fled Franco: a microcosm of conquered Europe. Although it is not known exactly what happened to Maria in the months she was there, we can be sure that she witnessed and was subjected to horrors. It was a place of inconceivable barbarism whose secrecy liberated its masters into a horrific inventiveness.

In the privacy of the camp the guards learned to conduct experiments; to find out what happened, for example, when they herded a group of inmates onto a cliff top and gave them the choice of being shot or pushing another prisoner off the edge. They would throw people, some of them children, down the side of a quarry which they nicknamed 'the Parachute Wall', the joke being that the prisoners had no parachutes. In the camp's gas chambers, quarries, hospitals, isolation units and crematoria, in its underground brothel and on its dissecting tables, a creative degeneracy blossomed.

On 5 May 1945 Mauthausen was liberated by the 41st Reconnaissance Squad of the US 11th Armoured Division. In total the Mauthausen-Gusen complex of camps was found to contain 85,000 inmates, and the death toll is thought to have been around 320,000. Among those liberated were Simon Wiesenthal, later to become the world's most assiduous Nazi-hunter, and Maria Nenning.

Three days later, on 8 May, the war in Europe came to an end. Its last shots were fired in Amstetten. When the German High Command surrendered in Berlin, SS troops guarding the labour camps were still fiercely resisting Allied forces; in one last air raid Russian bombers obliterated the railway junction so thoroughly that it was referred to for years afterward as 'the ploughed field'. At two that afternoon the commanders of the Russian and American troops shook hands in the town square, officially marking the end of the war. Four days later Wolfgang Mitteldorfer, Amstetten's mayor, was found dead in his holiday home in Gmunden, over-dosed on sleeping pills. And Josef Fritzl was miraculously reunited with a mother he had thought was dead.

Possibly Maria had been raped as well as starved and frequently beaten or even tortured. She returned to the house in Ybbsstrasse and those who came across her at this time described her as a small, unsmiling, friendless woman who never discussed herself with her lodgers. Whenever possible she avoided talking to them at all, communicating with silent nods or rapid-fire blurtings.

Maria was desperately poor and always wore the same clothes: a pinafore smock over a dark dress, a pair of rubber boots, and a black headscarf or a dirty straw hat, sometimes both. The frightening impression she made, particularly on the tenants' children, was intensified after she lost her eye in a fight with one of the tenants. After that, she always kept it covered with either her hand or a scarf, or later with a patch worn behind a pair of thick-lensed glasses: a figure out of a Dostoyevsky novel. Only very occasionally did she leave the house and when she did it was usually to sit aimlessly among the rubble and weeds of her garden. Nobody else was allowed there and she would fly into a rage if any of her tenants, even the children, dared to trespass. Gardens weren't playgrounds: as far as the landlady was concerned, the children could play in the street.

Number 40 had never been a pretty house but by the end of the war it had become one of the ugliest buildings in Ybbsstrasse: a gloomy, damp, dilapidated wreck with no proper toilets and holes in its internal walls, its old ochre paint peeling off in gashes which exposed the crumbling brickwork. Inside the house everything was either broken or falling apart: the electricity and plumbing had been badly installed and bandaged and rusty pipes and cables trailed along the floors at odd angles, dripping or spluttering. The windows were nearly opaque with grime and the whole place gave off a smell of mould that seeped into the clothes and hair of all who lived there. It was now carved up into four dwellings: a two-room ground-floor flat on either side of the front door and two upstairs. Maria and Josef lived in the larger upstairs flat at the back, looking onto the garden. The small outhouse for washing, containing a basin and a cold-water tap, and the bespattered and often blocked squat-toilet were shared. Yet, despite the stench and the appalling condition of the house, it wasn't hard to find lodgers, for Amstetten was full of poor railway workers and times continued to be hard. Besides, anti-inflationary measures aimed at landlords prevented Maria from either increasing the rent or evicting tenants, so some families remained in the flats for more than a decade, avoiding as much as they could their bitter, silently furious, one-eyed landlady, a woman profoundly disturbed by her experiences in Mauthausen-Gusen.

After her return the punishments Maria inflicted on her son seem to have gained a new imaginativeness. Slaps were no longer enough and now she used her fists, her booted feet – once she kicked him in the face until he bled all over the floor. Sometimes when Josef was disobedient, whether by accident or by childish design, he was made to sleep outside in the garden. Sometimes he was tied to his bed. A favourite punishment was *Scheitelknien*, a disciplinary practice that was still legal in parts of Austria and Germany. Children were made to kneel on the angle of a piece of wood so that the sharp edge was painful, and an hour on the board was considered normal. Maria kept her plank in the kitchen, using it often: there was plenty to punish. The child was too hungry, too clingy, too stupid. Too expensive too, the rate at which he grew out of his clothes. Obsessed with the story of his conception, she continually aimed her old refrain at him: 'I only got pregnant to prove a point!' And over and over she would relive her disappointment at discovering his sex: 'A boy!' she would say. 'And the very image of his useless father.'

The intensity of their relationship was more like that of a couple than a parent and child. They had no other family. Maria never found out the identity of her biological mother and her foster mother was dead; her abusive father was nothing more than a memory, she had broken contact with her two half-siblings, and her second husband, Josef's father, was still being held in a Russian prisoner-of-war camp – which suited her fine. Although she instinctively disliked Josef and treated him appallingly, she also clung to him. A jealous parent, she pushed him away and reeled him back in; monopolized him. She was working in farmers' households in the countryside and as a result little Josef would spend a lot of time on his own in the crumbling house. But, when at home, his mother would shout at him or slap him or pretend he wasn't there and the next thing he knew she was sobbing in a heap, extracting promises from him that he would never leave her. Even in her most violent tantrums she was terrified of his rejection. Would he abandon her like the others had? He was already eleven and she was paranoid that he was slipping through her fingers. Still a religious woman, she took him to church every Sunday to impress on him the consequences of sin. 'You're a criminal,' she would accuse him, 'a criminal that needs to be watched.' She claimed she could see the devil when she looked into his face.

Like the house in Ybbsstrasse, Austria was divided after the war. Lower Austria fell under Russian administration and remained so until 1955. Amstetten considered itself fortunate to house the regional administrative headquarters of the Red Army since the major in charge kept a relatively close eye on the men billeted there. Nevertheless, the early days of the occupation were turbulent and frightening. Virtually lawless Russian troops terrorized the countryside: there were seventy recorded cases of murder and manslaughter in Amstetten county in the second half of 1945 alone. Rape was so endemic in Kollmitzberg that a special hospital was set up to treat the syphilis and gonorrhoea that inevitably resulted: over a third of the girls and women who lived there became infected. Some women committed suicide to avoid rape: Amstetten's register of deaths records that at 9am on 9 May 1946 'all the females living in Gorch-Fockstrasse died. A mother aged 45 and her 19-year-old daughter shot themselves. The 78-year-old grandmother took her own life by hanging herself.' All the women in the family had committed suicide to avoid rape by Russian soldiers.

The privations of wartime continued. While those in the American zone, around Linz in Upper Austria, enjoyed luxuries such as chocolate and American cigarettes, those in the Russian zone lived off what they could grow – rationing continued there until 1950. Almost as bad as the privation was the double humiliation of having both lost the war and being occupied by communists. The first anniversary of the Russian occupation was celebrated by unveiling a monument to fallen Russian soldiers on the spot where a bronze bust of the Emperor Franz Joseph I had once stood. The town's children were bemused when their park, the Schulwiese, the only patch of land not covered in dust and rubble, was renamed. From now on they were to refer to it only as Park Stalin. But gradually the town was being rebuilt by the forced labour of former Nazis. By the autumn of 1947 one of Amstetten's schools, in Kirchenstrasse, which had been converted into a makeshift hospital during the war, had been scrubbed clean of all traces of its wartime usage and the camp beds and operating tables replaced by neat rows of desks. It was here that Josef Fritzl began his education.

To accommodate the demands of a growing population, the school operated in two shifts. Children from the town attended in the mornings and those who lived in the surrounding countryside in the afternoons, once they had completed their chores on their parents' farms, some of them cycling in every day, whatever the weather, from up to fifteen miles away. Josef was lucky in that he could walk to school: it took ten minutes, along dusty Ybbsstrasse, past the crumbling façades of the businesses that had survived the war, past Hans Schachner's construction firm and Johann Ekart the stove-fitter; past Anton Schillhuber's tavern ('Come In and Enjoy Our Lovely Ballroom!'), and into the centre of town and Kirchenstrasse. The school, squeezed between the St Stephan church and the old cemetery, which was visible from the classrooms, was his refuge from his mother and the squalor and loneliness of home. It was the first semblance of stability he had known.

In Josef's year there were thirty-two pupils: twelve girls and twenty boys, the girls along the internal wall and then two rows of ten boys each. His teachers, Herr Kuhn and Herr Bauer, were strict but compassionate men who taught their pupils the rudiments of the classics, mathematics, and German with a view to preparing them for a future that might in some way make up for the past. Josef sat on the outer row, next to the window, and at first struggled with his work. At twelve he was two years older than the rest of the class and turning into a tall, good-looking, dark-haired boy, although one barely registered by the girls. He was the quiet one by the window, in the shabby clothes.

Over the next five years the class would remain virtually intact. The friendships that were formed among these children would in many cases last through their lifetimes. Although initially introverted, Josef did begin to make friends with the other boys, who discovered in him a lightly cynical sense of humour and a talent for clever wordplay. He was known not as Josef but by its diminutives 'Pepperl' and 'Pepi'. His core group of friends – Karl Dunkl, Franz Cimanek, Otto Gatten-bauer, and Friedrich Leimlehner – called themselves the Dunkl Gang, after Karl, at whose house in Ardagger-strasse they would gather after school and where Karl's mother, who ran a grocery, would supply them with treats. Karl was always trying to impress the other boys with the story of his mother's bravery when Russian soldiers had held her at gunpoint while looters stole the shop's entire stock and smashed every jar of Herr Dunkl's pear jam. They played the games that boys usually play: cowboys and Indians and cops and robbers, and Josef, as at school, took on subordinate roles: he was the hench-man, never the hero; the Indian but never the chief. If the boys were lucky enough to find a football – footballs were beyond the pocket of most of their parents – or when they played ping-pong on a rickety old table, Josef would never join in but preferred to stand by and watch.

It was taken for granted that he was withdrawn because his mother was poor. Even the least well-off of his friends' parents pitied him and would often slip him small gifts of bread. Any boy in his situation would have felt humiliated. Friedrich Leimlehner's grandparents owned a farm and when the boys went round to his house they would sometimes be fed luxuries such as eggs and schmaltz, a type of lard that was delicious spread on toast. Everyone was poor, but the contrast for Josef, whose mother struggled to scrape together the money to buy basic food and fuel, was stark. He concealed his home life from his friends. Over the years of their friendship none of his schoolmates ever entered number 40: Franz

Cimanek once got as far as the entrance hall. But Maria forbade visitors and Josef was only too glad to comply with his mother's wishes.

In 1948 the Russians finally released their prisoners of war, including the fathers of three of the Dunkl Gang: Karl, Friedrich, and Josef. It was an unforgettable event in the children's lives: the day the fathers came back. Karl's father returned, gravely ill with malaria, to find that his house had been partly appropriated by a Russian major and his servant, who were occupying the two biggest bedrooms. He felt himself rather lucky to have the senior Russian officer in Amstetten resident in his home. Friedrich's father, exhausted and emaciated, weighed less than a hundred pounds on his return. As a carpenter he had been considered too valuable to the Russians to be allowed to go home and had spent the three years carrying out repairs inside the Kremlin. But at least he was now back home.

It would have taken a very hard-hearted person indeed not to have been moved by the sight of her common-law husband when he finally appeared on the doorstep of 40 Ybbsstrasse after six years away, unwashed, bedraggled, exhausted, and probably injured or sick. But he never crossed the threshold. Maria closed the door in his face. For a while he moped about the streets of Amstetten and made a number of attempts to see his son, but Maria blocked all his overtures. When, eventually, he began a relationship with another woman, this served only to vindicate his wife's feelings of outrage and injury. Josef

Fritzl had known his father only slightly in early childhood and he unquestioningly accepted Maria's version of events. He was the son of a feckless, weak, womanizing failure. He felt no sorrow when, in the early fifties, his father dropped out of sight altogether.

CHAPTER TWO

'A RESPECTABLE ENGINEER'

A school photograph of Josef Fritzl at 15 shows a good-looking boy in a class of forty, the handsomeness of his narrow, even-featured face only slightly compromised by his protruding ears and the cheerless seriousness of his expression. His blue eyes, black in monochrome, peep somewhat desolately at the camera from beneath eyebrows that will in later years lose all their symmetry, growing so wildly askew that they seem to hint at something absurd in the depths of his nature. His mouth, too, bears no trace of what it would become: an ironic mouth with a sugges-tion of a joke constantly playing about its lips. At 15 the mouth is earnest; compressed in a way that is peculiar to unhappy children whose feelings are communicated by the fiercely brave look they carry on their faces. Josef wears the blank, self-disciplined air of a soldier on parade.

The children in the photograph have been arranged in three rows and Josef, because of his height, made to stand at the back. He is a good head taller than the other boys, trussed up in a dark-coloured, high-collared, brass-buttoned coat, two years older than the rest of the class.

During those first couple of years at the school in Kirchenstrasse Josef had changed very little. He remained withdrawn and unsure of himself: nobody except for the headmaster, Josef Freihammer, expected him to do much more than languish at the bottom of the class. Freihammer was only 27 at the time and in the eyes of many of his students, his youth and unorthodox teaching methods somewhat undermined his authority. He taught German alongside his other duties and never resorted to the harsh, disciplinarian tactics then common in the teaching profession. He well understood the profound effect on his pupils of their recently turbulent family lives; he knew how poverty and, in many cases, fatherlessness had taken their toll on their self-esteem.

Had it not been for Freihammer, it is quite possible that Josef would never have overcome the intellectual deprivation of his childhood but gone on to scratch a living, much as his mother had done, in badly paid jobs in local farms or inns. But the headmaster recognized that what Josef Fritzl lacked in schooling he could make up for with brains, and so encouraged him, with after-school classes and fatherly talks, to 'work hard and make something of yourself'. Freihammer saw that the boy was more than averagely bright, that his aptitude for maths was particularly striking. And with his headmaster's encouragement he soon began to show signs of academic promise.

Other things about him began to change, most notice-ably his appearance. Shortly after his fifteenth birthday, as if having suddenly become aware of his own poverty he started to tie his shoelaces properly, paid attention to the state of his fingernails, and generally did whatever he could to ward off the pitying glances of his school friends' parents, which, in his teenage pride, he no longer felt capable of tolerating. The most dramatic outward manifestation of this new, more confident Josef was what he had done to his light-brown, naturally straight hair: one day he appeared in class with a *Schmalzlocke*, the lightly pompadoured, brilliantined style that was then popular. To his friends this was a turning point, a decisive gesture. The old, slow Pepperl had gone.

Amstetten in the late forties and early fifties was hardly a haven for young people. Nevertheless, teenage life still held its promise and by 1950 Josef's class in the school in Kirchenstrasse was alive with adolescent energy.

The boys all fell helplessly in love with Franzciska Woll, whose coal-black hair and even, pale features, previously unnoticed by the boys in school, now made her the class beauty; Karl Dunkl's cheerful good humour began to draw admiring glances from the girls. But it was pretty much still unthinkable in this still strongly conservative and Catholic part of the world for a young woman to be out on her own; an attitude strongly reinforced by the continuing Russian military presence in the region. The occupation had resulted in a good number of rapes, hospitalizations, and even murders of young women. (The young Karl Dunkl had been deeply shocked when his neighbour, Cilli Brandstötter, was shot in the back and killed, trying to flee a group of Russian soldiers.) And as a consequence, the freedoms the young women of Amstetten had enjoyed in childhood became forbidden: no more sunbathing on the grassy banks of the Ybbs or splashing about in the town's nineteenth-century wooden swimming pool. Throughout their early teens, wherever they went the girls of the school in Kirchenstrasse were closely chaperoned by an anxious parent. 'You'll only escape your father on your wedding day,' the old joke went.

Because access to girls was so difficult, the question of how to get one alone obsessed the boys. What little they could find out about sex, they learned in the Baumann, Amstetten's cinema. Not from *Casablanca* or the Hans Moser adaptations of famous novels that were regularly screened there – these were almost impossible to get into owing to their '18' certificate – but from *Schleichendes Gift* (Creeping Poison), a government-sponsored sex-education film and morality tale. Absent or dead husbands and the now semi-permanent presence of foreign troops in the country had led to a rapid increase in sexually transmitted diseases. And the poster – painted in lurid acid colours, it depicted a large serpent coiled around an attractive, naked, young starlet, her arms outstretched in terror – was alone enough to cause a sensation among the young Amstetteners. Repeat visits to the film were made by many members of the teenage audience who considered the parts where the amateur cast demonstrated exactly how these sinister-sounding afflictions might be passed on to be both informative and wildly erotic.

But even at 15, Josef was almost invisible to the girls, and he expressed no interest in them either, and despite

his looks, his age, his height, his newly discovered intelligence – all of which another, more confident boy might
have turned to his advantage – Josef was distinguished
among his peers only as a boy skilled at fixing things:
bored at home, he had taken to making small repairs on
the house, a pastime for which he had begun to exhibit
noticeable skill. He was turning into a driven young man,
a hard worker with his head in his books who seemed
more preoccupied with his studies than with going out.
Nor did the now-widening gap between Josef and his
core group of friends repair itself as opportunities for
socializing multiplied. When the Paradisl Garten, which
boasted the town's first concrete dance floor, or the Neues
Tanzcafe (whose dance floor was made of glass), or later,
the Nibelungen Hof, whose ultraviolet lights drew
crowds from neighbouring towns, opened their doors, his
class-mates would go and dance to Benny Goodman or
Glenn Miller tunes reworked as traditional waltzes, or
Schlager, a type of easy-listening music that had become
popular across Austria, Germany, and Switzerland. But
Josef stayed at home, oblivious to the light orchestral
tunes of the Mantovani Band and the sugary love songs
of Vico Torriani. He was frequently alone, barely drank,
never danced and spent most of his time inside the house
in Ybbsstrasse.

His relationship with his mother was also changing.
Maria hated to see her son grow up. Despite limiting his
freedom as best she could, she was helpless to stifle the
keen interest that he now showed in his studies, an interest she knew was largely generated by the knowledge
that a career would give him the independence he needed

to assert himself against her. And not only was he now physically much stronger than her (and she knew it was only a matter of time before he would begin to defend himself against her attacks), but she began to sense in him a growing embarrassment about her. And it was true that for the first time in his life Josef had begun to regard his mother with a feeling other than anxiety. He was old enough to recognize that she constituted a frightening sight, dressed in all weathers in her incongruous gypsy style of filthy headscarf and rubber boots, her left eye obscured by a rag she would press to her face, and he had grown to dread those rare occasions when she would leave the house to shuffle about the streets of Amstetten mumbling to herself incoherently for everyone to see.

He was 15 when he finally turned on her. Josef hit his mother on the side of the head with a punch so violent that it sent her reeling across the kitchen. For a few seconds she had lain sprawled on the floor, shrieking terribly. And things changed after that. His mother began to be afraid of him and he realized he had great power over her. It was, by the standards of how he had been used to living in number 40, a quite astonishing transgression.

Not long after that he began to exhibit other forms of unusual behaviour. He would never remember how it was that, late one evening, not long after the incident with his mother, he had found himself drawn to the ground-floor bedroom window of one of his neighbours. Barely open a crack, the window was lined on the inside by a thick, unevenly hung curtain. And somehow he had ended up crouching beneath the sill, just waiting there, listening. For many minutes he stayed there, straining to hear, and at last he caught a fragment of the private murmurings of what he knew, from an announcement in the Births, Marriages, and Deaths section of the *Anzeiger*, to be a recently married couple. He hoped, but for lack of experience couldn't be sure, that what he was overhearing was sex. But after that there wasn't a window in Amstetten that didn't seem to present itself as an opportunity for lurking and spying.

He became a talented snoop, familiarizing himself with the habits of his neighbours, making it his business to know just what time someone was undressing for bed, when so-and-so was most likely to have her weekly bath (the clattering of a tin pan being filled with water in the kitchen was the clue). Most of all he liked to watch women in their own homes, cosy, tidy homes with lit fires and comfortable furniture, places where he might have liked to have lived himself.

In the early fifties the Schlemmer Gasthof had became a magnet for young Amstettners, a fact that could be attributed neither to a dance floor nor a jukebox – it had neither – but to its position in the heart of the Amstetten woods.

Josef liked to find a hiding place among the shadows of beeches and oaks, a lookout post where he would wait for the swish of a petticoat or the click-clack of heels – in those days skirts were nipped in at the waist and flouncy, and girls tottered along on heels that were pencil-thin – on the stone path that signalled the approach of a young woman.

But he was growing bolder, more reckless: he began to follow women, or wait for them to cross his path, before stepping out of his hiding place. One day, in one of the 'spontaneous' acts that would characterize Josef's entire sexual life, he did something that shocked even him. He saw a woman, stepped into her path, and revealed himself. Solitary and one-sided, these were Josef Fritzl's first sexual experiences. He was 16.

Many years in the future only Friedrich Leimlehner would be able to look back on this period of time – their 'idyllic' (Dunkl's word) childhood – and remember anything concrete about the young Josef that might have indicated the direction his life would later take. To Leimlehner, Josef loved 'dirty jokes – he was never the initiator but the kind of boy who laughed too long when one was made and then somehow manage to keep the conversation focussed on the subject'. Nobody really noticed that anything odd was obscured behind the exterior of the ambitious young man. Here was a person, they felt sure, who had overcome the disadvantages of his deprived childhood to go on and make something of himself. Josef had exceeded his teachers' expectations in the three years since his former headmaster had taken him under his wing. Aged 16 he finished school, one of the few among his classmates to go on to further education. Behind his mother's back he enrolled on a two-year evening course in engineering, and he would support himself with a day job in metalwork. In 1951 he left Amstetten for the very first time. His destination was Linz.

* * *

Just 20 miles south of the Czechoslovakian border, Linz is Austria's third largest city, a prosperous place which had fallen into the American zone during the occupation. Unlike Amstetten, where people subsisted on food vouchers until the mid-fifties, Linz had Hershey's chocolate, Winston cigarettes, and a thriving black market. It was one of the few places in Austria whose economy had survived the trauma of war. Linz owed much of its comparative prosperity to Hitler, who grew up here. Hitler had earmarked his home town for rapid industrialization: whole factories, mainly chemical and metal-manufacturing plants, had been dismantled brick by brick in conquered Czechoslovakia, loaded on to trains, and reassembled in Linz. At the heart of this economic powerhouse were the city's steelworks, built with slave labour in 1938, and named the Reichswerke Hermann Goering, in honour of Hitler's putative successor. When the war ended the plant continued as one of the region's largest employers, and in 1952 the American occupation authorities renamed it. Reichswerke Hermann Goering became Vereinigte Österreichische Eisen-und Stahlwerke AG, or VÖEST.

In Linz he had found lodgings in a Catholic home for boys, Don Bosco, and, through a local job centre, he was taken on as an apprentice at the engineering firm Hüner und Ziegler, where he learned to design farming machinery and for which he was paid thirty schillings a month. But he was always aimed at VÖEST. It was only natural that Josef Fritzl, who was now proving himself to be a diligent, even gifted, worker with a flair for the construction of machines, would be drawn to the possibility of working for one of Austria's most rapidly expanding and successful businesses VÖEST had interests in far-away places, like Africa and Brazil. Four years passed without any particularly memorable incidents. He felt exceptionally proud when, in 1956, the company gave him his first real job.

Although excelling professionally, he still lagged behind in his personal life. It was usual in fifties Austria for young men to be married by their early twenties. He was 19 and had never even had a girlfriend, and stood little chance of finding one in the technical department of an engineering company. But early in 1956 he accepted an invitation from a colleague at VÖEST to a party in Linz, hosted by a lively, middle-aged couple and their three teenage daughters, Christine, Erna, and Rosemarie.

The Bayers had moved to Austria from what was then Czechoslovakia; they were among the German minority expelled from that country when the communists took power. Their party was largely a family affair, an assortment of cousins, grandparents, aunts, uncles, and their various children, and had an atmosphere vastly different from anything Josef had ever experienced at home. The second-youngest daughter, 16-year-old Rosemarie, a quiet girl with a tomboyish physique and not, by all accounts, the assertive type, spotted Josef the minute he entered the room and something about this handsome, distant young man must have lent her the courage to be bold. It was Rosemarie who asked Josef to dance, and she who initiated their first kiss.

The courtship was straightforward enough, as courtships tended to be in those days. For their first outing he took her to the cinema in Linz. Rosemarie sensed his ambition and felt fortunate to have met a man of such intelligence and drive. In return she could offer herself to him as a traditional wife and home-maker: she cooked well and would accept without question her husband as the head of the household. She understood that he had very firm ideas about marriage, that he wanted a large family, that he was keen to take on the role of the reliable patriarch, never abandoning his children as his father had done. He and Rosemarie wanted the same things: to have a lot of children and do well for themselves. In June 1956 they were married.

Financially it wasn't an easy start to a marriage. The young couple moved into one of the two-bedroom flats in Ybbsstrasse, where the rent was cheapest. Josef would continue to work at VÖEST in Linz, where he lived with Rosemarie's parents during the week, returning to Amstetten each weekend. And to supplement his income – and pay Maria, who still relied on her tenants' rent for her livelihood – Rosemarie worked in a bakery. Amstetten, although still a backwater, now boasted a bank, its own symphony orchestra, even its own cultural week, the Amstettner Kulturwoche, during which various municipal buildings hosted art exhibitions and concerts and plays were staged. But the house at 40 Ybbsstrasse remained as squalid as ever.

Josef and Rosemarie lived on the first floor. Their two-bedroom apartment was flanked on the left by a two-bedroom flat rented by a young couple, the Kaisers, and on the right by a small one-room flat where an elderly widow, Frau Klammer, lived on her own. On the ground floor Friedrich Setz, a poor widower and labourer who later found moderately better-paid work in an insurance firm, lived in the two-room flat to the left of the front door with his young sons, Peter and Friedrich. The flat to the right of this was let out to Peter and Aloisia Berger and their son. The top-floor flat with its view onto Ybbsstrasse was occupied by Hans and Herta Kaiser and their three daughters, Elvira, Gudrun, and Judith. Maria still lived in her flat on the top floor overlooking the garden. The house had not been improved since the war and would remain in a dilapidated state for another decade. There was only one tap and the tenants would bathe and wash their clothes and dishes only once a week with water heated up over the stove in a large tin bucket. The ground-floor toilet was still a pit latrine in the garden; upstairs the toilets were holes without flushes connected to pipes that fed into the outhouse, the waste washed down with water from a pail.

Maria much preferred her daughter-in-law to her son, and they got on tolerably well. But, manipulative, she was using Rosemarie as an excuse to stop talking to Josef. When Josef wanted anything at all from his mother she would pretend not to hear, so he would have to put the question to his wife, who would in turn ask Maria. In this way ordinary, everyday communication between mother and son virtually ceased. They lived in the same house, on the same floor, but rarely spoke to each other.

But Josef and Rosemarie's relationship remained good. He was overjoyed when, on 17 June 1957, she gave birth to their first child, a girl, whom they christened Ulrike. Just under three years later, on 11 May 1960, the couple's second child was born, another daughter, and they called her after her mother. That second pregnancy was complicated. But she was adamant she would have more children and so she ignored the doctor's advice, her husband's misgivings and on 7 September 1963, the couple's first son, Harald Günther, was born.

The second half of the fifties was a period of rapid and exciting change in Austria – the beginning of the so-called *Wirtschaftswunder*, or Economic Miracle. Finally there were signs of a better life ahead. After a decade of occupation Soviet, British, American, and French forces were withdrawn and on 15 May 1955 Austria became a sovereign state. The Austrian State Treaty had banned Austria from forming another union with Germany, and Nazi and fascist organizations were outlawed. But unlike the Germans, who were undergoing a difficult period of self-examination and guilt about the Second World War, Austrians wasted little time castigating themselves for their recent past. Their lack of accountability had been formally ratified by post-war propaganda in which the Allied powers had declared Austria to be a victim, rather than an accomplice, of Nazi aggression. By the fifties the unspoken consensus in Austria was that most of its citizens had been unaware of the crimes committed during the Third Reich and that only individual Austrians could be judged for their actions. While Germany prepared to pay millions in reparations and restitution, its neighbour

went about the task of restoring its self-image while culti-
vating itself as a victim nation. While elevating its small
wartime resistance movement to an heroic scale, Austria
also focused on the atrocities committed by the Russians.
Any mention of either the country's delirious admiration
for Hitler during the *Anschluss*, or the complicity of its
citizens in the atrocities that followed, was considered
irrelevant and in bad taste.

So the cream of Austrian politics and society remained
largely unchanged. High-ranking former Nazis formed
part of the new establishment after the war and became
members of the two most prominent political groupings,
the Social Democratic Party and the People's Party, the
second being the new incarnation of the old Christian
Social Party, which had changed very little except its
name. Former Nazis continued their lives and careers
uninterrupted by prison sentences or even demotions.
Among these were men such as Dr Heinrich Gross, a
leading Austrian psychiatrist and medical doctor, who
had personally killed at least nine disabled children at the
Am Spiegelgrund clinic in Vienna as part of the Nazi
euthanasia programme. Gross was a veteran Nazi Party
member but, because he had been captured by the Red
Army after the war, was unavailable to be tried at
Nuremberg in the late forties. On his return from the
Soviet Union he was convicted for manslaughter in an
Austrian court but his sentence was overturned on a tech-
nicality. He joined and became a trusted member of the
Social Democrats and returned to Am Spiegelgrund,
where he became chief physician and used the preserved
brains of children that he had ordered to be killed during

the war as the basis for his research. By the fifties he was carving out a reputation for himself as one of the best-known and best-paid psychiatric court experts in the country.

In Amstetten the *Anzeiger* became an organ of the Social Democratic Party. Its former publisher, Josef Rahmhart, cleared of charges of collaborating with the Nazi regime, bought the printing plant that produced the newspaper and became close to the Social Democrats.

Josef's career at VÖEST was progressing well. In 1958 he was made a full-time employee, working as an electrical engineer in the division responsible for the design of cranes, lathes, and other construction machines. His achievements within the company had given him confidence and all traces of the awkward, unhappy-looking boy he had once been were disappearing. He walked taller now, had an excellent posture, and wore a blue suit set off with a canary-yellow shirt. He was vain, there was no doubt, and a new expression took over his face, one of light irony; his lopsided grin looked, according to a friend, as if it were saying, 'The situation, although hopeless, isn't serious.'

He liked to go about his business alone and put no effort into maintaining his old school friendships. People who knew him around this time describe him as a respectable, almost impressive-looking man, a real 'sir'.

VÖEST was a great innovator in its field: in 1952 it had patented a process involving the use of oxygen in the manufacture of steel, and became a commercial giant. By the sixties the company had expanded worldwide, building and maintaining steelworks and ironworks, as well as other plants, in countries including France, Italy, Poland, the USSR, Brazil, India, and parts of Africa. The future looked exciting for both the company and its employees. Josef was seen as an up-and-coming young manager: he would continue to pursue his studies in his spare time at a technical school. Company business had taken him to Vienna, then Luxemburg for eight months in 1962, and now it was felt he was ready to oversee a project, at their new plant in the newly independent Ghana. Fritzl was delighted to be chosen. Not only would his income double but his food and accommodation would be paid for. After seven years of marriage and three children, and having lived his whole life in Austria, he found his first taste of Africa exhilarating, disorientating but full of promise. During the eighteen months he spent there Josef did not return to see his wife and there were no telecommunications. He was completely cut off from his family and, like many of his colleagues, had a series of short 'sexual experiences'. In many ways he was a fastidious man. He prided himself on the fact that while working abroad he never had sex with prostitutes, instead having what he called 'affairs' with local women to whom he would give gifts of food or money. They were the 'normal' extramarital affairs of a man away from home for a long time.

But when he returned home, in 1965, the first cracks in his marriage began to show. It was hard to tell what exactly had changed. Rosemarie was lonely, unhappy, and overburdened raising three children. And the children, now 8, 5, and 2, had forgotten him and regarded him with suspicion and a little fear. Perhaps he had become use to living the life of a bachelor and being waited on by servants. Perhaps he felt that, having improved his family's financial circumstances, he deserved their love and respect. Failing to get it, he became violent and would resort to the same disciplinary tools that his mother had used: *Scheitelknien*. He felt shut out by his wife who seemed to him entirely preoccupied by her children and, soon, by a fourth pregnancy. Josef hated fat women and pregnancy made Rosi fatter. The old feelings of loneliness and self-pity returned with a vengeance: 'If you don't do what I say,' he would threaten his wife, 'it will only get worse.' His sister-in-law, Christine, had never liked him and now she decided that his attitude towards his wife and children could only be described as 'despotic'.

Into this volatile household now came the couple's fourth child. She was born on 8 April 1966. They called her Elisabeth.

By 1967 many of the Mostviertel's pear trees had been felled in what was known as the 'Clearing of the Fruit Gardens' to make space for industrially grown crops. In Amstetten, every household now had water, gas, and electricity on tap. Two large construction companies, which had in Nazi times relied on forced labour, now became profitable again thanks to the growing influx of foreign workers, lured by the Austrian government from Turkey and Yugoslavia. Amstetten became both uglier and livelier. Roads were resurfaced, the town square was given over to parking, and Ybbsstrasse became a major artery leading out to the Westautobahn, the motorway that connected Vienna and Linz. The town's biggest dance hall, the Schillhuber Gasthof, opened at number 15, where government-sponsored parties, resembling conservative balls, were held for the town's youth. Even the fourteenth-century, gothic-steepled church of St Stephan, which had given Kirchenstrasse its name, tried to engage the interest of a new generation of young people by hosting jazz evenings in its public hall.

While some of the big events of the sixties passed Austria by – protests against the Vietnam war, widespread drug use – the sexual revolution did not. Women embraced their new freedoms, shocking traditionalists, and were blamed, along with jazz and pop and a growing lack of interest in religion among the young, for the rising number of sexual attacks on young women. And there was no denying it was a problem: the late sixties would mark the peak of violence against women in twentieth-century Austria. The case that most deeply shocked Amstetten in 1967 was the rape and murder of Rosa Laimlehner, a 41-year-old mother of ten, by a 20-year-old apprentice electrician in the nearby town of Ansfelden. The attack was shocking enough to be featured prominently in the regional press – an article by a Dr Schneider in the Linz-based *Oberösterreichische Nachrichten* newspaper gives a flavour of the contemporary responses: 'There have always been murders and sex murders,' Dr Schneider wrote. 'But it seems that the numbers of sexually motivated murders has been increasing since the end of the last war. Young people are being revealed as murderers more and more frequently. Criminologists, teachers, psychologists, and, not least, doctors, are trying to understand the reasons behind these murders. Probably the most common cause is the flood of sexual stimuli from magazines, novels, and films. Even fashion is being blamed and this summer people have earnestly warned girls about wearing mini-skirts, as they could directly provoke sexual assaults.'

In Linz, Josef had his room, his job, at which he excelled, and he had a bicycle. Much more about his existence there we don't know except that Rosemarie, feeling the emotional distance between herself and her husband, began to worry he was having an affair and confided her anxieties to Christine. Although Rosemarie was right to suspect Josef, her instincts about the precise nature of his infidelity were wrong. He had in fact slipped back into his teenage ways. In Linz's main park he had begun to expose himself. He had been cautioned when a woman had reported him to the police. A few months later he again came to the attention of the police, this time for the attempted rape of a young woman. Again he was cautioned.

It would seem likely that there were other incidents but these remained unknown to the authorities.

Shortly afterwards, in October 1967, when Josef was 32, he began to follow a young woman about the streets of Linz. Having discovered that she lived in Klein-münchen, the old garment district at the southern end of the city, he took to lurking outside her home, as he had done outside the homes of many of his neighbours as a teenager in Amstetten. He soon gathered the basic facts of her life: that she worked as a nurse, that she was married, and that she had a young child with her husband, a railway worker. The couple lived in a ground-floor apartment and their bedroom window looked onto the street. Josef noticed that the young woman slept with the window open every night, even when her husband was on a late shift at work.

Josef found himself drawn back to the house again and again. He familiarized himself with the young woman's habits: when she returned home from work, when she fed her child, when she went to bed, and how long after she had gone to bed she was most likely to turn off the lamp that stood on her bedside table. Eventually, one evening, he waited until he saw the light in her bedroom go out, waited for another half-hour, tinkering with his bicycle. Then he walked up to the young woman's open window and climbed in.

What happened next was reported in the *Oberösterreichische Nachrichten* on 27 October 1967. Having crept into her bedroom, Josef stood there in the darkness, observing the sleeping woman. Next he went into the kitchen, where he fetched a long-handled carving knife. He returned to the bedroom, and while she continued to sleep he removed his shoes, his trousers, and his underwear. From the waist down he was naked except for his socks. From the waist up he might have been on his way to work: he wore an ironed shirt and his tie was neatly knotted.

Waking her, he held the knife to her throat and said, 'If you don't do what I say, I'll kill you.' He had not needed the knife, or indeed the threat. He was a strong man, used to lifting heavy machinery in his job, and his weight alone would have been sufficient to overwhelm a woman struggling into consciousness. He raped the young woman while her child slept in its cot.

When it was over, he lingered for a while, slipping calmly back into his clothes and leaving as he had entered. Minutes later he was cycling home.

And that might have been the last of it had the nurse not telephoned the police. Josef was arrested, confessed, and appeared in Linz county court to plead guilty to the charge. 'Police Expose Family Father as Monstrous Sex Fiend,' the local papers said, but Josef Fritzl was sentenced to just 18 months in prison. It was more of a ticking-off than a punishment, a verdict that would have cemented Josef's idea of himself as the infallible patriarch, a real man, a hard-working, reliable provider who would never leave his children in the lurch, as his own father had done. There was plenty of evidence to suggest that the rape of a woman at knifepoint was the culmination of a string of sex offences, that his behaviour was compulsive, and that, once he got started he could not stop. But here was a man had worked his way up from nothing to become an engineer, a most respectable profession, and in conservative Austria this would have carried a lot of weight. Unlike the hippies and the drug-takers, who were regarded with great suspicion and unease, Josef Fritzl was considered a valuable member of society. There were mitigating circumstances for a family of four.

Josef Fritzl, dedicated family man: an image that he cultivated and that was now reinforced by the law. A violent
rapist and a good father. The lenient sentence said that he
could be both.

When Rosemarie visited him in prison she never once
mentioned the rape. It wasn't her way to embarrass her
husband. And so they never talked about what had
happened in Linz, or why, or how often, or whether it
was ever likely to happen again. To have brought it up –
and it was difficult enough for Rosemarie to even *think*
about what had happened in Linz – would have called
into question her role as a wife, a role which certainly did
not give her the right to put her husband on the spot in
any way, or question his authority by highlighting his
weaknesses. Besides, she was afraid of him. 'If you don't
do what I say, it will only get worse.' Afraid, too, of imagining her life without him. And so she invested all her
energy into trying not to think about what had happened
in Linz, hoping, in so doing, that the facts would magically rearrange themselves into something she could cope
with, and that he might change. The prison sentence was
a turning point for Rosemarie too; she had had to find
work in a bakery. She wanted to see the best in her
husband and tried to close her eyes to the rest.

She made sure their conversations were pleasant, and
they talked about the children and their future together
almost as they had done in the early years. They made
plans. Once he was out of prison Josef would move back
to Amstetten. He had been an absent father, he conceded;
the family needed him at home. They even looked
forward to trying for a fifth child. As far as she was

concerned, she couldn't have enough children: when she had first met her husband she had told him she wanted 'at least ten'.

They never talked about the incident in Linz and it was amazing what not talking about it could do. When Josef returned home in 1969 the past had simply gone away.

He was sacked from VÖEST, of course. But he had no problem finding another job almost immediately, at Zehetner, a family-run business of 200 workers based, conveniently enough, in Ybbsstrasse. The company manufactured building materials and was by far the most respected in Amstetten. Its owner, Mr Zehetner, knew about the rape – Josef himself brought it up in his job interview – but hired him anyway because he felt sorry for him and knew him to be an excellent engineer. 'Let's give the man a chance,' he told his wife Sieghilde, who was against the idea. 'He's a good worker.' Despite Sieghilde's objections, Josef was put in charge of the company's studio, where he designed the machines that made concrete pipes. He found the work interesting because it broadened his horizons. Having learned almost everything there was to know about electrics during his two-year technical engineering course in Linz, now he taught himself new skills: how to lay floors and pipes; sealing and plastering; insulation against noise, cold, or damp; the installation of doors, windows, and air-shafts. Concrete, cement, bricks, and mortar: he was excited by the many possibilities of these materials and the things he could build, and very proud to be given his own secretary.

It was fitting for a family man such as Josef Fritzl to have moved back to Amstetten to spend more time with his wife and children. Although some people in the town kept their distance – Sieghilde Zehetner, for one, avoided him as much as possible and warned her two young daughters to stay out of his way – his return to his home town was not the scandal it might have been. The crime of which he had been convicted was regarded as largely a private matter by local people and his sentence was not regarded as overly lenient. A 1968 editorial in the *Niederösterreichische Nachrichten* considered the five-year sentence of a man convicted of robbery and rape 'draconian', and his job at Zehetner lent Josef a certain dignity. More than twenty years after the war engineers were still in great demand for building projects, and Josef was particularly respected for what he had achieved. People would greet him in the street courteously, '*Guten Morgen, Herr Ingenieur.*' Life carried on much as it had done before. Josef was delighted when, in the summer of 1970, less than a year after he had completed his prison sentence and moved back to Amstetten, Rosemarie became pregnant again. This time she was carrying a boy and a girl. Josef and Gabriele were born on 5 January 1971, the same year he was poached from Zehetner by a Danish concrete-producing company, Rimas, to head up their Austrian division. He had over eighty clients, travelled, developed the company's business strategy, knew the market well. Just under two years later, on 28 December 1972, the couple's seventh and final child, Doris, was born. A large family, a well-paid job in a prestigious firm, and respectability: Pepperl had made it.

CHAPTER THREE

MASTER OF THE HOUSE

To apologize – if only implicitly – to Rosemarie for what had happened in Linz, Josef Fritzl bought her a house. It was the family's first holiday home. Officially the Seestern (the Starfish) was a bed and breakfast, but really it was more of a hotel: an enormous, three-storey converted barn with forty bedrooms, three terraces, a restaurant, and a bar. It stood beside Mondsee (Moon Lake) in the area known as the Salzkammergut, a network of lakes that stretches from Salzburg to the foot of the Dachstein mountain in the High Alps, one of the most magnificent regions in Austria. The last great Emperor of Austria-Hungary, Franz Joseph I, liked to spend his summers here, swimming in the clear, blue waters of the lakes and taking the pristine air that sweeps down off the surrounding mountainsides.

The Salzkammergut had lost none of its charm by the time the Fritzls came into possession of the Seestern in 1973. An hour and a half's drive due west from Amstetten, Mondsee is accessed by turning off the Westautobahn just before Salzburg. There follows a glorious, winding drive alongside birch, pine, and chestnut woods; past many roadside shrines of saints and the Virgin Mary; and through clusters of whitewashed, wooden-roofed Alpine houses whose window boxes are always spilling over with red geraniums. Like most of Austria's countryside, the Salzkammergut is both litter-free and immaculately kept, the water of its smaller lakes still pure enough to drink. And the region owes its flawless appearance to the importance that the Austrians have always attached to presentation, both as individuals and as a nation. One of the reasons why the local farmers keep their smallhold-ings so neat and tidy is that they are paid handsome subsi-dies by the state to do so. As a result their prettily cultivated meadows are as if copied out of a picture book: dotted, here and there, with a grazing Pinzgauer cow and framed with hedges so neat they might have been trimmed by a surgeon.

After Attersee, a 12-mile-long lake popular with sailors and water-skiers, past the town of Unterach, you come to Mondsee. Smaller than Attersee, it is considered the most romantic of the lakes. It appears around a curve in the road quite unexpectedly, a sedate retreat waiting to be discovered. On clear days, of which there are many in summer, the Seestern has a view of the magnificent Schafberg with its sawn-off, snow-dusted peak which is reflected, almost as perfect as the original, in the silky surface of the lake.

It is in every way an idyllic setting for a holiday home. But Josef bought it for purely practical reasons.

* * *

As a tourist destination the house had a lot of potential. In summer, the grassy beaches around the lake were full of Austrians on holiday. And Josef endeavoured to accommodate even those travellers whose budgets did not stretch to a hotel room by persuading a local farmer to rent him the piece of land which separates the Seestern from the water, a campsite with space for twenty caravans. So, although it was ostensibly a present for Rosemarie, the Seestern was more of a business venture, the first of several properties that Josef would invest in over the next thirty years. Rosemarie, he told her, was in charge of managing the place: that meant cooking, and cleaning all the rooms, on top of looking after the couple's children. Despite the extra work it entailed, however, the Seestern represented a significant step up from the Fritzls' lower-middle-class origins. From then on the family would spend the majority of their summers at their 'country house' at Mondsee.

No sooner had he come into the possession of the Seestern than Josef set about hiring out its rooms and caravan spaces to holidaymakers. Among them was Paul Höra, a stout man with a bushy moustache who spent most of his holiday, indeed all of his free time, in a football strip, shorts, and a pair of sandals. Paul was untypical of the tourists who regularly stayed in the area, in that he was German. He lived in Bavaria, where he ran a cleaning business in Munich. Every summer since 1969, four years before Josef bought the Seestern, Paul, his wife, Elfriede, and the couple's three young children had driven to Mondsee in their white campervan and occupied one of the spaces at the campsite. And it was while

out walking on the shore one day in 1973 with his children that Paul met the new proprietor for the first time.
The month was August, one of those perfectly languid
Austrian summer afternoons when the intense heat that
makes other parts of Europe unbearable at this time of
year is cut through by pleasant, conifer-scented mountain
breezes. Somehow the two men got talking, and although
appearances suggested they had little in common – Paul
overweight and laidback, Josef fastidious and energetic –
something, says Paul, 'just clicked'. The two of them
shared a similar sense of humour and called each other by
their nicknames. Josef was 'Sepp', Paul was 'Pauli'. Soon
they fell into the habit of spending their afternoons
together, sailing in Paul's British-built catamaran or
sitting on the makeshift veranda in front of his caravan,
a pleasant enough spot with a view of the lake. Like all
the other camping places, it had many personal little
touches that gave it the feeling of home: a miniature
wooden fence and gate separated Paul from his neighbours, while a neat, round bed of daisies and hollyhocks
did its best to disguise the ugliness of the caravan, its
assortment of garden gnomes keeping it colourful even
in winter.

Over time Paul came to know the basic facts of his
new friend's life: Josef was a married engineer, the father
of seven children, the two eldest of whom, Ulrike and
Rosemarie, were already teenagers by the time he met
them. Harald was clearly the more intelligent of the two
sons, but Josef detected in the younger boy, a slow, sham-
bling character he had named Josef after himself, signs of
unusual intelligence, and he was always urging Paul to

eavesdrop on their conversations for proof of this hidden brilliance. Of all the children Josef seemed to love Ulrike the most, for she was intelligent as well as confident, the only one to stand up to him. As for the rest of the brood they were so numerous that to Paul they all seemed to merge into one.

Josef joked to Paul that he had saved himself the expense of hiring staff at the Seestern by putting his family to work. As soon as they were old enough the children waited at table, while his wife, Rosemarie, was kept busy running the kitchen. This left him free to play the affable host with his guests or to sit with Paul during those long summer evenings swapping tall tales and cracking jokes. Gradually Paul gathered that, besides himself, Josef had no close friends, certainly no one he could really confide in, having let time and his work come between him and his former schoolmates. When Josef had returned to Amstetten after some years of working in Linz he had felt no great desire to rekindle old friendships, having come to regard what Josef called the 'provincial Austrians' as a little too strait-laced. Paul, flattered to have been singled out for friendship by a charismatic man such as Josef Fritzl, spent most of his time in his presence oscillating between admiration and gratitude. Wistfully he now says – for their friendship is over – 'I had so much fun with that man.'

Paul thought of Josef as a true man of the world: calm, authoritative, with a deep voice, cynical, but also possessed of a terrific sense of humour, 'always making jokes, always in a good mood'. 'He loved Tom & Jerry cartoons,' Paul remembers. 'He would cry with laughter at the parts, you know, when Jerry chops up Tom's tail with a cleaver or stuffs it into an electrical wall socket.' Dirty jokes too. Undeniably, Josef had a grubby mind, making lewd comments under his breath, devilishly raising one of his arched, mismatching eyebrows when a woman walked by. But to Paul it was just man's talk, nothing he hadn't seen or heard before. Dirty jokes and slapstick and practical jokes too. He would hide in Paul's caravan from Rosemarie's sister, Christine, a hefty woman with cropped, peroxide-blonde hair, whose relationship with her brother-in-law had, for reasons unknown to Paul, deteriorated over the years into one of mutual hatred. "'The fat pig," Josef called her: "Hide me, Paul. The fat pig's coming," or "That fat pig's here again!"' Josef's laugh was so infectious that sometimes the other holidaymakers would crowd around to find out what was so funny. He had that kind of magnetism.

Late one evening, while Paul's wife and children were away somewhere, and Paul and Josef were sitting around having one of their chats, two women from a neighbouring caravan, both in their mid-fifties, turned up at his caravan in their negligees. One of them, it was obvious, wasn't wearing any underwear and so was putting her cards on the table. Paul didn't mind but Josef screwed up his face. 'Frightening,' he said coolly, as if he had just witnessed an unpleasant scene in a horror movie. It was a joke but he meant it too. He didn't like fat women and he didn't like old women either. If they crossed his path when Paul was there he would grimace and, for his friend's benefit, affect a violent shudder.

Another thing Paul liked about Josef besides his sense of humour was his generosity. Sometimes Josef would invite him to eat or drink at the Seestern for free. Living over 300 miles apart as they did, their friendship evolved in intense bursts during Paul's annual summer holidays at Mondsee, with periods of months in between when they didn't see or talk to each other. But over the years a pattern established itself: to thank Josef for the free meals Paul would supply food for his restaurant as he could buy certain items much more cheaply in Germany. He would pack the campervan full of cans of whipping cream and other things that Rosemarie needed to run the kitchen of the Seestern and drive them illegally over the border. 'Not that I ever got caught.' One year, after Paul bought a new bungalow in Bavaria, Josef made the four-hour drive from Amstetten to install an electrical circuit. 'He was extremely clever with things like that. A genius at electrics. A genius full stop.' Another time Josef needed to move some wooden beams into the house from the hardware shop where he had bought them and Paul drove over from Germany in his campervan to help. It was one good turn deserves another.

Paul had never in his life met a man who could make him laugh so much. He and Josef became like brothers. They went together to the Oktoberfest, the Munich Beer Festival, a hilarious five-day escapade even though, Paul says, not much alcohol was consumed. And there were holidays: in 1975 Paul and his family travelled with the Fritzls to Lake Garda in northern Italy and the two men got on so well that they decided to do it again, only this time without their wives and children. Rosemarie had her hands full with the kids anyway, and with Paul's marriage on the rocks by this stage the two friends decided to go off on their own.

Paul had been to Thailand before, 'by accident', on the way back from a holiday in Malaysia in 1977 where he had become very ill on the second day. He felt so unwell – he suspected malaria – that he cancelled his hotel and jumped on the first plane back which happened to refuel in Bangkok. By the time the plane touched down in Thailand, however – or at least by the time Paul had had the chance to stretch his legs and take a look around – he was feeling much better. He decided to stay. Thailand was a lovely place, he thought, much nicer than Malaysia, and unbelievably cheap. Paul, who always had an eye for a bargain, could not believe the prices: fifty American cents a night for a hotel room.

So impressed was Paul by Thailand that he convinced Josef to join him the following year and even lent him 500 Deutschmarks to cover the costs. In January 1978 they took the cheapest flight they could find: Vienna to Bangkok via Moscow with Aeroflot. Their final destination, they had decided, was to be a simple fishing village on the east coast of the Gulf of Thailand: Pattaya. Well, a little more than just a simple fishing village. Even Paul concedes that.

In late 1959 five hundred GIs stationed in the neighbouring province, in the build-up to the Vietnam war, were driven to Pattaya for a weekend of 'Rest and Recreation', after which Pattaya became well known among all the American troops in the region. Hundreds of them, many very disturbed by their experiences of war, would stop off there to use the area's brothels. Back home, free love might have been booming in far-out hippy enclaves, but Pattaya was something else: a place of extremes where soldiers could find, so the joke went, not just R&R but I&I, 'Intoxication and Intercourse', in every conceivable form. When the war ended in 1975 and the soldiers returned home, Pattaya was saved from almost total economic collapse by the influx of tourists. Thousands of single men, mainly from Asia and the Soviet Union, were drawn to the town by its reputation as a no-holds-barred centre of prostitution where things for which a man would face a prison sentence in his home country were in plentiful supply. Visitors couldn't walk down a beach without being solicited: by women, by men, by men who looked like women, and by children. All in tropical surroundings that had been hastily modified to suit Western tastes: go-go bars, strip joints – whatever you wanted, it was here. And it was mind-blowingly cheap. But, Paul says, it was pure coincidence that they booked their flight just at the time when Pattaya's reputation had started to spread to Europe.

His version of that first holiday is this: they spent the whole three weeks at the Ocean View Hotel, where to save money they shared a twin bedroom but didn't get on each other's nerves. They were typical tourists. Paul was impressed by how enthusiastically Josef soaked up the local culture: he seemed to much prefer it to his own, which was unusual as his compatriots tend to be a defensively patriotic bunch. 'Josef must be the only Austrian on the planet who wasn't proud of his country and would avoid the other Austrian tourists if he came across them on the beach. He acted more as a German would do, as if he were above them: Austrians were "stupid" and "backward".' 'People from Austria,' he would often tell Paul, 'are generally all idiots.' Mainly the two men sunbathed, did the temple tours, and went shopping. It was a very cultural trip. And they ate: Josef had nothing against the local cuisine as long as he could avoid tipping. Before they left Paul bought himself a gold necklace encrusted with precious stones, in the shape of his star sign, Libra, which he wears around his neck to this day. But Josef, either because he was averse to spending money or because he was worried about paying customs duty on the way back, bought nothing for himself or his family.

On their way back they missed their connecting flight to Vienna and somehow ended up in Moscow for eight days in the freezing cold without a visa, which 'basically meant living in a Russian airport for a week, in winter, wearing our holiday clothes. For some stupid reason they're like that, the Russians: we had our suitcases confiscated.' Paul's teeth chattered as he waddled around in his shorts and sandals, Josef behind him, asking, 'Pauli, why are you walking like a geisha?' The unfriendly treatment by the Russians – Paul says that Josef was privileged because he could speak English and talk to some of their guards – caused a tension that led to the first and only fight the two men had in their thirty-five-year friendship. When they finally boarded the plane – they now had to take a flight to Munich rather than Vienna – they exacted their revenge. Four Russians sitting in a neighbouring aisle spent the whole flight poring over a map of the Ruhr area in Germany, 'which is an industrial area famous for its coal mines. So, not that we had any real suspicions, when we arrived in Munich I told the border police that these four guys were spies, and what do you know? They were taken in for questioning!' Josef had highly commended Paul for that particular practical joke.

Several pictures of Josef Fritzl survive this, the first of two holidays in Thailand the men took together. Most of the photographs were taken by Paul. In one he is splayed out, tanned, and asleep in a deckchair in tight, zebra-print swimming briefs, a heavily built man of just above average height with sturdy legs and butcher's arms, Pattaya's crescent-shape beach behind him in the distance. In another picture he is standing at a market stall holding a pineapple. He is smiling broadly because he knows that being photographed in a tropical holiday resort holding a pineapple is a cliché. He is wearing khaki shorts with a matching fisherman's hat and is, except for the chain that dangles from his neck, bare-chested. His hair and eyebrows have retained the dark-brown colour of his youth but his face has lost some of its discipline. At 48 he has grown jowly and wolfish, his open mouth cave-like and leering. He looks exactly what one would expect a single man on holiday in Pattaya to look like: mirthful, vigorous, and middle-aged.

Paul says that nothing of a sexual nature happened in Pattaya, explaining, 'The clap, it's just everywhere in Thailand.' But, knowing Josef as they did, many of their fellow caravan-owners in Mondsee took the view that he would not have travelled all the way to one of the world's most notorious fleshpots for no reason. He went there, it became a running joke, '*Um die Sau rauss zu lassen*', to use the crass German expression. 'To let out his inner pig.'

Several years passed. Paul's crumbling marriage finally fell apart. He spent some time pleading poverty, in a moderately successful attempt to avoid paying his ex-wife child support. There were girlfriends, some steadier than others, but, when he looked back on it, the one solid thing throughout his life had been his admiration for Josef. Over time he had come to think of him simply as a very funny man – a true character – who had achieved a great deal in his life.

If he had ever stopped to think about it properly, Paul would have said that Josef might have been a violent man behind closed doors. But personally he had seen him fly into a rage only once, during a disagreement with his wife in a supermarket, 'But you could tell the way that his wife and the children would do anything he said.' It was just understood: if the children misbehaved they'd get a beating; that kind of behaviour wasn't unusual among men of their generation. Austria was still a devoutly Catholic place, patriarchy was alive and well. Ulrike, the eldest, stood up for herself, Paul remembers, and some-how she would get away with it. When they were at Mondsee Josef would ban all the children from going to discos but Ulli would say, 'I don't care. I'm going to the disco and will stay late.' Not like the rest of the family, who just crept around him. Including Rosemarie – she was always in the background making cakes or some such. Or looking after the children. Being a mother of seven children – not to mention her work at the Seestern – kept her busy, that was for sure.

Paul never knew about the rape conviction. The case had never been reported in the German papers. And there were other facts about himself that Josef took pains to conceal from his friend. The indiscretions in Ghana: Paul never knew about them either. Or his friend's considerable wealth, amassed over the years but kept secret from those who thought they knew him. There was no reason for Paul to suspect that his best friend – the joker, the cool-headed raconteur with an astonishing arsenal of smutty stories – was a snoop, a stalker, an exhibitionist, and a voyeur, let alone a convicted rapist.

So it was a terrible, almost implausible surprise when, in April 2008, Paul turned on his television and saw Josef's face on the screen. 'Josef F', as he was referred to in the Austrian press for reasons of confidentiality, had been arrested. In a voice that betrayed her own feelings on the matter the newscaster remarked that once Josef F had stood trial it was unlikely that a criminal of this level of cunning and depravity would ever leave his cell. Paul did not sleep that night. In the morning he made his decision. 'That man is dead to me,' he said to himself. And that same day, the day after the story broke, thirty-five years after he had first encountered Josef Fritzl walking on the beach at Mondsee with his children, Paul sold all his pictures to the highest bidder. 'There are no mates when it comes to money,' he said. 'Especially not after what he did.'

* * *

Because the laws governing rent control prevented Josef from kicking out the tenants of 40 Ybbsstrasse, he refused to do anything at all to the house until they either died or moved out. He was a practical man: no electricity, no hot water – only cold water ran out of the taps. He refused point-blank to fix anything except one or two windows which he eventually replaced. And right up to the seventies, while all the other houses in the street were being done up and modernized, number 40 remained both dilapidated and chaotic.

Well into the second decade of their marriage the Fritzls continued to live in their two-roomed apartment on the first floor, next door to Josef's mother and two other dwellings: the single room occupied by old Mrs Klammer and the two-roomed flat rented by Hans and Herta Kaiser and their three daughters. When Mrs Klammer died some time in the mid-sixties – just after Elisabeth was born, when Ulrike was 8, little Rosemarie 5, and Harald 2 – Josef had finally been able to convert her room into a bedroom for his children. He wanted to take over the entire first floor but this was made impossible by the fact that the Kaisers could not afford to live anywhere else. This and the refusal of Friedrich Setz and the Bergers to move out of the two ground-floor flats led Josef to conclude that it would be a waste of money to renovate the house in any way, so he left it to sink into almost grotesque disrepair. Except for the new children's bedroom, the only thing that he changed in the first twenty years of his marriage was the upstairs toilet – the hole in the floor – which he fitted with an enamel 'English toilet seat'. The waste was still flushed down as it always had been, with a bucket of water. The garden, however, was a different story. In the garden he'd built himself a tool shed and was in the process of excavating a small area towards the back of the house which he wanted to convert into a garage.

He had to wait until the mid-seventies for his tenants to finally drift off. In the end a tragedy would precipitate the departure of the Kaisers from their two-roomed flat on the first floor. Hans had been spending his weeks in Linz, where he worked at VÖEST, and one night the coal-fired heating system in his room malfunctioned and he died in his sleep from carbon-monoxide poisoning. For a while Josef worried that Hans's widow might continue to live in the flat indefinitely but any fears he had on that count were assuaged when Herta entered into a love affair with Rupert Wenger, the son of her downstairs neighbour, Frau Berger. After accepting Rupert's offer of marriage she eventually moved with him to another part of Amstetten, leaving the flat free for the first time in over two decades.

For the first time in his life, the whole house finally became Josef's to do with what he liked: a paradise for a man whose identity was rooted in notions of control and ownership. He had left his job at Zehetner two years earlier, when, impressed by his now considerable knowl-edge of construction, the owner of a Danish concrete firm had approached him to help sell its products on the Austrian market. And, with the first floor rid of tenants, he could put to good use the many skills he had learned during his career. It became Josef's 'project'. His friend Paul saw the transformation in Josef, teasing him for being a *'Bastelfreak'*, a DIY fanatic: Josef was always building something, or tearing something down.

In his overwhelmingly practical, deeply repressed mind Josef Fritzl could only conceive of the house – as he conceived of most things – as a resource to be shaped to his will and exploited. And he began to make up for years of treating the house appallingly by making great plans for its future. Now he turned his focus to property development.

The following year, on 6 November 1978, a few months after returning from his first holiday in Thailand, he applied for and received planning permission from Amstetten Council to make major alterations to the house. He had managed to turn a profit with the bed and breakfast at Mondsee, and buoyed by this success, made plans to exploit the commercial potential of the house. The planners allowed him to make the three major changes he had requested: to construct a roof terrace, to build a colossal extension to the back of the house which would function as an apartment block containing nine near-identical flats to be let to tenants, and to add a cellar to number 40. Work began almost immediately.

He ripped up the house completely. He knocked down walls and made new rooms and connected them all with awkward winding corridors. He wired it, installed proper plumbing and electricity, and filled it with mismatching discount furniture and appliances. No two rooms were the same size or shape. The corridors that ran through the house would also connect it with the apartment block, once it was built: a massive, strikingly ugly construction designed by Josef himself. Although from outside it would look as if they were two separate buildings, inside there were corridors all over the place, which meant you could walk from one building right into the other. Josef moved the entrance from the centre of the old house to the right and painted it black. This was the main entrance to both the old house and the apartment block and behind the front door was a passageway that lead into a courtyard from which a central staircase lead either up into the two buildings or, beyond a locked door, down into the cellar. The tenants who would come to live at number 40 in the future would describe how easy it was to get lost or feel disorientated there, especially as the floors of the apartment block had been built at a slightly different level from those of the house. You would come into a room and there would be stairs in the middle of it. There would be little nooks and crannies which would give you the feeling that you never knew what was around the next corner. The whole thing felt like a rabbit warren. It would feel claustrophobic and you would want to go and sit in the garden. But that wasn't allowed. The garden was off-limits because Herr Fritzl's mother had a vegetable patch here and didn't trust the tenants not to steal from it.

* * *

Various factors combined to make number 40 a complicated place for a young person to exist. The previous tenants' departure made it more isolated. And because it would take four years for the new apartment block to be completed, there would be no lodgers in or around the house until the early eighties. And Josef was changing. He had become domineering with his family, a bully who would intimidate his wife and children with a vile, often violent, temper and threats.

The main casualty of his mood swings was Rosemarie. He had been a good husband to her for many years but by the time he started building the extension he was lashing out all the time, often in front of the children. He was pushing her about and he was punching her. He was keeping her in check with his rages. Any small thing could set him off. Rosemarie had never been a particularly assertive woman and this dismayed her sister, Christine, who saw how her brother-in-law had begun to control with his fists the movements of his entire family. As far as Christine was concerned, her sister 'should just pack up and leave'. But Rosemarie hadn't been strong enough. She didn't want to. Perhaps it was for religious reasons: Rosemarie still attended mass every Sunday.

It was difficult for Christine to watch the deterioration of her sister's marriage even if from the outside they seemed to be happy enough. She had been on the telephone once to Rosemarie and heard him smashing a plate of food against the wall. Once he began the works on the house, the violence was always threatening to erupt, with the result that Rosemarie was sinking into herself, busying herself as best she could with her household chores, the Seestern, and her children. And when her husband decided to include in his design of the apartment block his very own private flat on the first floor, Rosemarie was glad. He wanted the flat so that he could shut himself away from the rest of the family whenever he felt the urge to be alone. It meant he was out of her way for longer.

He was also violent with the children. He would be in a fine mood and then he'd just turn. Slaps, punches, kicks, death threats even. He could be terribly frightening. He couldn't bear to be disobeyed. A funny expression would come over his face and he would just let rip. Being a possessive man, he also watched them. He was always there somehow, even though he was forever travelling on business trips. The children always felt he was behind them, watching. It was creepy and very overbearing. They weren't allowed many visitors. And their father would check their post or confiscate their letters for no reason. He would make detailed inspections of their rooms when they were out and he would find out all sorts of personal things that weren't really any of his business. 'If you don't do what I say, it will only get worse,' was one of his favourite expressions. As a mark of his authority, as well as a demonstration of his view of under-age drinking, he had punched his eldest son, 15-year-old Harald, in the face after he had 'caught' him sipping from a glass of sparkling wine at a party. His treatment of Harald, in particular, was very cruel. But it was impossible to reason with him. It was always easier to give in. The best way to cope with it was grow up as quickly as possible and move out.

All this made 40 Ybbsstrasse a place from which its younger inhabitants could not wait to escape. One by one they left. First Ulli, then Rosemarie, married and left the family home. Next Harald dropped out halfway through an engineering apprenticeship and resumed his education as a trainee chef in the Tyrol. Which left Elisabeth, the eldest of the four siblings who remained at home, to defend herself from her father as best she could.

Elisabeth, Josef Fritzl's fourth child, lived upstairs on the first floor in the children's room next to her parents' bedroom and her grandmother, Maria. An undemonstrative girl, more obedient than her elder sister Ulli, and had a self-deprecating manner that had always rendered her somewhat invisible in a brood of seven. When she was 6 or 7 her hair had been cut into a page-boy style and was so richly blonde it was almost golden. By the time she was 11, however, it was longer and mousier. Her personality also seemed to have become more muted. Paul must have met Elisabeth at least a couple of dozen times during his long friendship with her father, but remembers her only vaguely as 'the quiet one'.

Elisabeth was not Josef's favourite but he was quick to notice that her meekness made her malleable. There were even times when he recognized in her traces of himself as a boy: the way she retreated into herself, her dreaminess. And he mistook these familiar traits for a special connection between himself and his daughter. Something about her preoccupied him to the extent that by his 43rd year, when his bald spot was just starting to show on the crown of his head, he started watching her. And soon watching had become spying. And spying had become a feeling that he wanted to get close to her in ways that he knew would make her profoundly unhappy.

His first overture to his daughter took the form of what he considered to be a practical joke. She was only 11. He was often in and out of her room anyway, snooping about, but one evening he hid a pornographic magazine under her pillow: a surprise to be discovered when she was alone at bedtime in the dark, when the shadows of the night creep up the walls and bring on terrible feelings of isolation and defencelessness. He hid the pornographic magazine under her pillow. Then, a few weeks later, he did it again. He thought of it as a joke. He thought of it in the same way as he thought about hiding Easter eggs in the garden for the children.

CHAPTER FOUR

ELISABETH

Between the ages of 10 and 14 Elisabeth Fritzl attended the *Hauptschule*, the basic-level secondary school in Pestalozzistrasse. It was a short walk from her home in Ybbsstrasse, past Stefan-Fadingerstrasse and third on the left. She was a quiet, pretty, neatly turned-out girl, who wore her thick, blonde hair shoulder length and her white, round-collared blouses tucked obediently into carefully ironed skirts, without make-up or jewellery: a picture of compliant, small-town conventionality. 'Sissi', she was called, short for Elisabeth in Austria, the most famous Sissi of them all being Elisabeth, Empress of Austro-Hungary. That was the Sissi of legend. This Sissi, however, was an average-looking student of average ability in a class of thirty-two pupils, always somewhat in the background, much like her father had been at the same age.

Elisabeth was an Amstetten girl, born and bred. So it was odd that she was practically never seen in the streets of her home town at weekends or after school. Nobody in

Amstetten really knew her. If people noticed anything at all about her it was that she never went out: never visited other students in her class after school or went about with them at weekends, as did other children her age, in the park or at the *Volksfest*, the funfair that occasionally swept through Amstetten. She was hardly ever around, especially during the summer months, when the whole Fritzl family would disappear off to the house at Mondsee.

Her seriousness did little for her popularity. The few children she knew at school – they weren't really friends – were never invited to her home and one of the very few people who ever came close to glimpsing the inside of number 40 was 12-year-old Susanne Parb. When one day she came to pick Elisabeth up she got only as far as the entrance hall, which was panelled with semi-opaque glass through which she tried but failed to make out a few unrecognizable shapes. There was a moment of tension while she waited to be invited in, but from the way Elisabeth stood there, not really saying anything, with a meaningful but not quite penetrable expression on her face, could tell she was not welcome and after that they drifted apart.

Only two friendships were ever destined to develop beyond the classroom. Christa and Jutta, twin sisters, lived not far from Elisabeth, and the three girls got into the habit of walking to and from school together, drawn together for obvious, if unacknowledged, reasons, the way people from similar backgrounds always seem to find each other instinctively. Like Elisabeth, Christa and Jutta were from a lower-middle-class family of seven children dominated by a punitive and irrational father. Like

Rosemarie, their mother had married very young, and had given birth to her first child at 16. She wasn't the kind of woman who dared stand up to her husband, although over the course of their marriage he subjected her and her children to many physical assaults. She had always felt helpless against his temper. But there was another part of her – the part that had grown up under the thumb of another volatile man, her father – that accepted her husband's casual violence and authoritarianism as an innate, perhaps even admirable, male characteristic.

Their father, like Josef, was an unapologetic advocate of corporal punishment. He beat his children with a stick, forced them to kneel for hours on a wooden board in *Scheitelknien*, and would make them hold a stack of books with arms outstretched for twenty, thirty minutes at a time. He restricted their movements as much as possible and was miserly too, preferring them to run around in scruffy clothes rather than spend money on new ones. The tiniest thing could inspire a terrifying physical retaliation. 'Medieval practices', the more progressive parents of Amstetten called this kind of behaviour, although there were many other people in this still very conservative and patriarchal country who seem to have generally accepted that 'strictness', even when enforced by violence, was a normal part of bringing up children.

If there was a feeling among many men (and many women too) that it was a father's role to keep order in the family, that was hardly surprising. The domineering patriarch was held up as the perfect expression of masculinity in Austria at a time when its hierarchical traditions were felt to be under threat from the wacky ideologies of the seventies. The sixties never really happened in Austria, so went the joke. If you were young and Austrian and living in the sixties you'd still rather listen to folk music than pop. It was a very conservative place then. And most people liked it that way. They were proud of the fact that the country had been left largely 'uncontaminated' by the hippie culture that was sweeping through much of Europe, the student uprisings in France in May 1968, or even the political radicalism of young Germans.

But the seventies were different, even in Amstetten. All of a sudden there was rock music and drugs and women's liberation. The conservatives didn't like it, nor did the dominant Catholic Church. There were articles in the paper almost every day about how traditional families were being destroyed. Typical of this attitude was an article in the *Anzeiger* which asked: 'Is so-called free love true freedom, when every marital union can be destroyed with no shame? Is it real freedom when one can murder a child in a mother's womb?'

And at the centre of this moral panic was the threat to the role of the father, the symbol of discipline and order. In a patriarchal society like Austria the father was an antidote to dissolution and chaos. Strong fathers were better than weak ones. This was certainly the feeling among contributors to a proposed scheme that was printed in full in one of Austria's leading law magazines: 'weak fathers' needed to be taught the basics of disciplining their children with corporal punishment. It was further suggested that the state should set up special classes in which an 'expert' would demonstrate, with a rod or stick, a ruler, or a belt, how it was done. So it is hardly surprising that right up until the eighties the word 'strict' still carried such positive connotations among the majority of the population. An Austrian man could be proud to hear himself described in this way. Better to be strong father than a weak one who could not or would not raise his hand to his children.

By the early eighties it was impossible for a young girl of 14 not to notice the vast changes sweeping through the town, now that Amstetten had once again established itself as one of the country's most important regional centres for the production of metals, chemicals, paper, and wood, and for construction. And although this dramatic economic progress had its disadvantages – two thirds of the Mostviertel's pear and apple trees had been sacrificed to intensive farming; and the River Ybbs, which now received the toxic waste of several dozen factories, had turned a fizzy, congested yellow – economic success had brought commerce, and with it life, to Amstetten.

Ybbsstrasse, for example, no longer had the feel of a dead-end street in the back end of nowhere but had been transformed into the main thoroughfare into and out of the town. Although the street was more than ever polluted by the exhaust fumes of cars and lorries, many young families had chosen to make their home there. At its south end was a gleaming new sports hall. And there were all sorts of small businesses springing up along Ybbsstrasse that made it a lively, if not particularly pretty, place to live. Next to the Fritzls' was a new bakery, and across the road a hairdresser, a florist, and a Spar supermarket. Around the corner in Wienerstrasse the bakery where Rosemarie had worked part-time when Elisabeth was a child had been replaced by a smart new café, the Eberl, which served cappuccinos for the first time in Amstetten.

There were, of course, casualties of this new era. The Schillhuber guesthouse, which since the fifties had more or less single-handedly catered for the leisure requirements of Amstettners, still existed. But its once-unbeatable formula of jazz and swing, performed by amateur local bands the Flamingos, the Pelicans, and the Melodiacs, and its menu of traditional Austrian food now failed to draw young people to its door. Especially now that the town's first discotheque, the Bel Ami, had opened at number 7, complete with strobe lighting, a large glittering disco ball hanging from the ceiling of the dance floor, and several other contemporary innovations never before seen in Amstetten. The Bel Ami had a 'disc jockey' – the Austrians use the English word – usually imported from one of the larger towns in the area, like St Pölten, who played whatever music was currently dominating Austria's Top Ten: songs like Queen's theme for the *Flash Gordon* movie, or, for the obligatory slow dance at the end of every evening, 'In the Air Tonight' by Phil Collins. And while the more extreme trends that were becoming popular almost everywhere else in Europe – punk, heavy metal, goth – would never catch on in this cosy enclave of conservative Austria, the feeling among young locals was that traditional Austrian pop music was for the middle-aged. The Bel Ami's DJs never played Peter Cornelius, the Austrian singer of sentimental ballads. Every Friday and Saturday evening a large crowd would gather at the disco and the noise inevitably drew complaints from the neighbours.

The neighbours kicked up a similar fuss a few months later when a tattoo and piercing parlour arrived in Ybbsstrasse. Sweet Pain, named by its biker owners in homage to the band Kiss, was across the road from number 40. Josef and Rosemarie Fritzl were among the concerned residents who felt that the stream of people now coming and going from the shop on motorbikes, with their strange haircuts and clothes, would bring the neighbourhood into disrepute.

The were only two things Elisabeth and the twins talked about on their journeys to and from school: marriage and how to get out of Amstetten. They would get jobs. Christa would train as a maternity nurse and marry a handsome doctor; Jutta wanted to be a chef. Elisabeth's aspirations were more modest: turning '18 as soon as possible' and leaving the family home. Every day for three years Elisabeth, Jutta, and Christa walked to and from school together without mentioning the things that were happening at home. It seemed natural to them to want to protect their fathers, cover up for them. There were things that were supposed to happen in families, and things that weren't. And the things that were now happening almost constantly to Elisabeth – Josef was coming into her room and touching her – had forced her into an involuntary intimacy: he showed her his frailty, which, in her dependence on him, she was forced to hide. She knew him well. She knew his moods and weaknesses, and she carried his burdens.

Because most of Elisabeth's friends had never been in her home in Ybbsstrasse, the facts of her life inside the house were unknown to them. And now that Josef had done it up to make it look like any other house in Amstetten, there was no reason for anyone to suspect that what was going on inside differed in any significant respect from what was going on in any other house in the town.

The new flat that Josef had built for himself on the first floor of the apartment block when Elisabeth was 13 was separated from the marital bedroom by two doors, a corridor, and a staircase. It comprised five rooms: an office, a bathroom, a living room furnished with two sofas and a television, a small kitchen complete with microwave, and another room which Josef left completely unfurnished except for a single bed. And although it had not originally been his intention to actually move into this last room full-time, he soon found himself spending days, then whole weeks, in the apartment. Meals he would take with Rosemarie in the old house.

In the days when he and Rosemarie still shared the bedroom in the old house, his wife's presence had been an obvious obstacle to any intimacy between Josef and his daughter. But with the new living arrangements there were suddenly plenty of opportunities to spend time alone with Elisabeth. He moved in to his private flat permanently in 1980, a few months after he turned 45 and Elisabeth turned 14.

* * *

The coy seduction phase, or, as Fritzl saw it, his daughter's initiation into the world of sex by a real man – the phase in which he would hide pornographic magazines under her pillow – was now over. He was touching her and masturbating in front of her. When they were alone in the car it would happen. When they were alone in one of the rooms at Mondsee, while Rosemarie was busy in the kitchen, it would happen again. He would masturbate in front of her and tell her afterwards that the police were idiots and that nobody would take her word against his anyway. Or that he would kill her and that she should do what he said unless she wanted to bear the consequences.

But worse than this was his watchfulness. His peeping and spying. His endless fascination with everything that was hers. He had taken to confiscating her letters, letters that she would never receive but which her father was now filing away in a special folder he kept in his office. He was following her and keeping her in check. He was reading all her letters and finding out about her private life. So that, no matter where she was, he always seemed to be standing right behind her, an overbearing and threatening presence, anxious now that she was growing up.

The abuse of his daughter was compulsive, because he could never seem to get it right. As with the house that he would spend his entire time endlessly fixing and remoulding – trying to give it the elusive feeling of 'home' by boring holes in its walls, or partly installing a new sink, or ripping down the wallpaper but never quite getting round to replacing it, so that the place was in the continual process of being renovated, not just for a month or two, but for the next thirty years of his life – the abuse of his daughter was a letdown. The feeling it gave him always fell short of the desired effect. No matter what he did or how far he went, it never felt right. The escalation of Josef Fritzl's sexual attacks on his daughter was a symptom of his perpetual disappointment. He was expelling his feelings but then they would come back. And he would find himself wanting to be near her for reasons that he chose never to explain to himself. It got to the point where he found it more or less impossible to leave her alone.

As was usual for students of the Pestalozzistrasse *Hauptschule*, Elisabeth was transferred at 14 to the poly-technic in Siedlungsstrasse for a year, after which, had her marks been good enough, her aspirations high enough, she might have continued her education at a *Realschule*, a superior secondary school. But, like most of the young men and women in her class, including Christa and Jutta, Elisabeth now faced the more immediate problem of how to earn a living. Of one thing she was sure: she had to break her financial dependency on her parents as soon as she could.

Even at this crucial juncture the question of what Elisabeth might like to do with her life was taken out of her hands by her father, who judged his daughter to be too young and wilful to make such life-changing deci-sions for herself. The same thing had happened to Christa: her dreams of becoming a maternity nurse had collapsed when they were vetoed by her father – and she was made instead to train as a cook, the kind of solid job for which there would always be a demand, and in which Christa had never expressed the slightest interest. Elisabeth saw Christa for the last time one afternoon in August. Christa was holding a cigarette, an unforgivable transgression in the house she came from. But Christa was rebelling. She was pleased that at least in the Tyrolean Alps she would be several hundred miles away from her father.

Two months after Elisabeth turned 15, in April 1981, she graduated from the polytechnic in Siedlungsstrasse. Over the summer months at Mondsee, where her friends imagined her lolling on the beach, Elisabeth worked in her father's bed and breakfast as a waitress, to save him money. She would start her course in Waldegg, a tiny market town 12 miles from Amstetten, in September, where she would train for two months every Autumn for the next two years. It was far enough away to warrant her living there rather than home. To support herself she would work as an apprentice waitress at the Rosenberg, the 'restaurant' attached to a petrol station on the north side of the Westautobahn at the junction for Strengberg. So as to build on her experience of waiting tables at Mondsee, Josef thought it sensible for his daughter to enrol in a course in tourism and gastronomy.

That summer, there was a fire at the Seestern, and the hotel was badly damaged. Josef was suspected of setting fire to the house where he and his family had spent every summer since 1973 in the hope of pulling off an insurance fraud. He was arrested, questioned, and spent a night in prison.

The police had good reason to suspect Fritzl of arson, as they had discovered a can of petrol next to the kitchen stove. This was his fourth arrest and it revealed a disturbing pattern: exhibitionism, attempted rape, rape, attempted arson. Back in 1973 there had been another suspected arson attempt on the Seestern by Josef. When the prosecutors threw this second case out for lack of evidence, Josef went about collecting the money from the insurance firm. If Josef had intended this second attempt to net him a handsome pot of insurance money, it was a very badly thought-out scam: he was underinsured and the house he subsequently built on the site of the Seestern was much smaller than the original. Burning down the house was either a premeditated but poorly executed plan or one of the 'spontaneous' and destructive acts that Josef would perpetuate throughout his life. His extramarital 'sexual experiences' in Ghana had been 'unplanned'. The attacks on three women in Linz had been 'spontaneous'. According to Josef.

To set it apart from other drive-in restaurants, the management of the Rosenberg required the waitresses to wear the *Dirndl*. This, the female counterpart to *Lederhosen*, had come back into vogue, along with other important symbols of Austrian culture – its dialect, its cuisine – when the post-war occupation ended in 1955 and Austrians began to express their rediscovered sense of national identity in a fierce attachment to tradition.

The hospitality business in Austria had adopted the *Dirndl* as the standard uniform for female employees. Its ruffled skirts and velvet bodice were an emblem of *Gemütlichkeit*, a concept fundamental to the Austrian way of life. The word translates literally as 'cosiness' but its meaning is at once broader and more subtle. *Gemütlichkeit* is harmony and warmth: a pleasant evening spent in genial surroundings, all disagreeable thoughts left at the door.

Elisabeth wore her *Dirndl* with great pride and dignity. This elaborate arrangement – a white frilly blouse, worn under a red velvet bodice drawn in tightly at the waist and set off by a red apron wrapped around a full skirt of thick green wool – was her first-ever uniform and represented a step into the unknown territory of adulthood and independence. And although her hours were sometimes gruelling and her lodgings in Waldegg cramped and basic – a shoebox really – she now became hopeful. She appreciated her freedom. And her loyalty to the place was best illustrated by the fact that she chose to remain in her quarters in Waldegg, not just on week nights, but on her days off and at weekends. It was incomprehensible to her fellow trainees, who could not understand why she would not prefer to return home to Amstetten, where, by all accounts, her family had a large house in the centre of town. The college, with its remoteness and strict rules on relations between male and female apprentices – even flirting was grounds for expulsion – was often described by those who lived there as 'a prison'. But for Elisabeth her shoebox in Waldegg was the very opposite. For one thing, it had a lock on the door.

And she made friends. She had met and befriended Brigitte Wanderer at the Rosenberg. Brigitte was a 'troubled girl', according to those who knew her, with problems at home. The two girls became confidantes. There were other friends. Behind her father's back Elisabeth began a relationship of sorts with 17-year-old Andreas Kruzik, a trainee sous-chef. They would meet during her lunch break, but at first they were so nervous in each other's company, Elisabeth 'serious and introverted' according to Andreas, that any conversation was impossible. They managed only to stutter awkwardly about teachers and lessons. But eventually Andreas plucked up the courage to ask Elisabeth out. Things between them intensified. A boyfriend: it was a minor achievement. She was moving forward.

In one of the roundabout conversations that Brigitte and Elisabeth were apt to have in the Rosenberg in those days, Elisabeth had plucked up the courage to tell her friend about her father. It had been the first time she had breathed a word to anybody about what was happening at home and she had been relieved when Brigitte's response had been sympathetic. And when Elisabeth had returned to the house in Ybbsstrasse after those two months away in Waldegg, and when her father had once again begun to creep into her room, she and Brigitte had started dreaming of leaving Amstetten altogether. Christmas was coming and the two girls concocted a plan. It involved taking the train to Vienna and never coming back.

Work on the cellar at 40 Ybbsstrasse had begun in 1978 and never really stopped. Whenever Paul rang the Fritzls, Josef was busy down in the cellar, rummaging around, doing whatever was involved in creating storage space for the tools and building supplies that were now spilling out from his garage. Rosemarie would answer the phone and say, 'He's in the cellar.' Or, 'He's downstairs again.' Or, 'He can't come to the phone …' Josef's preoccupation with the cellar had become a running joke between the two men. 'He's in the cellar' stood in for '*Er hat ein Vogel*', 'He's a nutter', although Paul respected his friend as one of the sanest men he knew.

The cellar wasn't under the old house. Josef had studied the architectural plans of the old house and these clearly showed that it had been built cellar-less: the house, according to the plans, sat directly on top of an impenetrable slab. So it made sense, instead, to build a cellar under the apartment block.

He had made sure to set the concrete foundations of the apartment block several metres into the earth, which meant that its supporting walls rose up from well beneath ground level, with large, room-sized hollows in between them. A perfect space, Josef Fritzl had successfully argued in his application for planning permission, to convert into a cellar. The whole space was so vast and his plans so intricate that what he was now in the process of constructing under the extension could more accurately be described as a warren of interlocking chambers, an orderly labyrinth, a burrow. There were seven rooms in total, each with a specific purpose: rooms to store tools and building materials in; rooms in which Josef would build a workshop; plus a room where he would install the furnace that would heat the entire building.

To get to the new cellar meant first passing through the front door of number 40 and down the corridor, past the entrance to the old house, beside which was a locked door to which only Josef Fritzl possessed the keys. Behind this door was a flight of stairs which led down below ground level to a second door which was also locked. This was the entrance to the cellar.

In excavating and refining the space to his requirements Josef followed almost to the letter the plans, neatly drawn in red and green ink, that he had submitted to the council. He started with 'the terrazzo', the rather grand title he had given to the cellar's dimly lit and L-shaped antechamber with its three doors, all with locks. One door led to a small, rectangular room where he installed the furnace; the second to the *Abstellraum,* a storage room; and the third door to the *Ersatzteillager*, where he intended to keep spare parts. Travelling anti-clockwise from the *Ersatzteillager*, one came first to another storage room, then to the workshop, the cellar's nucleus, where Josef built a shelf unit against the wall for tins of paint, plastic gloves, pliers, and piping, and which he used as a second office. His workshop was an intensely private space: much like the office he had built upstairs, it was off-limits to the rest of the family. Now there were two areas at number 40 that Josef could claim as entirely his own, two secret compartments containing different aspects of his life and reflecting the strict delineation of his roles: father, husband, engineer, builder. In the cellar he could be both at home and separate; contained as well as shut off. Seven rooms. Every time he was down there he felt exhilarated, as if he was moving towards something. He did not know what.

Whereas he tinkered obsessively with the cellar, the new extension that squatted above it had been completed some time around 1980, when Elisabeth was 14, and he had wasted no time installing tenants, turning it into a money-making machine. The current crop were hand-picked by him. Periodically an advertisement would appear in the local newspapers, and an assortment of students, stragglers, or part-time workers would appear at number 40 looking for accommodation.

Josef preferred his tenants to be strays and nomads, the jobless or homeless, those living on sickness benefit – all plucked deliberately from the sidelines of life. The majority had their rent paid by the state, which was a guaranteed payer, and their stays in Ybbsstrasse were dependably fleeting, sometimes lasting as little as three months. On their way to somewhere else or on their way to nowhere, it didn't matter to Josef. At any given time there could be up to thirty people living in the apartments at the back of the house. There were twelve buzzers on the front door and only one marked 'Fritzl'. Always there were people passing in and out of the house. The flotsam and jetsam of life on the edge, too preoccupied with their own problems to notice much else.

As a landlord Josef liked to take a back seat. He didn't like to interfere or come across as heavy-handed but, if something displeased him which was more than Rose-marie could handle – it was always Rosemarie who would apologetically amble forth from the kitchen to ask whether so-and-so could please turn down their stereo – he would let them know soon enough by changing the locks. And that would be it. There were rules: nobody in the garden, no pets, no photographs even. Firm but fair, friendly but never intimate. Moving into the extension at the back of the Fritzl house, big as that family was, never signified the beginning of any sort of friendship.

Like their predecessors, in the time whenMaria was the landlady, the tenants had no access to the garden, although many of their windows looked out on to it. And they could see that their landlord was obsessed with that cellar, given he worked on it like a mad man. He'd built the whole thing with his own two hands. He would constantly be lugging things in and out of the cellar and what was supposed to be the garden was rapidly turning into a building site. Bags of concrete, a cement mixer, saws, electrical equipment, paint brushes, pliers, planks of wood, spare bits of metal, pipes and tubes, were constantly being carried in and out of the cellar or in and out of the house by Josef.

By the beginning of 1983 Josef felt that the cellar might be nearing completion. Already he had called the planning inspectors from the council to give it a final inspection. His mood was good. And it would be amid this atmosphere of general satisfaction and contentment with his life that, one morning, Rosemarie asked him whether he had seen Elisabeth. Rosemarie hadn't seen her come in the night before; nor had anybody else.

Elisabeth, his daughter, was gone.

Elisabeth and Brigitte left for Vienna on an afternoon train on 28 January, sleeping rough on the benches of the main station, the Westbahnhof, the first night, before a friend of a friend offered to put them up in his flat in Donaustadt, a lacklustre, blue-collar patchwork of tenements and new housing just north of where the Danube flows through the city.

Two teenage girls with no aim except to stay away from home; happy to be in Vienna for the simple reason that Vienna was not Amstetten, and big enough, they thought, to absorb two vagrant girls into its heart without attracting the attention of the authorities. At 16 they were old enough and just about qualified enough to find jobs, and they viewed this – their great break for freedom – as the beginning of a marvellous adventure without end. The first heady days were spent in celebratory mood – parties, alcohol, cigarettes, even coy experiments with cannabis – a delightful release, a new beginning, all thoughts of home behind them.

On the fourth day another member of the Fritzl household took the late-afternoon train from Amstetten to Vienna and arrived towards early evening at the West-bahnhof. Harald Fritzl, Elisabeth's eldest and favourite brother, had been sent by his father to look for her, and his instincts led him straight to the Westgürtel. Along this stretch of the six-lane highway between the train station and the University Hospital, the pavements, shabby and forlorn in the daytime, glittered with the multi-coloured lights of brothels and sex shops at night. Harald went around with a photograph, like he'd seen them do in the detective shows, and when Elisabeth failed to crop up he headed further east, to the Prater, Vienna's sprawling main park. Here pimps and prostitutes of a lower order than those who hung about on the Westgürtel did business among the chestnut trees and makeshift bars that cluster around the Riesenrad, the giant Ferris wheel known worldwide from the Orson Welles film *The Third Man*. But nobody had seen or recognized Elisabeth there either, so Harald returned home to Amstetten in disgrace.

It now fell to Elisabeth's father to call the police. This he did on day five of her disappearance, explaining to the officer – in the same concerned, fatherly tone of voice he would employ one day many years in the future in the Intensive Care unit of Amstetten Hospital – that his daughter's whereabouts was of particularly grave concern to her family, considering her sheltered upbringing and innocence. The police, understanding from Josef Fritzl that here was a girl who was more than usually suscepti-ble to injury in a predatory city like Vienna, moved swiftly, sending out the alarm to the authorities across the country and alerting the media. By the beginning of February all of the regional papers carried a picture of Elisabeth with the headline 'Have you seen this girl?'

Many parties were held in the flat in Donaustadt but on the evening of 18 February the stereo was turned up so loud that that the neighbours called the police. Had the two duty officers, in their vigilance, not subsequently followed standard procedure to the letter – which was to examine the identity papers of every single person on the premises – it is quite possible that neither Elisabeth nor Brigitte would have ever resurfaced in Amstetten. Instead the two girls were escorted into the back of a squad car, driven to the police station, and thrown into a cell, shared with a man who had been picked up for drunkenness. While one of the officers telephoned the two girls' parents with the news of their haul – it made him proud to think that they would be returned to the safety of home because of the efficiency of the police – his colleague had turned to Brigitte and whispered, 'Did you come to Vienna to fuck?' It was the kind of sly joke that a certain kind of police officer felt entitled to make to a couple of 16-year-old strays who, he couldn't imagine, had much else in mind on an escapade like this. His face turned ugly when Brigitte replied evenly that if she had wanted to fuck she wouldn't have needed to come all the way to Vienna.

It was still dark when a black Mercedes pulled up outside the police station and the figure of a heavily built, tidily dressed, middle-aged man emerged from the car. The man – who failed to mention that, not twelve months earlier, he had himself been the subject of a criminal investigation – thanked the police, expressing, in the confidential tones that are used between adults, a father's embarrassment at having to collect his own daughter from a police station.

Before he packed Elisabeth into the car he said in a voice that was loud enough for Brigitte to hear, 'That's the last time you see each other.' Then he drove Elisabeth down the Westautobahn, through the outskirts of Vienna, through the darkness, towards the safety of Amstetten.

Twenty-five years later Brigitte would come home from work at the restaurant where she worked in Vienna, turn on the television, and recognize a picture of Elisabeth above a ticker-tape at the bottom of the screen that read, 'Breaking news'. It was the same picture they had used to report her disappearance in 1983.

In the instant it took her to turn up the volume Brigitte would remember that a couple of months after she and Elisabeth had run away to Vienna the two of them had lost touch completely, partly because of the intervention of Elisabeth's father, who had imposed a fearsome curfew on his errant daughter. She would remember also that she had bumped into Elisabeth one final time on the street in Amstetten, and Elisabeth had instantly brought up the subject of running away again: her father had clearly not been able to control himself. But by that time Brigitte had a boyfriend and an OK job and she felt she had grown out of adventures. And after that Elisabeth seemed to just drift out of her life. She had left town on her own, Brigitte had thought, and possibly fallen on hard times. It was what tended to happen to girls from those kinds of backgrounds: they run away from home only to bump into another kind of trouble, usually the same kind of trouble from which they had hoped to escape. Brigitte had vaguely assumed that Elisabeth had become a prostitute.

So when she switched on the television that April afternoon and heard what had actually happened to Elisabeth – to Elisabeth, her old friend; the girl she used to call Sissi – she was sick.

CHAPTER FIVE

'THINK OF ME'

Even Josef Fritzl had to admit that he had taken on an enormous task in excavating the cellar, but by the middle of 1983 he was beginning to feel convinced that this, his most cherished project, was finally nearing completion. The warren of rooms that had been mere lines on a scrap of paper in the seventies, when he had first sketched them out for the local council's approval, had been realized with satisfying precision, and at minimum expense.

Having wired the cellar for electricity and damp-proofed the concrete underpinning, Josef had carved rectangular vertical openings into the cellar's interior walls and attached to them doors, and to the doors locks. Next he illuminated each of the seven underground rooms with fluorescent wall lights he had picked up here and there at discount. A windowless cellar needed light – this much he was prepared to concede – but he refused to squander money on heating, preferring to work in the cold rather than rely on the wood-fired stove in the boiler room which kept the flats above so agreeably warm.

It pleased him that no two rooms in the cellar were alike in either shape or purpose. In the small room in the south-eastern corner designated as his workshop, for example, he had installed a shelf unit on which he had arranged most of his electrical tools – drills, saws, a sander – along with the odds and ends, such as tubing, electrical wire, spare plugs, and sockets, that are the builder's stock in trade. He had lugged most of the construction materials down from the garage and sorted them into compartments: planks of oak and pine stood stacked neatly against the wall in the room he had earmarked for storing wood; sacks of cement and sand for mixing concrete were piled up in the store rooms; and odd items such as spare window frames and sinks, a box full of ceramic wall tiles that he had snapped up at half price – things which he had picked up cheap but for which he had not yet conceived a purpose – were given space in the room allocated to 'spare parts'. Dimly lit and dank though the cellar was – damp-proofing it completely had proved impossible: it had no ventilation, so, especially in winter, the walls farthest from the boiler room were often slimy with condensation – it was a well-ordered, functional place.

Indeed Josef had been so convinced that the cellar was now complete that in the summer of 1983 he had arranged for the council to visit in due course and rubber-stamp it: a legally required procedure to ensure that any alterations made to a building conformed to the original plans. And on 14 November 1983 a man with a clipboard arrived at 40 Ybbsstrasse to make the official inspection. Josef was proud to be able to tell him, as they wandered from one dimly lit room to the next, discussing the expert job he had made of rendering the walls, or the fuel efficiency of the log-burning stove, that what the man was looking at was all Josef Fritzl's own handiwork. 'Five years it took for me to do this,' he said. The inspector went back to his office to write up his report and approved the cellar the same day.

But, proud as he was of his achievement, Josef couldn't help but feel there was something missing. Like the house that he had spent the past few years endlessly tearing apart and putting back together again, the cellar failed to live up to his expectations – it seemed to lack some indefinable thing. This uncomfortable feeling had first crept over him in the autumn of 1983, between the time he had asked the council to inspect the cellar and the day the official with the clipboard had appeared at his door. The cellar, it had slowly dawned on him, was not complete at all. It needed to be bigger, and his instinct told him that he would have to build two more rooms which would extend from his workshop in an upside-down P-shape, underneath the courtyard, in the direction of the old house.

Had Josef been given to contemplation he might have wondered what the extra two rooms would be for. Or why he had felt the need, at around the same time, to reinforce the courtyard with two layers of concrete. But his instinct would tell him only that seven rooms were now insufficient for his needs and further excavation was now essential. And if Josef had been predisposed to self-analysis he might have noticed that whatever was happening to his perception of the cellar had started to occur around about the time that Elisabeth had run away. Because it had been after she had disappeared – or, more precisely, once he had picked her up from the police cell in Vienna and driven her back to the safety of their home – that he had first fallen into the habit of spending long periods of time underground: accustomizing himself to the cellar's smells and atmosphere, to the point where it became by far his favourite area of the house.

But Josef Fritzl was not a man who thought very much about the significance of what he did. And had he been asked – as indeed he was, twenty-four years later in a prison cell in St Pölten – he probably would have said that, more than once in his life, he had found himself in a situation that had seemed to have come about 'spontaneously', entirely independently of his own will. For there had been times when he had found himself doing something or other – loitering about on a bicycle in the streets of Linz, say – without knowing why. And although it was inconvenient that Josef would now have to start work on the cellar again just when it appeared to be finished, he had set about making the necessary arrangements. A week before the official from Amstetten Council had come to inspect the cellar on 14 November, Josef Fritzl had sent further drawings to the housing department, seeking permission to excavate two additional rooms.

The council approved this second application on 11 November 1983, but because nobody there ever heard another word about it, it was assumed that Fritzl had abandoned the project. And when, five years later, a member of the council's planning team finally rang him to find out what had ever become of these two rooms, Fritzl would tell him that he had given up on the project because it had proved too complicated. Quite the opposite was true. He hadn't given up on the project at all, only decided it now needed to be carried out in secrecy. And he had spent the following nine months – from November 1983 to August 1984 – deeply involved in burrowing out and furnishing these two extra chambers. Because he trusted his instinct he continued to carry out what he now knew to be a vitally significant work without asking himself why and without breathing a word of it to anyone.

Elisabeth had always been a keen letter writer. And although it had been a long day at the Rosenberger restaurant, where still, after almost two years, she reluctantly worked as a waitress, she now felt the urge to commit her thoughts to paper. She had arrived back home in Ybbsstrasse after her shift some time in the early evening, far too exhausted to do much else but go straight to her room, flop into bed, and flick on the television. Somehow she had ended up watching the late film: *Duel*, Steven Spielberg's first feature, the story of a man who is stalked by an apparently driverless lorry. It was not usually her sort of thing, but she had surprised herself by enjoying it so much that she had watched it to the end. For several days she had been turning over thoughts of

Ernst, a friend from whom she had unexpectedly received a letter. And now she chose from a selection a pen filled with pink ink and a sheet of plain paper.

'Dear Ernst,' she wrote in a compressed, girlish hand. 'First I want to thank you for your nice letter. I was so happy to receive it. I hope you'll forgive me for not having written back straight away, but I'm having a very stressful time.' (Her sentences in letters were always brief and to the point, not the sprawling constructions typical of many German-speakers.) 'I didn't actually expect you to write. Because you said you didn't like writing letters.' And, because she liked Ernst and it seemed silly to rule out the possibility that he might one day become more than just a friend, she rounded off the paragraph with a question: 'Am I,' she asked somewhat playfully, 'your new hobby?'

In his letter to Elisabeth Ernst had complained about the poor marks he had received in his exams – three Ds – but Elisabeth now consoled him with the news that she had fared considerably worse: 'Five Ds. So you've got no reason to complain.' What was more, her finals were coming up in June. She had always been a mediocre student, very dreamy and prone to illness but the latest exam results had tipped her over into a period of more than usually profound anxiety. Theoretically she would complete her two-year course in tourism and gastronomy once she had passed those exams in the summer. After which she planned to move out of her home. The prospect of another five Ds was the only thing in her way.

'I hope,' she continued, changing the subject, 'you keep your promise to visit me once you've got your driving licence. On Saturday I went to a *Volksfest* with a couple of people from work … We only got back at midnight, and work the next day started at three in the morning. So I had a proper sleep on Monday.' Today was Wednesday. Thoughts of Monday brought her back to her studies: 'On Monday I found out that I have an exam on 28 June. I am already terrified.'

She went on to confide to Ernst that she intended to leave her waitressing job at the Rosenberger and move into her sister, Rosemarie's, flat in Linz: 'I'll send you my new address.'

Then it was 'Bye. Speak soon.' She signed her name with a large, swirling 'S', for 'Sissi', and added, 'Write back to me soon and don't worry yourself to death!'

The letter was dated 9 May 1984: three weeks after Elisabeth's eighteenth birthday. By September she hoped to be living with her sister in their very own flat.

Just over two years had passed since she had run away to Vienna. And although that drive back in her father's car remained frozen in her memory as one of her worst-ever moments – the sight of his corrupt, lopsided face staring at her in the rear-view mirror: even in a car he was a peeper – life for Elisabeth had not necessarily deteriorated. True, there had been an exceptionally bad patch in the Fritzl household after her forced return: her mother looking doleful, not daring to say much; her father trying to play the big man by slapping his daughter under some ridiculous curfew. That had cost her some friends. But Josef hadn't been able to get around the fact that she worked for a living. And work and curfews were incompatible. Working meant getting out of the house. And getting out of the house meant that she had gradually – not that it had been easy – won back a degree of independence.

And one of the good things that had come out of the trip to Vienna was that he wasn't touching her any more. He would stare at her and follow her around in his creepy way and he was still opening all of her post and probably not passing half of it on to her. But he wouldn't touch her. And it was obvious why not. He wouldn't come near her because he was frightened that she was going to tell someone. He had always been adamant that nobody would believe her against him anyway. But when she'd run away he had been taken aback. He hadn't known what else she was capable of. And, for her, just the fact that he was keeping his distance had suddenly made life so much more bearable.

She was still fragile. She was very thin. One of her colleagues at the Rosenberger had taken her aside one day and asked her if she was self-harming, and she had told him that she had fallen off a motorbike. But she was feeling more confident now. And although her father still tried to control her and standing up to him always required tremendous reserves of courage, she was steadier now and more confident. Day by day she grew more assertive. Until she got to the point where she could almost ignore him. She wasn't afraid to talk back to him. He'd tell her that she was going out too much or that she was going off the rails. And she'd tell him, 'I don't give a stuff.' When he was away on his business trips, she started having friends over to number 40 for the first time.

Besides, she saw less of him now that he was fanatically busy on one of his building projects. Doing whatever he was doing under the house. She didn't care what. As long as he was out of her way she was happy.

Value for money was his middle name and Josef had built the cellar with materials he had bought at a special rate from his former employer Zehetner. And whenever old Frau Zehetner or one of the odd-job men who helped her husband run the business asked Josef what he was planning to do with all this concrete, he would tell them that he was building a nuclear bunker. And in Austria during the Cold War, with Czechoslovakia to the north, Hungary to the west, and Yugoslavia to the south, this seemed like a fairly reasonable, even astute, undertaking.

Everybody was building them. Austrians had reason to be anxious, after all. The Cuban Missile Crisis of 1962; the crash of a US Air Force B52 jet carrying four hydrogen bombs into the frozen ocean off Greenland in 1967; the stockpiling of nuclear weapons next door in divided Germany; not to mention the ever-present risk that tensions between NATO and the communist members of the Warsaw Pact would erupt at any moment into some sort of catastrophic end-of-the-world scenario – all this had convinced neutral Austria, geographically unlucky to be in the thick of it all, that, when it came to it (and most Austrians spoke of when, not if), the country would find itself at the centre of the nuclear crossfire between East and West. In 1969 an editorial in the *Amstettner Anzeiger* had starkly pointed out that 'the prospects for a nuclear war are becoming more and more terrible and the chances of survival smaller and smaller'. And the following year the Austrian government had passed a law which obliged its citizens to equip any newly built house with a nuclear shelter, a law which would remain in force until 1997. Meanwhile anybody who wanted to convert their cellar into a bunker was entitled to state subsidies.

In the early eighties the fear was still very real. So, although Frau Zehetner remained instinctively suspicious of Josef Fritzl, she saw nothing out of the ordinary about his intention to build a bunker. She suspected that many of the firm's clients were doing the same. Indeed, the only thing that had surprised her at all was his willingness to discuss it so openly: a bunker was something that most Austrians chose to build in utmost secrecy, so much so that even the government was never able to determine with any real accuracy how many of these radiation-proof hide-outs existed across the land. Something in the region of 2.7 million, it was estimated, of which at least half were thought to be privately owned. This tendency to furtiveness where bunker-building was concerned had its roots in two causes. First, there was something vaguely unseemly about admitting to your neighbours that you were frightened – or paranoid – enough about the future to want to carry out such major alterations to your home. And second, if nuclear war did break out, anyone in possession of a bunker wanted to be able to retreat to safety discreetly, without any last-minute moral dilemmas as to who to take in, who to leave out.

Every few days or so Josef would stride into Zehetner. 'How's the bunker going?' Frau Zehetner would ask, not entirely without irony – she had never liked him, nor forgotten his rape conviction. 'Fine, it's fine,' he would reply with a wink, then disappear with another sack of cement. He did not tell her that 'the bunker', as he himself was fond of calling it, did not refer to the original seven rooms of the cellar, but to the two extra rooms that he was now excavating in secret. Nor did he correct her assumption that the cataclysmic event towards which he was moving in his mind was based on some private conviction that Amstetten might one day become the casualty of a nuclear attack.

Now the two extra rooms began to take shape. To get to the first room, which was long and thin – a corridor, really – Josef had punched a hole in the wall behind the shelf unit in his workshop and enlarged it so that it was big enough for him to crawl through. Then there was the corridor through which he could access the second room, which measured 18 metres squared. The farthest wall of this second room backed on to the foundations of the old house.

Within the foundations of the old house he now excavated another two rooms which were, however, not connected to the P-shaped rooms but were accessible through the boiler room. Two rooms: he tiled them and filled them with the excess rubble and building materials and would leave them as they were for almost a decade.

* * *

A second letter to Ernst, a longer and more revealing one: Elisabeth sent it two and a half weeks after the first. This time she chose a blue fountain pen and baby-blue stationery, her hand sloping with the effort of writing neatly for the first paragraph, then reverting to the squashed, rounded style of her previous letter.

The date was 29 May, a day of brilliant sunshine which had burst forth unexpectedly after forty-eight hours of heavy rain. But Elisabeth had been unable to enjoy it: she was cooped up in Ybbsstrasse, off work, brought down once again with the unpredictable bouts of illness that had dogged her adolescence. 'I only sometimes have pains, and occasionally I also still feel sick,' she explained to Ernst. And, a few sentences later, 'I'm sorry about my handwriting, as well as being ill I'm also completely stressed. My nerves have never been the best.'

In a roundabout, oblique way it might have been an appeal for help, but Ernst would never detect it.

She had not been idle during her illness. In fact, she had come to an important decision. After a disagreement with her supervisor at the Rosenberger, a man she dismissed to Ernst as 'dim-witted', she had decided to find another job in Traun, a small town in Upper Austria some 35 miles west of Amstetten. With this in mind she had spent many hours combing the newspapers and sending off applications. There had been an opening in a restaurant for kitchen help. She had even written to a dentist who required an assistant. On Monday, she told Ernst, she would travel to Traun for interviews. And, for the second time that month, she promised to send him her new address, just as soon as she had moved.

There were other things that concerned her besides her job. Her boyfriend, Andreas, for example, whom she now mentioned to Ernst for the first time. 'I've been together with him since we started the course. Only it's difficult at the moment because he is from Lindabrunn. That's, of course, quite far away and it makes me quite sad.'

In his last letter, among tales of late-night parties and heavy drinking, Ernst had been bold enough to ask Elisabeth to send him a passport photograph of herself. She had searched around for something suitable and settled on a recent Polaroid. The picture shows Elisabeth beside one of her father's more frivolous additions to the house: an enormous, prefabricated swimming pool. Made of blue plastic, it takes up most of the roof terrace that Josef had recently built on the roof of the apartment block and squats there entirely out of place in its surroundings, looking more like an enormous vat – the kind one might expect to find in a factory for processing liquids – than a pool. Like many things about the house, both pools were practical, cheaply made, and strikingly ugly.

In the picture she sent Ernst an aluminium ladder is draped over the outside rim of the pool and Elisabeth is seated on one of its rungs, wearing jeans and a blue tartan cotton blouse cut off at the shoulders. Her hair has not kept its blonde colour but has turned light brown, and on a recent trip to the hairdresser's she had insisted on having it chopped into short, feathery layers the style of the day. And, although her posture is slightly hunched, she is smiling: her heart-shaped face has lost the prim seriousness of her early youth. It is an image of a blissful

early-summer evening, marred only slightly by the
evidence of her father's never-ending construction work.
Behind Elisabeth one of the gentle hills of the Mostviertel, densely covered with trees, is just about visible above
the high wooden fence of the terrace. And, strewn across
the decking are assorted unidentifiable objects, trussed up
in several layers of unravelling plastic sheeting – stored
here temporarily on the terrace until they were taken
down to the cellar.'

Before enclosing it with her letter to Ernst, she had
scrawled on the bottom of the Polaroid three words:
'*Denk an mich!!!*' 'Think of me!!!'

He had discovered what he was going to do with the two
extra rooms – the 'P-shaped bunker', the secret cellar – in
May 1984. Not before. Not even the prosecution, one day
long in the future, could find any evidence to suggest that
the crime he was about to commit had been premeditated
by more than three months. The years spent planning the
cellar, the excavation of seven rooms, the subsequent
excavation of other, secret rooms: all this he had done as
a sleepwalker who knows his way around his own home
without opening his eyes. Part of his mind – his instinct
– knew where it was all leading; the other – the conscious
part – did not.

It had finally come to him in an electrics shop which
sold remote-control devices for garage doors. It was there
that he realized what the secret cellar was for. The technology he was looking at was fairly new, but, as a trained
electrician, Josef saw no reason why it could not be

applied to other kinds of doors. And that got him thinking.

At this point he regarded what he intended to do with the cellar as a purely temporary solution. But it was a plan that nevertheless required careful preparation. Because time was against him, he hurried. He worked day and night to get the job done. The hole behind the shelf unit in his workshop he kept small so that it could be obscured, like a safe hidden behind a painting. Being a practical man, he attached one side of the shelf unit to the wall with hinges so that it could be opened and closed like a door.

Next he carried a king-size mattress and a bedframe down into the cellar and laid them out on the floor of the square room. He wired the cellar for electricity and bought other paraphernalia: two items from an electronics store, and, some plastic knives and forks. These he carried down to the secret cellar and carefully arranged them so that they were ready.

A third letter from Elisabeth to Ernst, dated 9 August 1984:

'I had the day off on Sunday which meant I left as soon as I could on Saturday. How drunk do you think I was?? First we went to a couple of discos.

'So: I usually work either from 7 to 3 or from 3 to 11 or from 10 to 8 p.m. There is also some other shiftwork … I usually have two days off a week and go swimming, play tennis or football. I like listening to music and I like being on my own and daydreaming. But if life was made of dreams then, well, I don't really know.'

* * *

To all appearances Elisabeth Fritzl came from a loving family, earned a decent living, and was looking forward to moving in with her sister in the autumn. None of which stopped her from disappearing a second time, on 28 August 1984.

Of course, her parents were beside themselves with worry. When his daughter failed to materialize the following day, Josef Fritzl marched straight down to the police station in Mozartstrasse to report her missing. It was a delicate situation for the officer in charge, having to explain to a man as sure of himself as Josef Fritzl, a man used to getting his way, that he was without legal recourse now that Elisabeth was 18, an adult, who could come and go as she pleased. And although he reassured Fritzl that the Amstetten police could be relied upon to do its utmost to find her – and hadn't they played a significant role in tracking Elisabeth down the last time she had run away? – he felt obliged to remind the father that his daughter had presumably disappeared through choice.

Now the officer took out his notepad. Had Elisabeth seemed troubled recently? It was Josef's turn to feel embarrassed. Reluctantly he admitted that, yes, her behaviour in recent months had given him grave cause for concern: her drinking, smoking, and, he suspected, solvent abuse; the late nights (only the other day she hadn't come home until five in the morning); his and Rosemarie's growing suspicion that their daughter had involved herself with the wrong crowd. He shook his head. It had, in all honesty, been very difficult to keep track of her. She showed little respect for her parents and, although she lived at home, cared little for their rules. He suspected his daughter might have joined some sort of commune. She had recently started expressing an interest in alternative religions. Behind his desk the officer silently took notes. He didn't say so at the time, but it was clear to him that Elisabeth was an easily corrupted, unreliable girl. He reassured her father that he was sure she would turn up eventually. They usually did.

PART TWO

CHAPTER SIX

THE CELLAR

Now the air grows stale and everything becomes obscure. Now things darken. Now we enter a place where little is known and we are forced to imagine. We are forced to imagine what we can hardly imagine.

What do we know? We know what Elisabeth told investigators: that on 29 August 1984, the day she went missing, the day she was thought to have run away to join a cult, that her father asked her to help him with some heavy lifting. Everyone else was out: Elisabeth's sister, Rosemarie, who had just had a baby and was visiting from Linz, was shopping with her mother. Another sister, Doris, was out for a walk with her baby in the pram. Except for Josef and Elisabeth, the house was empty.

He asked her to help him carry a door into the garage and this she had done: father and daughter together had carried the door down into the garage and set it down against a wall. You could enter the garage through the garden at the back of the house. It sloped down into the earth and was connected by a door to the cellar. A second entrance to the cellar. The other one was near the old house, next to the main entrance to the apartment block. But it made sense to be able to get into the cellar from the garage. It meant that Josef could carry whatever was inside his car straight into the cellar without having to haul it across the garden first.

They were still in the garage when Josef remembered that there was something he wished to discuss with Elisabeth, and so he had unlocked the door in the garage and ordered her into the cellar, saying that he wanted to talk to her somewhere private. Together they had walked down a dimly lit corridor and, through another locked door, into Josef's *Werkstätte*, his workshop, which he used as a second office. Elisabeth had never been down here before, nor had her mother, nor had any of her brothers or sisters. They had ceased to be interested and, even if they had been, the cellar was strictly off-limits: its doors were always locked and Josef carried with him the only set of keys.

Once they were in his office Josef asked his daughter to take a seat and, having done so, Elisabeth waited to find out what she was in trouble for. He had gone back to the garage to fetch something. He didn't say what and she hardly noticed: she had locked herself up into that dreamy, inaccessible way of hers which he hated. She was sure she was going to get a lecture. Her father had decided long ago that she had 'gone off the rails', what with her moods and answering back all the time. He hadn't liked it at all, the way she was turning out. So she waited impatiently for him to come back and give her a lecture, so that it would be over and she could go.

Only two days previously there had been an enormous row between Elisabeth and her father: the day she had broken the news to him that she was going to live with her sister, Rosemarie, in Linz. She had already moved most of her belongings out of Ybbsstrasse by this point but when she had told him that this was it, she was going, he had flown off the handle in a way she had never seen him do before. She had explained to him that she and Rosemarie had agreed that she would move in over the weekend and that it was fine because her sister had a spare room in her flat. But he had gone mad. He had lost all his self-posession. He was shouting and swearing and red in the face – he was so furious that half of what he was saying hadn't made any sense. 'You won't get out of it like this,' he was shouting, along with other things about how she was a drug addict and couldn't just go wherever she wanted. And she had just stood there, inert, trying to switch off and ignore him. All she had wanted to do was get on with her packing.

While she waited for her father to come back to the office she noticed for the first time a gun lying on one of the shelves on the wall: a small handgun that was lying there in among the tools. It had made her feel uneasy. The whole place was giving her the creeps.

He said that he wanted to talk, but this had been a lie. He had not wanted to talk; had no intention of talking; and the next thing she knew he had clapped his right hand around her face. He must have crept up and lunged at her from behind, because she hadn't seen it coming;

hadn't noticed him there, suddenly so close; hadn't seen that he was holding something. He clapped his right hand over her mouth and nose and in his hand was a piece of cloth. A faint smell: something like glue and alcohol. She found out later that he had soaked the cloth in chloroform; most probably he had bought it from a pet shop. Vets still use chloroform to render animals unconscious before an operation. He clapped his hand over her face and she didn't stand a chance. She was tiny – she weighed barely more than six stone – but she had struggled. She had kicked him and flailed about with her arms. But he was strong and well over twice her weight and she had started buckling in the chair. He had needed to hold the cloth to Elisabeth's face for a few seconds: for as long as it took for her to pass out.

When she awoke she didn't know where she was or what had happened to her. She felt disorientated from the anaesthetic and was seeing double. And she had never been in the cellar before, so at first she didn't understand the place she was in was a cellar at all. All she knew was that it was dark and that there was a smell of mildew and that she was alone. She could hardly move because she felt so nauseous from the chloroform. But there was another reason too. She realized, as gradually she emerged from the chaotic depths of an artificial sleep, that her hands had been tied behind her back with a chain.

It must have shocked and frightened her very badly to find herself in that unknown place. But worse than waking up alone in a strange cellar with her arms tied behind her back with a chain that, she could feel with her fingertips, had been wrapped around her upper arms and wrists in two figures-of-eight, then secured with a padlock; much worse than this, was the fact that the cellar had obviously been prepared for her arrival. Much thought had gone into its design. It must have been very frightening indeed to realize that this room had been done up specially. That it had in fact been expecting her to turn up for weeks.

She had awoken slumped, not on the floor, but on a bed. And it was a proper bed, not just a mattress: a king-sized mattress on a bedframe, made up with pillows and other bedlinen. Behind the foot of the bed an iron post had been screwed to the concrete floor and attached to it was one end of the chain that he had used to bind her arms behind her back. From her wrists to the post, the chain measured about half a metre – which meant that even when the nausea lifted, her movements were very restricted. She could get on and off the bed, that was about it.

Although it was very dark, she could establish some basic facts about where he had taken her. She was in a small, but not claustrophobically tiny, square room with low ceilings – roughly the same size as the courtyard of the house, directly overhead. It was quiet: no footsteps could be heard from above, the voices of the lodgers were very far away; the familiar sounds of everyday life barely penetrated the ceiling, which was low and clammy and yet less clammy than the walls and the floor. As well as the bed there were other objects in the room, and these she could just make out in the darkness: the reflective surface of a television screen; beneath it, the silver panel of a video recorder. There was a sink, too, and a toilet: he had gone so far as to plumb the cellar. But, chained up as she was, she was unable to reach the toilet, or even undress. He had tied a gag around her mouth which she now noticed for the first time: it had slipped down and was hanging around her neck.

The door to the room, she now realized, was ajar with a set of keys dangling in the lock. She had wanted to grab them but they were too far away and the next things she knew there he was beside her tightening her chains. He didn't say very much. He only told her that it was all her fault and that he had never wanted to resort to this. '*Der Krug geht so lange zum Brunnen bis er bricht*,' he said. It was an Austrian proverb: 'The pitcher that goes to the well too often gets broken', meaning Elisabeth had pushed him too far this time. She had no idea what he was talking about. Then he left, locking the door behind him. For twenty-four hours she was left there, not knowing where he was or why she was there. Shackled, afraid, not knowing what had happened to her or what was going to happen to her, whether this was a punishment, and if so, how long it would last.

What else do we know? We know, from the plans of the house that Josef had submitted nine months earlier to Amstetten Council, something about what had happened between the time he drugged her and the time she woke up alone in the room; that once she had passed out, he had laid her on the floor so that his hands were free to lift the shelf unit off the wall, the same shelf unit where, minutes earlier, Elisabeth has caught sight of a gun. The unit had been pushed up against the wall to cover the hole that Josef had made there; a hole that didn't so much resemble a door as the entrance to an animal's burrow: a narrow opening carved out roughly through the concrete wall: barely 3 feet in height, it came up to his waist. A tiny hole. A concealed, miniature entrance to a second, secret cellar that had never come into being as far as Amstetten Council was concerned, and so did not officially exist.

If you looked into this hole to find out what was beyond it, you could see only blackness.

Beyond the hole is a crawl space, big enough for him to crouch and pass through but it proves difficult with his unconscious daughter in his arms. So he enters the hole bent over double with her bunched up in his arms. Or he pushes her through the hole, then creeps in behind her. Or pulls her in after him, moving backwards as a badger or a fox drags its prey into its den. Once through this hole, he makes his way along its narrow passageway. One final door: he unlocks this, then bolts it at his back, his daughter lying unconscious in his arms. They are very deep in the cellar now, as deep as it is possible to go; they are inside the room where he had secured an iron post to the floor.

Her designated bedroom – what else could you call it? And in some grotesque way it does resemble the bedroom in 40 Ybbsstrasse in which she has lived, on and off, throughout her young life. The room he has allocated for her in the cellar has a bed and a television in it, just like her bedroom upstairs. He has equipped it with a washbasin, a toilet, and, she finds out later, an electric stove – just what you would expect to find in any ordinary household. There is a permanence about it, an attempt at homeliness even, as evidenced by the knives and forks he has provided – if these had not been made of plastic. Real knives – he knows from raping at knifepoint a young nurse in Linz – can be turned into weapons. So the knives and forks are plastic and the doors only lock from the outside. A place that could more accurately be described as an inverted version of her room upstairs: where there should have been light, there is darkness; where there should have been windows, there are cracks in the walls, through which seep the only source of ventilation: sour air contaminated by the smells of earth and mortar on its long journey into the cellar from above. The water that flows from the tap is unheated. The bare lightbulb that hangs from the ceiling can be turned on and off only by a switch on a wall several rooms away, so that Josef can leave her in darkness whenever he chooses.

There is something irreconcilable about the room, if you could call it a room: its atmosphere is closer to that of a cave; a low-ceilinged, damp, and stinking cave that sweats moisture from every surface. A cave within which he has nonetheless assembled an enormous bed, a stove, a sink, and a toilet – as if these were things that in any way belonged here. Josef bending the facts. Trying to make the cellar into something it's not. Taking what's upstairs and burying it here under the house. The room he has chosen for her is absurd. For it isn't a room at all. It is an impersonation of a room: an uninhabitable, secret, underground hovel where he wants his daughter now to live.

* * *

What else do we know? To get to the cellar on the second day of her captivity, the same day he goes down to the police station to report his daughter missing, he used the main entrance, the one that was accessed through a locked door in the courtyard of the house. He unlocked the door and descended the flight of stairs that lead into the cellar. At the foot of the stairs is a second door, the entrance proper to the cellar. Having unlocked it, he stepped into the first room: the *'Vorraum Terrazzo'*, he had called it in neatly aligned, squashed capital letters on the application form to the council. *'Vorraum'* means 'entrance hall' and *'terrazzo'*, borrowed from Italian, referred to the faux-marble flooring: a complicated procedure in which chips of stone or glass are embedded in a layer of concrete and then, when this is set, polished smooth with a grinder. For centuries the technique has been used in Venice to make inexpensive floors out of fragments of marble salvaged from other buildings. Just as Josef had used odds and ends left over from the gutting and refurbishment of number 40 to make the floor of the cellar. *'Spare in die Zeit, dann hast du in die Not.'* 'Waste not want not.' 'A penny saved is a penny earned.'

Josef, never throwing anything out; recycling everything. He had grown up poor; grown into a man obsessed with notions of property and ownership. He was always drawn to the solidity of buildings, of bricks and mortar, the illusion of stability they gave him. And he had learned to conceive in every last chipped tile or cracked brick another use. He was always fishing things out of skips, stopping his car by the side of the road if ever he saw discarded rubble in one, collecting odds and ends, broken pieces of furniture, lumps of things that were unidentifiable; all of them went into the boot of the car to be hoarded in the cellar and eventually turned into something else. '*Vorraum*': a rather grand title to give a room in what was essentially a storage facility; a name more appropriate to a room in somebody's home than a cellar. Rather a lot of effort to put into a place that was to be seen by only Josef and once, nine months earlier, by a council inspector who had been so impressed by his handiwork that he had issued a permit for the cellar that same day.

From the *Vorraum Terrazzo* Josef passed through the third door into the second room, the *Ersatzteillager*, the room for spare parts; and from there through the fourth door into another storeroom: perhaps carrying a battery-operated torch; perhaps not. He knew the place so well, having constructed every room himself, it is more than likely he would have been able to negotiate its passageways in the dark; he knew it like the back of his hand, as if it were a part of himself. Josef striding from chamber to chamber. He was not a man who liked to be rushed. The sounds of keys jangling; his footsteps; the sounds of doors opening and closing; the click of keys turning in locks; the drip of condensation on the concrete floor; the drone of the wood-fired furnace, very close by now. Josef moving deeper and deeper into the bowels of the cellar, travelling always anti-clockwise from the house. The bowels of the cellar, or, some would argue, its womb; away from daylight, away from fresh air, away from other people and the constraints – moral, physical, statutory – of civilized life. A million miles away from where Elisabeth had been packing her things into a suitcase just a day ago. But at the same time not far at all: just 9 or 10 feet, if there had been a way of tunnelling up.

To comprehend the intricacy of the cellar, one must imagine a maze of chambers and passageways, some dimly lit by overhead strip lights, others not lit at all. At its very heart lies the room he made for Elisabeth, separated from everything that went on above it by several feet of concrete and many doors, including the hole in the wall of the workshop which Josef would soon make into a door more impenetrable than every other door in the cellar, than every other door in Amstetten. And it's not difficult to see what many psychiatrists would later make of this construction, the effort he put into its assembly, the thought he invested in the configuration of this warren of rooms with its doors, keys, and locks, its underground location; and its almost mythological resonance: Hades abucting Persephone into the underworld; the many-doored castle of the murderer Bluebeard; the Minotaur trapped in his labyrinth. The dual nature of both man and house, part revealed and part hidden: a metaphor that underpins the psychoanalytical theory of Freud, of Jung, and the philosophy of Gaston Bachelard; and, before them, the stories of Poe, the fairy tales of the Brothers Grimm, the poetry of the Greek philosophers. For Freud and Jung the cellar represented the unconscious, the darkest and most mysterious entity of the mind. Above ground, in the airy light of day, our fears are easily rationalized, the experiences of our waking life release us from the fears of night. But downstairs in the cellar darkness reigns. Its walls are buried, encased in earth, the air is heavy, and we feel we are in the grip of subterranean forces. In the cellar there is no sunlight, therefore no measurable passage of time, and even with a candle we are afraid of what we might encounter in the shadows. The creatures that live here do not scamper away, as they might in the light; they move mysteriously, retreating to their holes only reluctantly.

'*Unheimlich*' was the word Freud used to describe both the cellar and the unconscious. Strange and yet familiar. Uncanny. Powerful too, because of its secrecy. From the outside it is impossible to tell whether there is a cellar at all, and how deep and dark it is.

He has brought a plastic salad bowl in case, as he delicately puts it, she needs to 'answer a call of nature'. And he unties her wrists. But not before he has wrapped a longer, equally heavy chain around her waist – this so that she can reach the toilet and the washbasin and the stove. He unties her wrists but not before he has slapped her and punched her and kicked her many times. He is not afraid to use his booted feet in order to penetrate that dreaminess of hers, to break her down. Breaking her down and building her back up again into something that better suits his purpose. Setting fire to the house at Mondsee and building it back up again. As he was with the things he owned, so he behaved with his children. 'He thought of her as his property and used her as if she was his possession,' Elisabeth's defence counsel would say of the relationship between father and daughter in a courtroom in St Pölten many years in the future.

And so the physical attack on his daughter on the second day of her imprisonment lasts about 40 minutes. He's hitting her in the face and chest, she's crying and struggling. He's putting his hands over her mouth and nose, gagging her with his thick builder's fingers. Suffocating her. She's trying to shake him off but it's almost impossible with the chains and the weight of him. And she's frightened. She knows very well what he's capable of. 'One day that pig will kill us all,' Harald, her favourite brother, once said of their father. The level of fear in that household, always very high, had become a kind of terror in recent years. Josef would come at his children like a bull. Out of the blue he would turn. Punch Harald in the face. Hold him by the scruff of his neck up against the wall so his feet dangled off the floor. Smash things up. Use his belt, use his shoe, use any old thing, whatever happened to be lying around. It wasn't beneath him to threaten to kill members of his family when he was on one of his rampages.

Very little noise penetrates the cellar from above; and the reverse is also true. Flatly, factually, he tells her, 'They can't hear you. So there's no point.' Still, she tries to defend herself. And this goes on until she's left defeated, bleeding, and cowering on the bed. Trembling uncontrollably as if she's been in an accident. Only then does he remove the chains from her upper arms and wrists to tie the larger chain around her waist.

He feels no need for explanations and gives none. He says, 'If you don't do what I say it will only get worse.

You can't get out of here anyway.' Words that he will repeat many times over the course of her imprisonment, until they become a sort of mantra: reassuring himself as much as he is threatening her. And, of course, he is right. She cannot leave. Nor can she be discovered. She is undiscoverable, given the circumstances above ground: her mother is an incurious woman, naive, afraid of her husband, getting through life by putting one foot in front of the other.

Equally incurious or naive are the Amstetten authorities. They feel no impulse to conduct a rigorous examination of this girl's disappearance, the second in two years; to explore in greater depth the clues that are laid out before them. Clues that are predominantly to be found in Josef's criminal record: the rape in 1967; two further sexual offences in the same year; a suspected arson in 1982. Clues that will before long disappear altogether. Time is against her. For the crimes of Josef Fritzl will remain on the police files for just three more years. After that they will be automatically deleted. Some of them have already been deleted as a matter of course because, despite any evidence to support their view, Austrian lawmakers are of the opinion that sexual offenders rehabilitate themselves of their own accord. They just get better. Time heals, so goes the thinking. And it is on the basis of this view that the law has decreed that any conviction for a sexual crime is to be held on record for exactly ten years, after which the ugly blot is simply erased. It is 1984. For a while the suspected arson attempt case will remain on file. But the record of sexual assaults have already vanished from police files. Most of the traces of Josef's criminal past now exist only in newspaper archives in dusty old libraries.

And, of course, in the memories of some of the citizens of Amstetten. Friedrich Laimlehner will not forget. Nor will Karl Dunkl. Both of them will, many years in the future, feel uneasy at school reunions about the things they once read in the paper about Josef. It's not their job to investigate the vanishing of young women. That is the police's job, and yet within days of Elisabeth's disappearance the police will accept the hypothesis – Josef's hypothesis – that she has run away to a join a cult, although you can count all the sects and cults in Austria on one hand: there is Otto Mühl's cult in Burgenland and there are the various international groups who are well known to the authorities and whose presence in Austria is negligible: the Scientologists, the Jehovah's Witnesses, the Hare Krishna, the Moonies. None of them has a history of making people disappear. It is a country of just eight million people.

Elisabeth is gone and the police seem not to have made a serious effort to find her. They do not cross-examine her father, they commiserate with him. They do not speculate about why a young girl would want to run away from home. And perhaps the reason they do not do these things is for lack of experience. Amstetten is a small town, after all, its citizens are obedient, and its police force seldom encounters serious crime: they imagine hardened criminals to be easily identifiable figures, outsiders, foreigners maybe, drawn from Austria's burgeoning Turkish and Yugoslavian populations who have been invited into the country to carry out its menial work. Or perhaps they do not do these things because they are unwilling to look beneath the surface of things. A horror of looking for which the officers at Amstetten police station cannot wholly be blamed. For it is a habit endemic in the culture they live in, this aversion to connecting the past with the present. It is a trait for which the whole nation is well known. Especially where it concerns a man as decent, as responsible, as well turned out as Josef Fritzl, an Amstettner born and bred. 'Give him a chance,' says the head of the construction firm Zehetner when, in 1968, fresh from prison, Josef returns home looking for a job. At Zehetner he learns to mix and lay concrete, techniques he later uses to build the cellar. 'Give him a chance,' says the law a decade later when, just at that point where he begins work underground, his criminal files are destroyed.

On the second day, he rapes Elisabeth. He has untied the chain from her around her wrists so that she can reach the toilet and basin; but also so that he can more easily force her to have sex with him. We know from what she told her lawyers that the rape goes on for hours. Then he rapes her again. The first rape goes on for hours. And so does the second. Perhaps there is a gap in between when he returns upstairs to the house to wash: he always paid fastidious attention to his personal hygiene. Perhaps he needs to check on his building work, make a telephone call or two. Tidying up some business. Placing some orders. There is nothing about his behaviour that day that alludes to his guilt. He rapes her once, and just as his shadow disappears from the wall, there he is again, to rape her a second time. He doesn't speak to her at all because, she will later say, he now knows 'he could do whatever he wanted … He was acting out sexually everything that had built up in him,' ever since she had come back from Vienna when, for fear that she would tell someone, he had reined himself in for two years. And these protracted desecrations of his daughter's body, her will, are a blueprint for how things are going to be from now on. The same thing happens the next day, and the day after that, and the week and the month after that. 'If you don't do what I say it will only get worse.' But it gets worse no matter what she does. Whether she screams or scratches his face or flies at him in her rage and hatred, whether she shuts her eyes to shut him out, it makes no difference. Over and over it happens. Twice-daily rapes of a daughter by her father. A routine. A system.

After a while he shows her what the television is for. He has bought the television and the video recorder with a specific purpose in mind. And to this end he has also spent some time in the little shop with blacked-out windows on an industrial estate not far from Amstetten. There he has bought several video tapes. And along with the videos he has bought props that he has seen women in pornographic films use. Next to where he has neatly arranged the plastic cutlery he has placed a vibrator and a whip. The knives and forks are for eating and the vibrator is for sex. Mixing things up: mixing the banally domestic with the overtly sexual, the acceptable with the forbidden; jumbling up his life above ground with what went on below in the cellar, where there were doors but no boundaries. Mixing them all up in the way he mixed cement, gravel, and water to make concrete: a process that had always fascinated him. The television is for watching pornographic videos and the props are there to help. Not long into her imprisonment he starts making Elisabeth watch the videos with him. She must use the props – the tools – the way the actors do. Right from the start he is there in the cellar for hours at a time. Mornings and evenings he sits down with Rosemarie for meals as if nothing has happened. What do they talk about, this couple who have grown so alienated from each other, during those first few months of their daughter's disappearance? 'Where is Elisabeth?' They have many conversations about that. She has always been wilful. Oh, she was wilful. Typical of her to have run away.

A month into her imprisonment. It is September, the temperature has dropped, and outside, on the hills surrounding Amstetten, the leaves of the pear trees have already started to lose their colour. Autumn is on its way. Down in the cellar, where there are no seasons, he gives Elisabeth a pen and a piece of paper and dictates a letter. Addressed to her parents, it implies – and hadn't he predicted as much to his wife and the police? – that she has joined a cult. *'Dort wo ich bin, geht es mir gut,'* the letter concludes. 'I am happy where I am.' Elisabeth's handwriting but Josef's words. And it's true, he is happy here. To him the cellar, like no other place he's ever been, feels right. Twenty-four years later the press will call this room a dungeon. But to Josef it was always a 'bunker', that is to say, a shelter. And it is quite possible, considering his wartime experiences as a child, that he does not think of the cellar as a frightening place at all. As a 9-year-old he had spent much time feeling safe and protected in the bunkers, the bomb shelters, that were set into the hills around Amstetten; burrowed deep in the earth like a woodland animal. Safe. And it is quite possible that, although the cellar is, by almost anybody's standards, a repellent place, Josef feels calmer and more comfortable here than he does anywhere else. Unlike the house which he would keep tinkering with and refurbishing in an attempt – always a failed attempt – to make it feel like home. The house was never right, no matter what he did to it. But the cellar was something else. It felt right. Even though the things that now went on inside it were all upside down and the wrong way around.

After she has finished writing out the letter – and it takes a whole week of threats and violence, of leaving her alone in the dark, of starving her, to get her to do it – he tucks it into his pocket and drives 100 miles to Braunau am Inn, Hitler's birthplace as it happens, and drop it into a postbox. Why he chose to send it from there is unclear: possibly he was there on business. When the letter arrives the next day at 40 Ybbsstrasse, Josef immediately shows it to his wife and then to the police. Many times they pore over it, searching for clues.

Autumn turns to winter. It grows cold in the cellar. Outside the temperature sinks to −10 degrees Centigrade. Snow creaks underfoot; it lies thick on the roofs of houses; when the wind rattles through the town it drops in soft clumps from the branches of trees. One of their children has built a snowman with a potato for a nose in the Fritzls' garden. Winter makes even the region's uglier factories dainty and picturesque. Even the plainest front door bears an advent wreath. Inside the cellar the only thing that has changed is the temperature. It is much colder – still there is no heating, nor warm water, and often there is no light. Already he has proved himself to be a resourceful jailer. And he punishes her for her wilfulness, for her repulsion of him, by starving her and leaving her in the dark for long periods of time. Not hours but days. We know from what Elisabeth later told her lawyers that it gets so cold in the cellar that she is forced to improvise an extra layer of clothing. At first he took away her clothes and would just leave her there naked, for weeks. So having any clothes at all is a comfort. Christmas she spends alone and chained up in darkness wearing a smock made out of bedlinen. Not many metres away her family is gathered together. Rosemarie and some of her other children have attended mass and together they now share a family meal. The first Christmas without Elisabeth. Her brothers and sisters are resentful. She hasn't even bothered to call.

In spring 1985 he acknowledges that the chain around her waist is becoming a problem. When he rapes her he often gets entangled in it, so he decides that the time has come to remove the chain altogether. But this thought throws up questions about security. He is afraid that she will escape through the door, bolted from the outside though it is. So for many weeks before he removes the chain he wrestles with the problem of how to make the cellar more secure. And, having spent a great deal of time reading all the latest literature on the subject and spending several hours in hardware and electronics shops, finally he finds a solution which makes use of his skills as an engineer. In an electronics shop one day he finds himself drawn to the new technology they're using for garage doors: remote-control devices. He sees no reason not to apply this to the cellar. He buys two hollow steel doors and reinforces them with poured concrete. They are the same kind of impenetrable, soundproof doors used in nuclear bunkers. The first door is for the hole in the wall of his workshop and the second is for the entrance to Elisabeth's room. To these doors he adds locks and bolts operated by remote-control pads that he fixes to the wall. On the same principle as the doors of a bank vault.

But just to make sure she won't even attempt to escape he tells Elisabeth that the doors of the cellar have been fitted with photo-sensitive alarms: if she opens the door from inside she will be electrocuted and gassed. He's lying of course: there is no such mechanism. But that doesn't stop her from believing that any attempt to escape from the cellar is suicide. He tells her there's no point in even trying to get out: she will be dead in the cellar and nobody will be any the wiser.

What else do we know? We know what he told the court and his psychiatrist. That he had never *intended* to keep her there. That what he claims started out as a temporary measure – a 'solution' for the many worrying behavioural changes he thought he had seen in her would eventually drag itself out over twenty-four years. He had totally convinced himself that she was on drugs and he had used this as a reason to keep her there. 'If she hadn't been taking drugs I wouldn't have needed to lock her up,' he said when, twenty-four years later, he was arrested and tried. There was no way out for Elisabeth. And no way out for her father either. The first lie – that his daughter had run off and joined a cult – had now been compounded by so many lies that it was impossible to backtrack. There was nothing he could think of except to carry on, to get in deeper. The answer had been to keep her there.

It had given him much pleasure and satisfaction to build the cellar: to transform it into what he imagined to be an inhabitable place. And, once his daughter was inside, he was quick to exercise the new freedoms it gave him. Those first forty-eight hours were the first step in Josef's deliberate and systematic humiliation of his daughter. The cellar as an isolation unit, a torture chamber, a porn film – all rolled into one.

Decades later one of the doctors who treated Elisabeth would compare her father's treatment of his daughter to what the Vietcong had done to American troops captured in combat in Vietnam. Well known for their cruelty – deprivation of food, water, light, deprivation of everything was their speciality – they tortured prisoners and held some of them for many years. 'It's easy to die but hard to live. And we'll show you how hard it is to live': this is perhaps the best-known quotation from that dark period, said by a Vietnamese fighter to one of his captives. Throughout that first year of her imprisonment Josef Fritzl was showing his daughter how hard it was going to be to live.

CHAPTER SEVEN

BIRTH

In the early days of her imprisonment, she does not comprehend the hopelessness of her situation. For the first two years she thinks only about escape. Plotting and scheming, watching and listening: all she needs to do is catch him off guard. Then she pictures herself grabbing the keys, unlocking the doors, scrambling through the corridors; bolting up the stairs, like a cat into daylight. She has a life to be getting on with. A future: a job, a husband, children. They are there on the outside, just waiting for her to show up.

In the very beginning, during those first few terrifying days of late August 1984, she had lived in a state of total bewilderment. But almost immediately after the shock had worn off, when she had gathered herself enough to grasp where she was and who had done this to her, she had made a decision. She was going to fight him. She had turned 18 in April. And with her teenager's faith in the future it had not occurred to her to think that he would want to keep her there for more than a few days. And then, when days had become weeks and weeks had become months, still her optimism had blinded her to the possibility that, eventually, months could turn into years. The cellar was an intermission as far as she was concerned. In her mind it had no permanency. Soon this will pass, she told herself. Soon this will be over. That he should want to keep her down here for ever was completely beyond her understanding.

Always, in these early days, her mind was working on some plan to escape. How hard could it be? Back then the possibilities seemed infinite: there were locks to be picked, secret tunnels to be unearthed – maybe she would discover in the ceiling a patch of discoloured mortar which would – what's this? – magically come loose in her hands, then with a plastic knife she would chisel a hole, bore up into the apartment above ... Other people had managed it. Famous cases. Every now and again there were reports of such things on television. Prison breaks. Inexplicable disappearances. Harry Houdini, the 'Handcuff King', escaping from straitjackets and chains. He has left a chisel here. 'He', as she would always refer to him. 'He', or much later, when it became plain that she had no hope of escape, 'papa'.

Although she lived in a state of almost constant pain, crying about what was happening to her, terrified of what the future held, anxious that the wounds he had inflicted on her body would not heal and become infected, none of this distracted her from her purpose. She knew him well, after all, better than any other member of his family did. And fighting her father is what she had been doing for most of her life. It was what she was used to. Father and daughter had been engaged in this battle ever since she had turned 11. He wanting to get close. She pushing him away. And yet never quite able to leave. Or else leaving, and after a while coming back again, despite everything she knew about him, everything he'd done.

Words and deeds that contradicted each other. 'I'm your father. Lie still.' And then, after it was over – when for days she would refuse to speak – he would wrongfoot her again: 'Why do you hate me?' The sincerity on his pouchy hangdog face. 'Is something wrong?' It was very confusing, his knack of being able to undermine everything she thought she knew about herself with a single word or gesture. 'Oh! Lisl's in a bad mood again! That's my daughter. Selfish and sullen as usual.' He had been obsessed with the idea – a complete fantasy – that she was on drugs. Or that she was going off the rails and it was his paternal duty to rein her in. Often she would doubt her own memory. Had it really happened the way she remembered it? She would see him and all her confidence would just go.

And now this. Ridiculous as it sounded, she had been abducted. Not by a stranger, not by a lunatic who stalks the street in search of his victim. No, surely the most grotesque aspect of her predicament is the fact that it is her own father who has taken her and now keeps her in this hole. She remembers how, as a young girl, her parents often warned her about the dangers that lay outside the house: the threat of the unfamiliar; the unpredictability of the unknown; anonymous men lurking late at night in bars or on street corners. 'Don't talk to strangers,' they would tell her. 'Make sure you're home before it gets dark.' Far better to be at home, where the strong, protective walls of the house could keep at bay the incalculable dangers of the world beyond. Home, where it was supposed to be safe. But who had warned her of the dangers of home? Because, going back as far as she could remember, the threat had been there, biding its time, not on a street corner, but right there beside her, inside the house: a threat that appeared in a guise that seemed neither dangerous nor unfamiliar. Her father. The most familiar thing of all. Who had protected her from him? Her father is both commonplace and mysterious. Ordinary and yet unsettling. He has her eyes and many of her mannerisms.

In the early days of her imprisonment the fight between father and daughter takes many forms. Constantly they are trying to outwit each other. Traps are laid. Promises are broken. No sooner has one strategy failed than another is put in its place. In the beginning she flies at him in her rages but when, chained up as she is, she realizes it is useless, she meekly promises to obey him. And then, in May 1985, nine months since she had last felt the sun on her face or breathed fresh air, he removed the chain from around her waist, and for several days there was a duplicate chain there – a chain of pinkish-brown blister-scars – and not long after he removed the chain she went back on her word. Scratching his face, determined to win. She continued to fight him and each time he retaliated so violently that there were times when she feared for her life. A big, hulking bully of a man with densely cartilaged fists, grown powerful from physical work. He didn't hesitate to use them. He would punch her in the face, in the stomach, come at her like a wrecking ball. There were times when, after a beating, she would lapse into prolonged illness. Just lie there for days, shaking and feverish. And once or twice, when she got so sick that he started to worry that he would lose her, he came to the cellar carrying a bottle of aspirin. She would see the pills and her thoughts would turn immediately to drugging him. Collecting the pills, grinding them up into a lethal dose. Slipping the powder into a drink. Poisoning him. Killing him even. She was not above murder. Her hatred was so intense she would have liked to attack him with a knife. But the knives were all made of plastic and the pills … Each time he brought her the aspirin he would count them out one at a time, parsimoniously, as if they were pennies. Then, handing her a glass of water, he would make her swallow them in front of him. Always he would sit very close. He was vigilant. Both of them were at first.

For a year she slept with one eye open all the time, looking for her chance. Determined to be brave. In the darkness that sometimes stretched out for days, sometimes for weeks, she mentally prepared herself to face him again. No matter what state she was in – whether she was starving, or shivering with cold, or stuttering with pain, or all three at once (the word the prosecution would later use to describe her physical condition during those first few years in the cellar was 'pitiful') – she remained on her guard. Counting down the days. For the situation she now found herself in was like a war. She spent much time preparing and revising her battle plan. Plotting. Not that it's easy to think straight when you are groping about in the dark, deprived of air and light. Not that your mind doesn't play tricks on you when, living among mice and rats that you can hear but cannot see, you inevitably start to wonder: how big are they? How many? Waking from a half-sleep, the sight of a spider hanging in what appears to be empty space between ceiling and wall, immediately suggests the possibility that the cellar may be inhabited by many other creatures; bedraggled, faceless, unnameable creatures, drawn by the dark and the moisture. The invisible threats of the cellar. Far worse than the pain. Always this terror of the unknown. Because the worst thing that can happen to you in the cellar is not the physical deterioration of your body: it is the inroads the cellar makes into your mind. She cried often then. It was a continual process of pulling herself together.

For a year, two years, she fought him. Then, in August 1986, something changed. Her body felt different. Her body no longer felt like her own. When her period didn't come she knew that she was pregnant, a secret she could keep from her father for no more than a few weeks. Her period didn't come and, because he was as captivated by the mechanics of her body as he had always been captivated by the workings of the drills, the metal-working lathes, the concrete block-making machines that he had spent his entire career working with and designing, he noticed the difference almost right away. He could tell, he said, because her body temperature was up, the same as it had been with his wife. And he was pleased. Upstairs in the house, during what he regarded as the happiest years of his marriage to Rosemarie, a new child was always the source of great joy. A new beginning. And he saw no reason why it shouldn't be the same down here in the cellar. He was pleased that his daughter was pregnant and told her she should be grateful. A baby is what every woman wants, he told her. He has given her the gift of a child.

For two months her body does what it is supposed to. But in the tenth week of her pregnancy – she is 20 years old and it is November 1986 – she miscarries. And from then on she is no longer the same. She miscarries, wretched, filthy, frightened, and, although she survives the shock physically, she is altered.

Winter approaches. Cold grips the cellar. The scuttling noises of vermin are more frantic now than in summer: starved, they are bolder now, their presence in the cellar more intrusive. One day, with a broom, she kills a rat: it measured 20 centimetres, she will later tell the prosecution. And the presence of this matted, dead thing beside her makes her panic. In sudden bursts of fright she will leap out of bed and rush this way and that in the room, meet with the iron door, claw and hammer at it, and then run back and throw herself at the wall, over and over again, until she is so exhausted she can only collapse on her bed and wait for the scuttling sounds to resume.

The temperature drops, then drops again. Pipes freeze and groan. Where there used to be condensation a furry coating of frost clings to the brickwork. Her body aches dully. Even wrapped in blankets, her hands and feet are numb. In the cold the cellar seems to contract, to shrink into itself, less visible than ever, and more difficult to find, clasping her in its grip. One of hundreds of thousands of cellars in Austria: who will think to search for her here?

For the first time she lapses into hopelessness.

Now she sleeps a lot and wakes up no longer caring what time it is. What difference does it make? If you live without sunlight, does it matter if it is five in the afternoon or two in the morning? When there is no sun to guide you. When the chronology of your waking life is marked, not by numbers on a clock, but by the movements of your own metabolism. Years could pass and nothing would change. She would grow older, or die, but the cellar would stay the same.

Christmas comes and goes again. Snow crunches underfoot; roads are salted and gritted; children heave stones into the Ybbs for the sheer pleasure of watching them plunge through the thick layer of ice that has formed on the surface. Then the thaw sets in, making way for spring. The skies turn from grey to a light, powdery blue. Hats and scarves are packed away. In the garden, where her father has planted cherry and apricot trees in an attempt to persuade his wife to make jam from the fruit, neat clumps of swollen buds burst chaotically into flower. Soon it is summer, with its languid weekend excursions to the lakes. Days spent living in shorts and T-shirts. Long evenings at a picnic, or at a *Heuriger*, a wine tavern, for a glass of wine, maybe two. The heat of the sun still imprinted on arms and faces many hours past dark. Then it is autumn, with its extraordinary smell, not unpleasant, of root vegetables flecked with soil and harvested fields burned down to the stubble. For miles around columns of smoke rise from bonfires, spreading into the air. Pumpkin season. For an entire month the compact, orange flesh finds its way into every soup, goulash, and strudel. Leaves curl and fall. The winds begin again. The first snows, thick, soggy flakes of sleet that barely touch the earth before melting. Then thicker flakes. Then the dead, white silence.

Another year has passed.

She remembers how it is outside but cannot see it. Cannot smell it. Instead she eats and sleeps and, in between, her father descends to the cellar: buoyant when she is compliant, brutal when she is not. The rapes carry on. Twice a day. It has become his routine, his lifeboat. Purging himself in the cellar. Up above ground there is no more peeping or spying. No more sexual assaults. There is no need.

When he is not there she observes her shadow dancing on the wall: it is like another person with giant arms and legs. Or dwarfish, with a squashed head and plump little deformed legs. It is her body but she has become afraid of it. Ever since the pregnancy, even her own body seems to be turning against her.

It is the same with her mind. All the assumptions she had about how her life was supposed to unfold, she must now review and discard. Now she regards hope, for so long her ally, as her enemy. Hope is a joke. Hope is dangerous for someone in her situation. There are only so many disappointments a person can take.

And all the while her depression deepens. All her thoughts are turning black. She gropes for an explanation. She fumbles around for a solution. But there is none. No remedy, either, for her loneliness. How will it end? Will she die here? Many times the thought has occurred to her to kill herself. She has wanted to cut her throat with a knife but he has made it impossible. Is it a sin to take your own life when your life is no longer your own? Would death now be preferable to death ten, twenty, years in the future? Her terror of waking is accompanied by an equally terrible fear of sleep. The spectre of another pregnancy. The fear of giving birth. The dread of what would happen after the birth – because another pregnancy, she now knows, is unavoidable. Her father refuses to use contraception: 'That is nothing for me,' he tells her. It will happen again. The horror of raising a child here. What would she tell it? How could she explain?

And alongside her doubts about whether she will ever escape, other doubts have crept up on her, a whole army of doubts: questions and fears that terminate in a fundamental uncertainty about who she is. 'Was there something wrong with *me*?' She has lived in the cellar for over three years. How can she be sure that she is not in some way to blame? The punishment fits the crime. What was her crime? Why had she been forsaken? There is no precedent. No example in history from which she can take comfort. This has never happened to anyone else before, ever.

If in the early days she thought of herself as a prisoner, now she knows that really she is a slave. A slave with a slave's habit, she has noticed, of deluding herself that she is choosing to obey when, really, she is obliged to. A slave who lives in a hole. 'Hole': prisoners' slang for solitary confinement. But her 'hole' is worse than any prison cell. And within the hole in which she lives there is another hole, a nothingness, growing inside her. An unwillingness to keep up the fight. When her father rapes her she no longer feels much. There is no room for manoeuvre.

'Post-traumatic shock' is the wildly inadequate technical phrase the prosecution will later use to describe the psychological state she now lapses into, a condition whose symptoms include confusion, memory loss, hallucinations, nightmares, flashbacks, and a psychological detachment from both one's surroundings and physical self. It is a severing, a disconnect. A waking sleep. Her clothes are rags. And inside the rags is a person going through the motions. Half-human, half-marionette, is her body now: he does with it what he likes. Many years in the future, under-cross-examination by state prosecutors, he will explain that in his daughter he had found an ideal partner. He desired her and she could not escape. He could have sex with her and she could not refuse. He had given her life and would think of her always as his possession, not much different from the things that he owned, to do with what he pleased. Like the house, he would knock her down and build her back up. In the cellar she belonged to him completely: 'A person all to myself.'

Now her hopes dwindle. Now her aspirations grow modest: not to be beaten is enough. One day she wakes up and realizes she has lost the ability to cry. The tears won't come. Christmas Day 1987 marks the turning point. Her will was broken.

By January 1988 Elisabeth is pregnant again.

Some time in the early Eighties, before he had locked Elisabeth in the cellar, Josef had bought himself a gun. Guns are legal in Austria and manufactured there too: the Glock 9mm semi-automatic pistol, for example, is Austrian-made. Any Austrian citizen who is deemed reliable – that is to say, any adult over the age of 21 without a criminal record or a history of alcoholism, drugs, violence, political extremism, psychiatric treatment, or carelessness – is entitled to own a firearm, and to purchase a gun you need only apply to the federal police. Josef had bought two guns: the first was a rifle that he kept on a shelf in his workshop, and the second was a 22-millimetre Bernadelli pistol. He kept the Bernadelli in the marital bedroom, 'for protection', he would later claim, although it is difficult to know what he thought he was protecting himself against. The threat was surely imagined. Amstetten, with its sleepy police station, its loosely knit community of law-abiding citizens, was an exceptionally safe place in which to live. Break-ins and burglaries were almost unheard of and when they did occur were splashed all over the front of the *Anzeiger*. It is the kind of place where dropping litter on the pavement, or crossing the road before the red man has turned green, count as vulgar offences, not only in the eyes of the law but among the local people themselves.

Josef had little use for the gun outside of the family home. But within 40 Ybbsstrasse he had often brandished it in front of his wife and children. There were other times when he beat Rosemarie so badly that her children

could hear her being thrown from one end of a room to
another: dull thumps from the other side of a wall or
closed door, the sounds of whimpering and shouting. As
a result of these attacks, once or twice she had ended up
in hospital, Elisabeth or one of her other daughters –
never her husband – at her side. There would be bruises
all over her body, open skin. Once, and this had happened
in front of Elisabeth and her brother Harald, he had sent
his wife flying across the room. He had fractured her
femur and Elisabeth had had to take her mother to hospital. Yet, even in the comparative safety of an emergency
ward, Rosemarie would make up some excuse about
falling down the stairs. Because she knew what would be
waiting for her at home, knew that by the time she
returned he would be even more worked up than when
she'd left. A time bomb. He could be lethal then. There
had been quite a few episodes between husband and wife
where he had ended up threatening her with the gun.
You never knew with him if he meant it as a joke. Often
he'd laugh. Then he'd turn on her again. Throw crock-
ery all over the floor. There would be food and broken
plates everywhere and then he would say, 'Where's
dinner?'

So, in buying and brandishing the gun, Josef sought to
protect himself against any threat to his own authority,
real or perceived. With a gun in his hand he felt safer.
The big man. Even at the best of times he had difficulty
trusting people, and always felt burdened by the feeling
that he was on the verge of being betrayed: by his family,
by the people he worked with, by just about anyone,
unless they were firmly subordinated and under his

thumb. It was always power games with Josef. Trusting no one, he liked to have one up on other people. He liked to know something they did not know, have something over them. He liked to keep secrets. Not that it was obvious from looking at him. 'Helpful', 'energetic', 'entertaining', 'bright': these were the words most often used to describe Josef Fritzl by the people he worked with and his neighbours. Amstetten's police and social workers would always think of him as an easy-going, upstanding man, 'one of us'. They were completely unaware of his watchfulness. They did not guess at the profound split inside him. Josef feared and distrusted other people all of his life. Other people were the threat. And the biggest threat of all was other men.

Other men, according to Josef, had corrupted Elisabeth in her youth. The root of the problem that had resulted in his having had to lock Elisabeth in the cellar could be traced back to her childhood, he maintained. Many years later, under cross-examination by the police, he would claim that she had been molested by an 'uncle Franz'. He may or may not have existed. 'Franz Fritzl', a '*Kindlerfummler*', or 'kiddy fiddler', had an unnatural interest in children and when she was just 8 or 9 he had turned his gaze on the fragile Elisabeth. Somewhere along the line, on some holiday, or in some secret place when her parents were busy doing something else, Franz had 'done something' to Elisabeth. Josef wasn't sure what. He had touched her, maybe more, in a sexual way and then paid her money not to say anything. And whatever uncle Franz had 'done' to Elisabeth had messed her up in the head, had made her sexually precocious. So by the time she was 12 or 13 she was wild. She would 'have sex with the builders' who occasionally came by the house. She would have 'sexual experiences' with boys who came to visit. She was having 'sexual experiences' with just about anyone who came near her. He had found letters once, addressed to Elisabeth from a married man. On another occasion he had caught her in bed with a boy. She was flagrant and out of control, if you believed Josef. Any father would have been concerned.

And so when, aged 16, she had run away to Vienna, he had been beside himself with worry. He sent Harald to search for her, and when Harald failed, he called the police. Thank God they had found her. But he wasn't satisfied. He wanted to reassure himself and so resolved to find out exactly what had happened in Vienna, exactly what sort of trouble she was in. And he drove all the way back there to talk to the boys in the flat she had been staying in, and discovered they belonged to a gang called *Die Lederjacken*, the Leather Jackets. And they were dangerous, this gang with which she had involved herself. More of a crime ring than a gang, they had intended to turn her into a prostitute. They were waiting until she had turned 18, then they would pimp her out to whoever and live off her earnings. Already they had introduced her to glue-sniffing and illegal drugs. She was out of control already: hysterical, volatile, angry, a trouble-maker with no respect for authority. She had gone off the rails. Tripped off the deep end. What kind of father wouldn't have been worried? And the only reason he had put her down in the cellar in the first place was to teach her a lesson. He hadn't intended it as a long-term arrangement: he had

just wanted to talk some sense into her. It was only afterwards that he, in his words, 'began to see her as a
woman'. If you believe Josef.

Years later it would become clear that he had made it
all up. There was no gang, no glue-sniffing, no imminent
descent into prostitution. These were people and events
that Josef had manufactured in his mind. They were
things that he had gleaned from television and, in his
paranoid imagination, they had calcified into fact. Elisabeth would remember him, in the early eighties, getting
very worked up about a government-sponsored anti-
drugs campaign that was showing on television which
featured two young girls getting high on cleaning products. And it is likely that the image became imprinted on
his mind. When she came back from Vienna he had
pestered her for information: 'Where did you stay? Who
were those boys? Did you have sex? Whose bed did you
sleep in?' For weeks he went on at her until her mother
told her to tell him. And so, in the end, she told him, and
off he went in the battered old Mercedes to Vienna. But
the 'information' he had come back with, it was all pure
fiction, right down to the gang's name. At that time
young men everywhere were wearing leather bomber
jackets, so he had called them *Die Lederjacken*. There was
no gang, no plan to prostitute her.

There was no child abuse at the hands of an uncle; no
married man, builders, or boys in her room. Most likely
these were all projections of his own desires. Josef the
trusted relative, molesting his young daughter. Josef the
married man, making sexual overtures to Elisabeth. Josef
the builder, having sex with her all over the house. Other

men: that old threat. Different versions of himself from which he wanted to distance himself. She always had the feeling he wanted to project things on to her that had nothing to do with the truth. At some point in her mid-teens she had written letters to her brother Harald about what her father was doing to her. And from the Tyrolean Alps, where Harald was then working as a cook, he had sent a ten-page reply to his sister in which he made clear his anger with their father. The letter still exists: it was found by police in April 2008 in among many other letters that had been sent to Elisabeth but which she had never received. They had been intercepted by her father. He had always needed to make up reasons and justifications for his behaviour. It was because of what he had allegedly found out in Vienna – a criminal gang – that he had needed to buy a gun. 'Protection'. He had no real use for a gun. But he was a man obsessed with his own virility and a gun was a symbol of that.

Elisabeth later said she never took drugs but believed he might have liked it to have been true – then at least he would have had reason for his actions.

On 30 August 1988 a child is born in the cellar of 40 Ybbsstrasse. It is born in the dark, without medical assistance and without complications. But, because the mother is alone and lacks experience in such matters or recourse should something go wrong, the labour is a terrifying ordeal.

She is quite unequipped for the birth: she has at her disposal one pair of scissors, one blanket, and a packet of nappies. It was Josef who gave Elisabeth the scissors and the extra blanket. And it was he who had travelled several miles out of Amstetten to buy nappies at a super-market in Linz where nobody would recognize him. In response to her repeated panicked entreaties he had even, seven months into her pregnancy, bought her a book on childbirth. It was from studying its contents that the young, terrified mother-to-be had gathered the basics of birth and child rearing. She had read all about what it might feel like when her waters broke; and she had known what to do. She had taught herself how to breathe and push once the contractions had started.

She has never done this before; does not know where it will end. Then, after it is over, she must cut the umbil-ical cord herself, and for this purpose she has been given a pair of kitchen scissors. She has read that severing an umbilical cord appears a straightforward procedure but may have deadly consequences. In days gone by, thou-sands of new mothers before her died of puerperal fever, a form of septicaemia, through lack of basic hygiene. The cellar is filthy. The scissors may be filthy too. Exhausted and blinded by the darkness, she boils up some water on the portable stove and douses them in the pan. Once the water has evaporated from the scissors – she dares not dry them on one of the unwashed bed sheets – she cuts the cord. Once it is over she can't quite believe that she has managed it. At the foot of her bed lies, gasping and shout-ing for breath, a tiny baby girl. The mother looks at her with ambivalence.

Then she swaddles her new-born child in a blanket and for a little while the baby sleeps. The heavy, late-

Above and right: Josef Fritzl, aged 16, posing for a photo with his secondary school classmates, June 1951.

The widely circulated police photo of Josef Fritzl, taken on 28 April 2008, the day he confessed to holding his daughter Elisabeth captive for 24 years.

Elisabeth Fritzl as a young teenager.

Austria

Amstetten

Ybbsstraße 40

800m

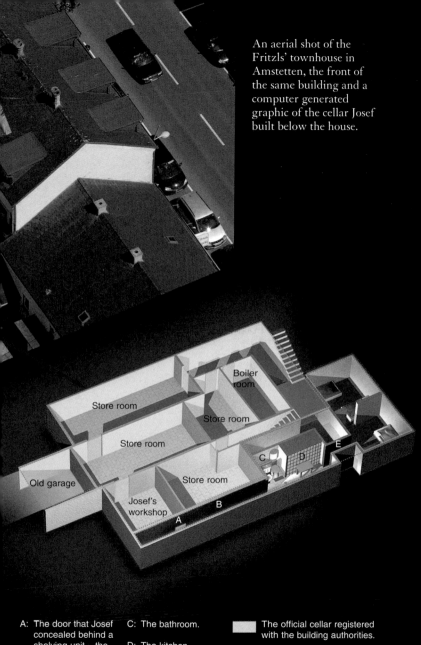

An aerial shot of the Fritzls' townhouse in Amstetten, the front of the same building and a computer generated graphic of the cellar Josef built below the house.

Boiler room

Store room

Store room

Store room

Store room

Old garage

Josef's workshop

A

B

C

D

E

A: The door that Josef concealed behind a shelving unit – the main entrance to the dungeon.

B: The corridor leading to the dungeon.

C: The bathroom.

D: The kitchen.

E: A narrow corridor to the bedrooms that were added in 1993.

The official cellar registered with the building authorities.

The secret section of the cellar that was not registered and was used to imprision Elisabeth and her children.

Police handout images of the cellar Josef Fritzl constructed beneath his house.

Seen here are the bathroom (*top left*), the cellar entrance (*top right*), and the narrow corridor along to Elisabeth's bedroom (*left*).

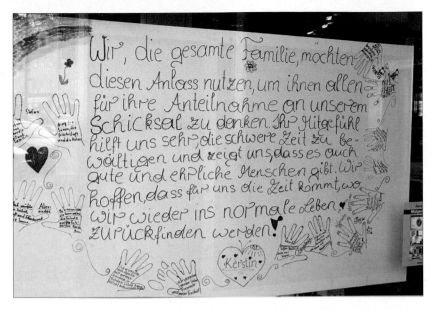

A poster painted by the family of Josef Fritzl and hung in the main square of Amstetten to thank the public for their support. This is the first and only statement made by the Fritzl family. Elisabeth's section *(below)* reads: 'Wishes: Recovery of my daughter Kerstin, love of the children, protection of the family, warm-hearted people and understanding.'

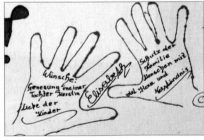

Thousands gathered in the main square in the weeks following Josef's confession to show their solidarity with the victims. People demonstrated all day and held vigils all night *(left)*.

Dr Albert Reiter, the doctor who oversaw Kerstin Fritzl's medical treatment.

Chief police investigator, Franz Polzer.

Defence lawyer, Rudolf Mayer.

Elisabeth Fritzl's lawyer, Christoph Herbst.

Journalists taking their positions on a media platform outside the front of the provincial court house in St Pölten.

Josef Fritzl covers his face with a ring-binder as he takes his seat in the St Pölten courtroom on the first day of his trial, March 2009. The prosecutor, Christiane Burkheiser, is on the far left.

Josef Fritzl in court, March 2009.

summer air has somehow percolated down into the cellar. Elisabeth is twenty-two years old. Four years ago, almost to the day, she woke up for the first time in this dank and forgotten place. Now it is her infant daughter's turn. What will become of them, mother and child? For ten days they sit in the dark and wait.

The child's father is also her grandfather. This 53-year-old man has lived in the house in Ybbsstrasse since his own childhood, and his solid marriage, his brood of seven children, and his career – first as a mechanical engineer and more recently as the Austrian representative of a Danish concrete firm and owner of his very own B&B – has earned him considerable respect in the local community. He is the kind of man about whom it is often said, '*Er hat alles im Griff*': 'He has everything under control.' A man to be counted on: meticulous, punctual, diligent, capable. A 'doer'. The child who has just been born in the cellar is his eighth.

Yet, despite his reputation for dependability, he has been conspicuously absent from the birth of this child. Normally he is down in the cellar every single day. But he hasn't shown his face during the birth, nor will he show his face for the next ten days. We may never know why he chooses to disappear from the cellar at this time and for so long, but it seems likely that, wishing to shield himself from responsibility for the death of mother or child, or both – should these have occurred – he simply absents himself. He is a man allergic to being morally implicated in any unpleasant scene. And so, for ten days, he happily potters about in the world above, no more or less preoccupied than usual, no more or less agitated, or short-tempered, or lost in thought. Nothing about his behaviour suggests that there is anything unusual or untoward going on in some secret part of his life. And such is his capacity for shutting himself off from unwanted thoughts that he spends these pleasantly warm days of late August and early September busying himself with building projects, ordering cement, updating his accounts, collecting rent from his tenants, and making little trips to the local nursery to buy plants for his garden while, beneath his feet, his daughter heaves and struggles with the agony of birth. As with the mother – who whipped him and beat him without apparent remorse – so it is with the son. Something is missing from his personality: not there where it should be. When he breaks the law, or crosses a moral boundary, or inflicts on another person some mental or physical torment, it does not make him feel wicked or depraved – although he is more than aware of what the law would say. It makes him feel courageous and unique. Indestructible and above the common man. Divine, almost: for he is always quick to condemn the villainy of others. When rapes or abductions are reported on television, or when he reads about them in the newspapers, he shakes his head in disgust. It makes him very nervous to think that such people exist in the world.

Josef Fritzl was not burying his feelings when, in late August and early September 1988, he went about the garden of 40 Ybbsstrasse, digging up the earth to plant raspberry canes and blackberry bushes. There were no feelings there to be buried. There was no guilt. No remorse. There he is contentedly forking the soil with the sun on his back: a watchful, controlling, paranoid man who is quite able, when he so chooses, to exist in a state of deliberate obliviousness.

Two years after Kerstin is born there is another child, a boy. Stefan comes into the world in February 1990. And then, two years later, Lisa is born, in August 1992. Monika, the fourth child, arrives in February 1994. A conveyor belt of children. Twins, Alexander and Michael, are born in April 1996. Finally, in December 2003, Felix. Seven children in total. Born, one after another, over a period of fifteen years. At some of these births the father will be present, at others not. He won't remember which. Some of these children will be more fortunate than others. But whether they will become ill and die, or be happy, be destined to live down in the cellar or above ground in the light, will depend entirely on the whims of their father.

CHAPTER EIGHT

THE DARKNESS

Some time around the birth of her first child in August 1988, when Elisabeth was 22, Josef gave her a notepad. He hadn't paid for it, of course. It was the kind of notepad banks give away free to their customers. The Raffeisen Bank, in this case, which has a branch in the centre of Amstetten, around the corner from Wiener-strasse, where, in the early, cash-struck days of their marriage, while her husband climbed the corporate ladder at VÖEST, Rosie had once worked in a bakery. Josef had been a loyal and valued customer of Raffeisen for over two decades. And although the notepad was nothing more than a flimsy giveaway, he presented it to his daughter, in one of the generous moods he was apt to fall into more and more frequently as his double life evolved, as a favour and a gift.

Elisabeth had been terribly grateful, of course, for the arrival of the notepad in the cellar was to be a life-changing event. She had been living beneath 40 Ybbsstrasse for four years now, chronically disorientated. Her father liked her best when she was helpless, she would later say, and one of the many things he had done to keep her in a position of complete subordination and vulnerability was to refuse her requests for a watch or a clock. Often he would stage week-long blackouts in the cellar, but even with the lights on she had existed in that murky place with no real sense of time, wholly detached from the rhythms of ordinary life, dependent on her father for much of her information. She had the television but for many months she had been unable to watch it at all. She had always considered it an alienating presence, telling her very little about her friends, her family, or the small-town life she had been forced to leave behind. And, except for the rising and falling temperature of the cellar and whatever Josef chose to tell her, the years had gone by, marked not by times and dates, but by the physical and mental events of her imprisonment. Moods and phases: cycles of illness and comparative good health; long, empty stretches of loneliness and anxiety; blank periods of numbness, violent episodes of confusion. She had no idea how long each phase or mood had lasted.

'Four years': the phrase was almost meaningless. There was summer, when it was swampy and hot in the cellar, and winter, when it was cold. In between there were the things that had happened, the significant events of the cellar: the first pregnancy, then a miscarriage; a second pregnancy, the miraculous birth of a child. And the less significant and yet memorable occurrences she would store up in her head for years to come: a toothache for which Josef had been persuaded to buy her a bottle of camomile mouthwash from the local pharmacy; the tick that she had found on Kerstin's belly and had eventually managed to remove with a pair of tweezers. He had gone on holiday once and left her alone for two weeks and she had panicked when the electricity supply had cut out. It had been very cold and she and the infant Kerstin had spent ten days in complete darkness, under a mouldy blanket, with Elisabeth trying to warm up the bottle of formula milk with the heat of her body. All of this set against a background, when he was there, of casual violence, frequent rape, and pornographic videos. Four years which in many ways didn't feel like four years. Time expanded in the cellar. It could just as easily have been ten.

But the notepad changed all that: she had decided to use it as a diary, dividing it up, on both sides of every one of its pages, into months and weeks and days. And her diary put her back in step with the world above. With the diary, which had Raffeisen's yellow and black slogan, *'Wir machen den Weg frei'*, 'We Pave the Way', stamped on all of its pages, Josef had granted his daughter a degree of autonomy. His gift. Her reward for having given in. Nineteen eighty-eight: the year the then president of the former USSR, Mikhail Gorbachev, initiated Perestroika, an overall reform of the Soviet communist system; the year that Kurt Waldheim, formerly Secretary-General of the UN and the then President of Austria, was implicated in the Second World War deportation of Jews to death camps. Irrelevant events to a young woman scratching out an existence underground. And the first thing Elisabeth had done with the diary was to write in the birthdays of all her brothers and sisters. Innocuous little reminders to herself to which Josef was unlikely to object. But still she was careful. And she kept the diary hidden under a pile of dirty washing.

Up until then she had been keeping a record of sorts on scraps of paper, old receipts he had left in the cellar, strips of cloth torn from bedsheets, anything she could get her hands on: roughly scribbled secret notes that she would screw up into little balls and secrete in corners of the room. In time she would begin to commit her thoughts to the diary instead. And she would later say that she started to think of the diary as a kind of historical 'document'. A chronicle of her life underground. Something that she hoped, one day, to be able to pass on to her children. Many years later the prosecution would use what Elisabeth had written in the diary as evidence against her father. But she would always maintain that it had never been her intention to incriminate him. That hadn't been the point. By the time she started scribbling little entries into the diary she had given up all hope of escape.

When, in April 2008, the police would finally raid the cellar of number 40 they would find a total of 15 diaries stacked neatly on a bookshelf covering the period between 1988 and 2008, with some years missing. The diaries dating from 1989, 1990, 1991, and 1992 would be improvised notepads. The rest were of the corporate variety that Josef had taken to picking up for free at the bank. And it would be clear to the police from the contents of these diaries that not only had Elisabeth been aware of how life was unfolding for her mother and siblings above ground, but that the things that were happening in their lives had become terribly important to her. Above ground, many of the people who had known her as a teenager would eventually write her off and come to think of her as a lost cause. Hardly any of them had bothered to look for her. But, downstairs in the cellar, they had always been on her mind. During her years in the cellar they had existed for her more vividly than it was possible to imagine.

Most of her entries are mundane, no more than a sentence long – annotations, really – with exclamation marks if she had been particularly pleased about whatever had come into her head that day. No mention of rapes, nor of beatings. No references to 'Josef', only of 'Him' or 'He' and latterly 'Papo'. Short and discreet. Nothing too emotional or descriptive. Nothing that was likely to bring on one of his rages. And it was to become something of a ritual between the two of them: his gift every year around Christmas time of a free notepad or diary, and her hiding it under the dirty clothes, where he seemed unlikely to look but would always end up finding it. Many diaries filled up over the years with the tiny events of her life: her bother's birthday; milk running out; Josef buying them ice cream, sausages, and liver dumplings.

* * *

With cheap gifts and news from above Josef kept her alive. With stories of his life outside the cellar he thrilled as well as tortured her. He would tell her when one of her sisters was expecting a baby, or how fast her little nieces and nephews were growing up. He would talk to her in particular about his construction work, his many plans, the pool with a sauna he had recently started to build on the terrace to replace the plastic one that used to be there. He also told her about how he had built a second, all-weather pool in the garden and had decided to fill it with salt water. In summer it had become his habit to go for a swim in the downstairs pool, then stretch out in the garden to get a tan. He was terribly proud of the pool and described it in great detail to Elisabeth. In summer temperatures in the cellar often exceeded 30 degrees.

Elisabeth, his confidante. Towards the fifth year of her imprisonment this would become another of her roles. 'My wife', as he now began to think of her. By the early nineties, with the approach of the couple's fortieth wedding anniversary, Josef and Rosemarie were still on 'friendly terms', he would later say, but their interactions had become practical and distant. He would show up only for meals, working the rest of the time or disappearing on 'business trips' that were often, unbeknown to the rest of his family, spent overnight in the cellar.

It was one of the defining characteristics of his personality that Josef would never have a problem with holding two contradictory ideas in his head and accepting them both as true. He could be a caring father who beat up his children. A stalker of women who found himself peeping through their windows 'by chance'. A control freak who tended to think of himself as a victim of circumstance whenever his sexually delinquent behaviour came to light. A philanderer and convicted rapist who, when he was eventually interrogated by the police in late spring 2008, would claim that 'one woman was enough for me'. The more Josef had alienated himself from his wife during this period, the closer he felt to his daughter. It was to Elisabeth that he started to open his heart, sharing all his hopes and fears, discussing with her his many plans for the future: property empires, more work on the house – it was impossible to tell whether he meant it or not. This transfer of 'wifely duties' from Rosemarie to his daughter started to happen after the birth of Kerstin in the autumn of 1988. He was raping Elisabeth and pouring out his heart. He was entrusting her with all of his secrets. In time there was hardly anything she didn't know about her father.

Her awareness of what was going on above her head was to have a very specific effect on Elisabeth. The desired effect, as far as her father was concerned: she began to live vicariously through him. It is not difficult to understand how the stories he told her about the world above made her existence more tolerable; how, furthermore, she began to crave these stories; and how life as she imagined it upstairs felt in many ways truer than her own. Downstairs in the darkness was her body, upstairs in the light was her mind. And through this process of story-telling, of opening himself up to her, of throwing her scraps of information about the life upstairs – her alternative life – he was assimilating her. Breaking down the boundaries between himself and his daughter, drawing her into the double life. A secret is only powerful so long as it isn't shared. And Josef's secrets had made him feel very powerful indeed. But he had been lonely in his secret life, existing on two levels at once. He had longed for a person with whom to share both his lives, and he made his daughter an accomplice.

She would go about the cellar in 'a trance', he would later complain. It was her way of coping. And in her trance-like state, after the birth of Kerstin, a strange thing began to happen to her way of thinking. She had started to settle in. She had started to accept all the privations of the cellar as a normal part of her life: partly because she had given up hope – 'You haven't got a chance,' he had told her often enough for her to believe him – and partly because of the new responsibilities that came with motherhood. With the birth of her children, Elisabeth's priorities had changed: not to fall apart, not to commit suicide, this now became the aim. And, seeing this change in his daughter, he had at last presented her with the gift of an alarm clock, which she took to setting each day for 6.30 a.m. Up at dawn. In bed by 10 p.m. The everyday routines of domesticated life. The cellar, which by 1994 had begun to hum with the rhythms of everyday life. There were good days and bad days, petty annoyances, just as in any household. The day the colour in the television stopped working. Mould had infested the electrics. For a while it stuttered on in black and white, but eventually Josef was persuaded to replace it. More proof that 'I was a good father', he would later claim. 'I provided for my family.'

There were food shortages: there were times when all they had to eat was stale bread and Elisabeth would have to chew it up with water to feed it to her babies. When there was water. One exceptionally cold winter the pipes had frozen and the water hadn't come out of the taps at all. And as much as they hated him there, they were also afraid in case he never came back. Always there was the fear that something would happen to him or that he'd leave them there and they'd never be discovered or they'd suffocate: the air was stifling at the best of times and they relied on an electric fan. Of course, when he'd punished them by cutting off the power supply, the fan would stop and they would be afraid that they wouldn't be able to breathe at all.

There were other gifts beside the alarm clock, at five- or six-month intervals but gifts nonetheless, her only possessions. One of these was a weighing scale. Her weight had teetered at just over six stone in her teens but was now stable at around ten. And he would bring pictures of the rest of the family, doing whatever they were doing, upstairs in the house, in the garden or at Mondsee. The lives of Elisabeth's siblings documented in photographs by her father from one month to the next; from year to year: information upon which she became dependent. When the police raided the cellar in April 2008 they would find its walls covered with photographs. Among other things – sex toys, pornographic videos, handcuffs, a whip – they would confiscate from Josef a total of five cameras, as well as a photograph album that he had given to Elisabeth. Of all the evidence the police and lawyers would have to sift through in the run-up to

Josef Fritzl's trial, the contents of the photograph album proved to be the most difficult to look at. In the front of the album were pictures from upstairs: brightly coloured snapshots of a normal family. At the back were some very different photographs: badly lit pictures of the family Josef had made live in the cellar, their faces bone-white, their expressions uncanny. Two very different existences lived practically side by side for twenty-four years. The only thing connecting them was Josef.

In the cellar Elisabeth often found herself worrying about becoming pregnant. Then these concerns were dashed when she discovered once again the worst had happened.

And towards the middle of 1989, a few weeks before Kerstin's first birthday, Elisabeth conceived for a third time. Stefan, her second child, was born in the cellar of number 40. Another child born in darkness without assistance or even the presence of the father. Another miraculous survival. It was even more astonishing that Kerstin and Stefan grew up and developed into relatively healthy children as, despite the obvious hazards of living in the cellar, the children and their mother had no access to any medical help.

Two years after Stefan, there was another child, another girl. Lisa was born in August 1992: like her sister Kerstin, her birth happened to coincide with the anniversary of her mother's abduction. Little Lisa was born a healthy baby but became inexplicably distressed by the time she was eight months old. She wouldn't stop crying no matter how often her mother carried her in her arms to and fro between the walls of the cellar. A screaming baby didn't do much for 'Papo's' temper: he feared that the noise of the child might be heard upstairs, just as the noise of the lodgers playing their music too loud travelled all over the house. Before he kidnapped Elisabeth he had tested the cellar for soundproofing by bringing down a radio and playing it loud, then going upstairs to check if he could hear it. But now he was always worried about the noises of the children. He had already hit 2-year-old Stefan in the face and split his lip because he was crying. But, no matter what her mother did, Lisa wouldn't stop crying. It soon became clear that she wasn't at all well, although the cause of her distress remained a mystery to both her parents. Only after her father had laid Lisa in a cardboard box, taken her upstairs, and made a convincing show of having discovered the 'abandoned' child on his doorstep, would she be rushed to hospital, to undergo emergency heart surgery. Below ground it was a torment for her mother who felt she would go mad with worry.

The year 1993 was to be a period of frantic activity in Josef's life, above ground and below. The apartment block was full of tenants: drifters, students, and unemployed people mainly, people who lived at life's margins, a ragtag bunch of builders and waiters drifting from job to job, distributed among the five ground-floor flats and the four smaller flats on the first floor. Among them were two couples, the Seiberts and the Swobodas, about whom nothing much was known; three female students who shared an apartment; Ludwig Jedlinek, a Slovak lorry driver; and Sepp Leitner, a waiter and part-time builder who had moved into one of the flats with his Romanian wife in 1990. Leitner's marriage had collapsed not long after his arrival at Ybbsstrasse, but he would continue to live in the flat for four years, eventually giving up his restaurant job for a more lucrative living as the manager of a strip club in the nearby town of Haus Menning. Although spiralling debts would eventually finish off that business in 2007, to this day he is affectionately greeted in the streets by the girls who once depended on him to earn their living.

Behind the garden of number 40, old Frau Danielzyck was often to be seen planting or picking fruit in the plot of land that she had been renting there since 1979. She had moved to Amstetten back in the fifties with her husband, a former hat-maker who had fled Communist Poland to make a new life for himself as a manager with the local concrete producer Umdasch. You could hardly call the patch of land attached to their own tiny house a garden, so Frau Danielzyck had rented one here, in Ybbsstrasse, from the woman who owned the house next door to the Fritzls but who spent most of her time in Linz. She had told Frau Danielzyck that she didn't like to stay overnight in Amstetten, mainly because of stories she had heard in the town concerning Josef Fritzl's criminal past. She had been equally ambivalent about the Fritzl's son Josef junior, who seemed to her to be *'ein Sonderling'*, an 'oddball', and 'not all there'. Frau Danielzyck herself had once caught sight of the boy, when he was still a young teenager, stuffing red and brown ants into a plastic bottle and watching them kill one another. When she had asked him what he was doing he had replied, 'I like to watch them fight.' There had been other incidents: the time, for example, Josef junior had stolen a moped and driven, hopelessly lost, to Bruck an der Mur, a good 40 miles south of Amstetten. Frau Danielzyck had heard that the boy had spent much of his young life in trouble with the police: they had arrested him once after some sort of car-wrecking spree, suspecting him of taking a hatchet to some cars and starting four fires – all on the same day, police would later reveal. This had been near Mondsee, where his own father had himself twice been arrested and charged with arson, but never convicted. When he was arrested the authorities had taken the view that the boy was not mentally competent to be held responsible for his actions, and there had even been a suggestion, never followed up, that his compulsive fire-starting might have been the acting out of some kind of trauma. 'A cry for help?' one of the officers investigating the case had scribbled in his notebook. Many years later, in 2008, the same year his father was finally arrested for the rape and enslavement of Elisabeth, Josef junior would be put in a home for the mentally impaired. Until then he would live in the house in Ybbsstrasse, the only one of the siblings who remained at home, carrying out odd jobs for his father on the many houses that Josef would come to possess.

Like many of her neighbours, Frau Danielzyck had over the years pieced together the bare facts of Herr Fritzl's own criminal past. She knew about the rape conviction and had heard from a friend about an earlier offence during which, in her friend's words, he had become 'excited' in the presence of a young pregnant woman and 'done something indecent'. Not that there was much evidence of this sexual delinquency in his actual behaviour. Indeed, it was only with great difficulty that Frau Danielzyck had been able to square the image she had in her head of what a convicted rapist might look like with the capable, well-turned-out, often helpful man she would see pottering about with a wheelbarrow in his garden. 'Hello, Frau Danielzyck,' he would call over to her with a wave. 'How are those strawberries coming along?'

In truth it was hard to fault him as a neighbour. He'd fixed Frau Danielzyck's lawnmower once. Another time, when her elderly husband had collapsed in a faint, it had been Herr Fritzl who had immediately rushed over and not only lifted him to his feet – quite a task in itself considering what a large man Herr Danielzyck had been – but practically carried him into the house. Herr Fritzl chaotically planting tulips; Herr Fritzl bedding down an apricot tree in one of his many attempts to persuade his wife to cut costs by making her own jam rather than buying it. He had dug a pond in the garden, more of a ditch, and filled it with goldfish. He had built a green-house – 'a touch of sophistication', he said – next to the pool on the terrace and was building a second pool out in the middle of the lawn. A very powerful man, always in motion, who seemed to run on thin air. 'I don't need much to eat,' he had once told Frau Danielzyck. 'A vegetable soup and an aspirin will do me.'

If there was one thing Frau Danielzyck disliked about Josef, it was his tendency to put himself on display: loung-

ing about in the garden half-naked every summer in a
pair of tight red swimming trunks. He was vain, that was
obvious, the kind of man one could imagine admiring
himself at great length in the mirror. A middle-aged
narcissus, always 'immaculately' turned out. Frau
Danielzyck didn't know how very self-conscious Josef
had been about the bald spot that had appeared on the
crown of his head in the late seventies, but she wouldn't
have been surprised. And in fact Josef had been made so
anxious about his thinning hair that he had been
persuaded by his friend Paul Höra to drive over to
Munich to try out some 'miracle' hair-regenerating cream
that had recently come onto the market in Germany. And
when that hadn't worked he had travelled all the way to
Hungary to have a hair transplant, where the procedure,
although just as painful, was cheaper than in Austria:
Josef's *Zweite Frühling*, his 'second spring' or 'mid-life
crisis'. He'd undergone the hair transplant in the early
eighties, around the time that Elisabeth had disappeared,
although, of course, neither Frau Danielzyck nor Paul
Höra could have guessed at the deep connection between
these apparently unconnected two events.

In retrospect, Frau Danielzyck would say, the only
clue to Herr Fritzl's dual nature was to be found in his
garden in the years before 1993. It seemed strange to her
that a man who paid such close attention to his personal
appearance would allow his garden to fall into such a
state of chaos. It was a tip, that garden, overgrown with
weeds and littered with the evidence of his building
work. Grass, unevenly mowed, poked through heaps of
cement and sand. Scattered about, along with a child's

tricycle or two, a couple of old footballs, were spanners and other tools, plastic sheeting, all sorts of junk.

And in the corner of the garden sat the solitary, rather bedraggled figure of Maria Nenning, Herr Fritzl's mother, now in her late eighties. Weather permitting, she was always out there, beneath the shade of a nut tree, a 'miserable-looking' woman in black, whose crooked frame and tramp-like demeanour seemed to emphasize the overall atmosphere of decay. She hardly, if ever, spoke, partly because she had lost all but one of her teeth, but mainly because she hated conversation. Towards the end of her life she would be packed off to a nursing home in Krems, an idyllic little town on the Danube close to Amstetten. And Frau Danielzyck would always remember the day Maria died because of what she would see Herr Fritzl doing with his mother's belongings. On the day of Maria Nenning's death her son had carried all of her clothes and possessions out of the house and dumped them in the garden. There they sat for days, amid the rubble: his mother's most precious possessions left to rot in the wind and the rain as if they were nothing more than a great pile of refuse.

As for Rosemarie, from her allotment Frau Danielzyck would often catch sight of her in the garden hanging out the washing and, naturally, the two women would often exchange a friendly word or two over the fence that separated the properties. Women's talk, which would often drift in the direction of Rosemarie's never-ending exasperation with her lodgers. She wanted them out, as they

were far too much work. If it had been up to her, she
would have evicted them all a long time ago. She didn't
like the lodgers but she had to put up with them. 'All
these funny people around the house,' she would
complain. 'You know what they're like: they get their
relatives to come round for a bath or a shower and it's us
who end up paying for it.'

Rosemarie wasn't a particularly discreet woman, that
much was clear. She never said no to a good gossip, or for
that matter, a good moan. Another of her pet peeves was
her bad treatment at the hands of her husband: his stingi-
ness, his cruelty, the shame she feared he had brought on
the family for raping that woman in Linz. She had
confided in Frau Danielzyck all about the rape conviction. 'What will people say?' she had said. 'You know
how people talk.' Rosemarie, a woman very conscious of
her own reputation. Very attached to convention, with
her pinafore dress, her hair modestly 'done', and no
make-up, she was not much different in appearance from
any other woman in Amstetten.

For all its surface harmony, Rosemarie assured Frau
Danielzyck, hers was a difficult marriage. Even though
they still lived in the same house, once the children were
grown, their lives had started to evolve in two very different directions. They still sat down together for most
meals but Josef spent most of his time absorbed in his
work or off on one of his business trips – to Denmark,
Hungary, Luxembourg – and days could go by when she
wouldn't see him. Not that these periods of absence had
necessarily come as much of a disappointment to Rosemarie. She suffered from health problems, which meant

that she had taken advantage of the week-long stays at medical spas that the Austrian state makes available to the chronically ill and infirm. And the relief she had felt in the first such week away from her husband had been one of the reasons behind the couple's subsequent decision to take separate holidays: Rosemarie would go off to Italy with one of her sisters; a few months later Josef would disappear to Thailand with Paul Höra, or once even to Kenya on safari.

What time the couple did spend together was often fractious, because of, according to Rosemarie, Josef's 'tyrannical' moods. Frau Danielzyck had witnessed these for herself only twice: once when Josef had stormed out of the house because Rosemarie had mislaid the money with which to pay an odd-job man; and another time when Rosemarie had apparently lingered too long over the preparation of the couple's evening meal. The two women had been chatting over the fence, when Josef emerged from the house red-faced and shouting. Rosemarie, visibly upset, had immediately scuttled back into the house and Josef had later attempted to smooth the whole thing over with Frau Danielzyck by turning it into a joke. He could be terribly charming when he wanted to make a good impression and she soon forgot the whole episode. Wives and husbands, and how they interact behind closed doors, are one of life's great mysteries – and certainly not, as far as Frau Danielzyck was concerned, any business of a neighbour.

But it did occur to her to wonder, what with the rapes and the violence, why Rosemarie had never divorced him. Frau Danielzyck had never quite felt satisfied with Rosemarie's explanation that her husband had threatened to kill her if she left. 'He'll shoot me,' she had told her. 'He's got a gun.' And, although Amstetten is the kind of conservative Catholic enclave where couples tend to stay together no matter what and divorce is often looked down upon as a failure of will, it seemed that the reluctance of this couple to separate lay just as much in Rosemarie's unwillingness to go as in her husband's insistence on her staying. Because, for all her complaining, Rosemarie never showed any real intention of leaving. She was a listless woman, just a touch self-pitying, with that ability, common in many women, to make other people feel sorry for her: the good mother, the put-upon wife, she would drift through her days quite passively, wrapped up in her role of nurturer. The family was her whole life. Her children were her identity. What life was there for Rosemarie beyond 40 Ybbsstrasse? She had hardly any experience of earning money herself. And either because the personal cost was too high or because, like many couples, Josef and Rosemarie were in some unknowable way enmeshed with each other, life, despite its difficulties, continued largely unchanged for her, a succession of days spent cooking, cleaning, looking after her children and grandchildren. You couldn't have described her as an imaginative woman.

It was Frau Danielzyck's understanding that Frau Fritzl had not been altogether devastated by the abrupt departure in 1984 of her third daughter, Elisabeth. And there had been signs that Rosemarie might even have felt relieved to see the back of this problem child who had spent most of her teens having weight issues and who would have been sacked even from her waitressing job at the service station had it not been for her mother's repeated interventions. And it was not difficult to see how in some ways it might have been easier to live in the house without Elisabeth's constant stubbornness and volatile moods. Relations between mother and daughter had been delicate at the best of times and, many years later, Elisabeth would refer to the relationship that she had with her mother during her teens as 'not particularly good'.

'Elisabeth is different,' were Rosemarie's exact words to Frau Danielzyck whenever the subject of her daughter had come up. 'Josef doesn't like her,' she had once said to Paul Höra's wife. 'It's just the way it is.' Not exactly spelling it out, but one sensed a coolness there between mother and daughter.

CHAPTER NINE

THE DOORSTEP

Dear mamma and papa
I pass on my little daughter Lisa to you. Look after her
carefully. You're probably wondering why you're only hearing
from me now, especially because this letter comes with a big
surprise. I have been breastfeeding her for six and a half
months. Now she only drinks milk out of a bottle and she eats
everything else off a spoon. I'm incapable of caring for her. I
hope she won't be too much trouble for you.

In the late spring of 1993 Rosemarie had started
appearing in the garden with a small child in her arms.
The child, a girl, must have been a year and a half old at
this stage, a good crawler but not yet able to speak. Lisa
was her name.

The tenants and neighbours of 40 Ybbsstrasse were used
to seeing various Fritzl grandchildren about the house
and garden and so the arrival of this new child hadn't
attracted any particular attention. One day she was just

'there' and it was generally accepted that she belonged to Ulli or Harald or formed part of the Fritzls' large extended family, many of whom would visit the house at weekends or on holidays. And none of the lodgers, nor any of the neighbours, would recall feeling particularly surprised when they learned that the child that Rosemarie had taken to carrying about with her everywhere she went had in fact been found abandoned in a cardboard box in front of the house. Perhaps the neighbours' lack of curiosity was in some part due to Josef's air of *Selbstverständlichkeit*, his nonchalance, his matter-of-factness, the feeling he gave you that everything he did, everything that happened in and around that house – even when it seemed to be at odds with the normal run of things – came to pass as a matter of course.

In any case – so it would emerge in dribs and drabs over the summer months – the girl had been discovered by 10-year-old Doris, the youngest of the Fritzls' seven children. Doris had found her on the doorstep and tucked in alongside the child had been a note from Elisabeth in which she had declared herself incapable of coping with the demands of motherhood. Ybbsstrasse was by then a busy thoroughfare even at night, and it was taken for granted that either Elisabeth or one of the strange 'cult people' she associated with must have crept into the town in the small hours of the morning: indeed, it was amazing that nobody had seen or heard anything. And it had been Josef who had marched straight down to the children's welfare office, where he had explained the situation to a social worker and signed a written statement which read: 'Today at 6.20 a.m. our daughter Doris found a baby in a cushioned cardboard box on our doorstep.' The social worker had promptly set up a case file on Lisa and noted that the child had been properly dressed at the time of her discovery and that there had been a letter in the box which seemed to indicate that Josef Fritzl and his wife were the grandparents of the girl.

There followed many communications between the Fritzls and the children's welfare office and, five days after Lisa was discovered, another social worker visited the couple at home where Josef had expressed his suspicions about the whole incident: although he and his wife were more than willing to take the nine-month-old girl under their wing, he wanted to make sure that the child was Elisabeth's and one way of doing that, Fritzl had suggested, was to have the letter analysed by a graphologist – luckily he still had a couple of Elisabeth's old school textbooks lying around against which to compare the handwriting. He also suggested that Lisa herself should be examined by a doctor. In his report the social worker surmised that Herr and Frau Fritzl had recovered from the initial shock. They were increasingly convinced that Lisa was their granddaughter: her appearance and various features alone indicated a great similarity to their daughter, Elisabeth. He could see no argument against allowing Lisa to remain for the time being with her grandparents.

The next day Lisa was taken to a doctor, who noted that she was unusually small, weighing just 5.5 kilos, but well taken care of, with a clean appearance and well-trimmed fingernails. It was the doctor's view that Lisa had probably been born in a hospital because her umbilical cord has been cut and clamped with expert precision. Meanwhile, it was noted by the children's welfare office that the local police were 'attempting' to find the mother. The Fritzl family was taking loving care of Lisa and would like to keep her in their custody, their social worker had observed. Later that week a graphologist confirmed that the letter found with Lisa had indeed been written by the Fritzls' long-lost daughter.

Just before Christmas the same year, social services paid another visit to number 40. Lisa was learning to speak and had become the focus of the family's attention … The social worker observed her grandparents claim that she was very similar to their daughter, Elisabeth, and also resembled her mother in her character. During this second visit Josef said that he and his wife would be happy to return the girl to her mother should she, in his words, 'exhibit an appropriate change of lifestyle'. But when Elisabeth failed to materialize it was decided that Lisa would be formally fostered by her grandparents, who, for their troubles, would receive income support of around 400 euros a month.

Although they didn't like to say it to the Fritzls, most of the people who knew them felt that Elisabeth was a *Schlampe*, a slut, and a *Raabenmutter*, a bad mother, to have conceived and abandoned her child in such murky circumstances. And their views will almost certainly have been heavily coloured, not only by the straitlaced attitudes that predominate in most small Austrian towns, but by the trial, just two years earlier, of the well-spoken and charismatic Austrian artist Otto Mühl. Mühl had been all over the papers for months after he was sentenced to seven years' imprisonment for the sexual abuse of children in a commune he had set up in the Burgenland province in eastern Austria. The case had caused a scandal, all the more so because, as an artist, Mühl had for several decades been an established figure in Austrian life. In the seventies his commune had survived on handsome state subsidies and Mühl himself had enjoyed the support of liberal politicians who liked to align themselves with a man who was one of the protagonists of an avant-garde artistic movement, Vienna Actionism, whose controversial photographic work and performances often involved the use of blood, faeces, and sadistic imagery. By the eighties, despite a near-constant stream of rumours and bad publicity surrounding Mühl and his cult, many of its members had become successful businessmen in the fields of insurance, agriculture, and property investment and the commune had amassed an estimated £15 million in various accounts in Luxembourg. It was already widely known that Mühl had founded his commune on the principles of free sexuality, creative expression, and the abolition of both private property and monogamous relationships; that passports and personal documents were confiscated; and that children born there were raised by the whole community. But it was only in the early nineties that the Austrian authorities uncovered the lengths Mühl had been prepared to go in order to fulfil his artistic vision.

The cult was strictly hierarchical and Mühl, as its undisputed leader, would enforce order with routine

corporal punishment and humiliation. He would make
lists of the men women were permitted to have sex with
and forbid any man and woman to sleep in the same bed
for more than one night, with the result that the children
conceived there often did not know who their natural
fathers were. Mühl himself had fathered, it was estimated, over fifty children, some of them the product of
his self-appointed right as cult leader to sexually 'initiate'
any young girl. Police found video footage of him sexually abusing young children. So terrible was the evidence
laid before the state prosecutor that he claimed in court
that never before in his career had he witnessed a case of
such barbaric oppression. 'We all know what a concentration camp is,' he said. 'What the girls in the ... cult
experienced was just as horrifying. Otto Mühl experi-
mented with human beings, he manipulated them ...
These young people weren't there of their own free will.
He took them from their parents so that there was no
possibility they could escape the commune. They didn't
stand a chance.'

'You don't stand a chance': the strikingly similar words
spoken by Josef Fritzl to his daughter Elisabeth after he
had locked her in a cellar and forced her into an existence
that bore striking resemblances to Mühl's cult. As a keen
newspaper reader Josef would undoubtedly have come
across the reports of Mühl's excesses that had made headlines not just during the nineties but throughout the previous two decades: a stream of reports concerning sexual
excess, ideas of patriarchy, authoritarianism, and deprivation. Josef might have seen newspaper pictures of exam-
ples of Mühl's work – naked women smeared with blood

or excrement, tied up with ropes and wires – and taken them literally, incorporating them into his vision of the cellar, just as he had incorporated pornographic images from video tapes and magazines.

The two men had some things in common. Both spoke in what has been described as a low, almost 'hypnotic' tone, they were charismatic and persuasive, and their prime interest in other people lay in the possibility of manipulating them. Like Mühl, Josef was a respected figure in the community, a successful business-man, and the recipient of state subsidies. Both men were described by their wives as 'patriarchal' and 'possessively jealous', and they shared a lifelong preoccupation with their sexual performance: Mühl publicly referred to himself as 'the Olympic champion of sex', and later, when police interrogated him after his final arrest, Josef would go into great, often irrelevant and yet boastful, detail about his erections, the number of times he had achieved orgasm, his unwillingness to use condoms because he found them emasculating.

It had been Josef's – not the police's – theory that Elis-abeth had left home to live in a 'cult', and it is more than likely that he had copied the idea directly from news reports about Mühl. Possibly Josef identified with him. Like Josef, Mühl saw himself as an exceptional man to whom normal moral codes did not apply. 'The artist is a man who cannot be judged by conventional standards,' he said after former cult members alleged that he had molested children. If a woman in the commune became pregnant, Mühl would decide what course the child's life would take, just as Josef would do with the children his daughter bore him in the cellar. The existence that Josef was attempting to create for himself below ground uncannily resembled what Mühl had already achieved in the world above: both men sought to create for themselves, through intimidation, isolation, and control, a sort of alternative civilization in which they would act as god-like beings, free to realize their fantasies of domination without the slightest risk of criticism. By the time Mühl's commune was raided by the police, Mühl had elevated himself to such a figure of fear and awe among the members of his commune that the teenagers who lived there would queue up at the toilet door with tissues to wipe him when he had finished.

Mühl remains a notorious figure to this day. And it is almost certain that the same headlines that are likely to have inspired Josef Fritzl left just as much of a mark on his fellow Amstettners, but for different reasons. This would help to explain why both the police and the social services took for granted the fact that Elisabeth was living in a 'cult', despite the lack of any evidence. It may also account for the assumption among those who knew the Fritzls that cults were places where carefree sexual anarchy, and therefore accidental pregnancies, prevailed. Whatever the case, the view of many Amstettners, including the police and social services, remained that, even though Elisabeth remained a 'slut' who had brought shame on her family with her promiscuity and 'degenerate' behaviour, she was extremely fortunate to have been able to fall back in times of crisis on two such understanding and responsible parents as Josef and Rosemarie Fritzl.

* * *

Sepp Leitner's recollection of the events surrounding the appearance of the child on the Fritzls' doorstep is more or less identical to Frau Danielzyck's. However, as a tenant of the couple, Leitner had, unlike Frau Danielzyck, known Elisabeth since she was a teenager, and he was still in touch with Brigitte, the friend with whom she had run away to Vienna. From Brigitte he had heard that some 'funny stuff' had been going on between Josef Fritzl and his daughter in the years before her disappearance. 'Funny stuff' as in sexual stuff. It wasn't remotely surprising to him that Elisabeth had wanted to escape that family. The further away, in his opinion, the better.

So when that baby had come along, it had all fitted into place. With her history, it was not surprising that Elisabeth had mixed herself up in some kind of 'wretched' business. There were rumours circulating in Amstetten that she had become a prostitute in Holland. It was sad, but as he hardly knew the girl, Leitner, to his profound regret in years to come, didn't dwell on the whys and wherefores of the child who had been so unceremoniously dumped on the doorstep of number 40. He had other things on his mind: parties and his campaign, with Ludwig the long-distance lorry driver, to persuade Herr Fritzl to allow them to have barbecues in the garden. Herr Fritzl had said no to that. Leitner had been successful, however, in overturning his landlord's 'no pets' policy when he brought home Sam, a Labrador-cross, to live with him in the apartment. He had convinced Herr Fritzl that the dog had belonged to his mother who had recently passed away. Leitner's mother was alive and well and had always hated animals, but he had sensed in Josef a sentimental streak and exploited it. Every now and again, Leitner noticed, the dog would for no reason start pawing the floor of Sepp's ground-floor flat and begin to whine.

The year after Lisa had appeared the neighbours became aware of another child. Again Rosemarie was seen nursing it in and around the house. Like Lisa, the child had been found abandoned on the doorstep of number 40 – this time by her grandmother and in a pram rather than a cardboard box. This was in December 1994 and, considering the sub-zero temperature outside, it was a miracle that the child had not frozen to death. Inside the pram Rosemarie Fritzl found another note from Elisabeth in which she had written the child's name – Monika – along with an apology for her continued absence. Like her sister, Monika was at first a restless and unhappy baby. It would be Rosemarie who would discover the cause of her troubles: a tiny hair had somehow wound itself around one of her toes. It had been invisible to Elisabeth in the dim light of the cellar, and had became ingrown and painful. Certainly it rescued Monika from the cellar, perhaps it had saved her life.

The precise details of Monika's discovery by Rosemarie were mystifying to everyone who heard the story. Rosemarie had woken up to the sound of a child crying shortly after midnight on 16 December. Minutes later she discovered the pram on the doorstep. She had only just about carried the child into the house when the phone started to ring. Rosemarie would tell the social worker that she had heard 'a female voice, obviously recorded', and that this voice described herself as the mother of the child and my daughter Elisabeth. Several minutes later the phone rang again and the same message was played down the line. The whole episode, said Rosemarie, was 'completely inexplicable', especially considering that the Fritzls had only very recently changed their phone number: it wasn't listed and nobody except for her and her husband had known it. But the curious circumstances surrounding the discovery of a second child on the Fritzls' doorstep seemed to trigger no particular concern among the authorities.

Nevertheless, the case of the two foundlings was unusual enough to attract the attention of the papers. Mark Perry, a British-born journalist then working for the Austrian tabloid the *Kronen Zeitung*, would later remember that: 'It was a bit of a spectacular case as it was unheard of that a mother would just disappear and then start sending her children to her own parents. People in Amstetten were pointing fingers: Elisabeth was seen as a bad mother.' Perry's article appeared bearing the headline 'Mother Gives Away Second Baby'. Josef had been happy to be interviewed by Perry about the matter and was quoted as saying, 'Our daughter has been missing since 1984 and we suspect she has fallen into the hands of a sect.'

* * *

Having proved themselves to be loving and devoted parents, the Fritzls now received permission from Amstetten Council to foster Monika. Earlier in the same year they had also looked into the possibility of formally adopting Lisa. And, although it is forbidden by Austrian law for any couple to adopt a child without the consent of both of its natural parents, in view of what the authorities decided were mitigating circumstances surrounding the birth of Lisa, these legal technicalities were, it seems, disregarded. A Lower Austrian court approved the adoption the same year but, owing to a clerical error, Lisa's adoption permit would for ever list the names of her adoptive parents as Josef and 'Maria' Fritzl. 'Officially' Elisabeth Fritzl had never been named as their mother. Notwithstanding the fuss the press had made over the story, Amstetten's social services and police department remained convinced of the story of the cult. In their minds, Elisabeth had managed to abandon her children in one of the busiest streets in the town without having attracted the slightest notice because 'it wouldn't have been difficult for a member of the sect to give her a lift'.

There were only ever two serious disagreements between Sepp Leitner and Josef, the second of which would result in the tenant's abrupt and unexpected departure from number 40. The first argument concerned Leitner's tendency to play his music too loud in the early hours of the morning. Josef knocked at the door and angrily told him to turn it down. He was shouting and it was the first time that Leitner had witnessed this other, bullying side to his landlord, the side he would normally only show women or children. Leitner threatened to 'smash his face in'. And that had been enough for Josef. The next thing Leitner knew, Fritzl was disappearing back up the stairs and into his office.

The second argument happened towards the middle of 1994 and related to Leitner's electricity bill, which for no apparent reason had risen to a level that he considered exorbitant. He was already paying a relatively high sum for his apartment and when he confronted Josef about the electricity bill the two men ended up having a stand-up row. Down in the cellar Josef had by this stage wired Elisabeth's room to the electrical circuit of the apartment block above. It was very like him to drain his tenants' electricity supply for his own ends in this way; to get something for nothing; to pull the wool over the eyes of others and to extract from this hidden advantage some secret pleasure and private feeling of power. But when Leitner had complained about the rising cost of the electricity, Josef took it as a warning. He wanted him out. And the day after their fierce argument Leitner returned to his flat to find that his landlord had changed the locks on his door. When Leitner called the police they arrived on the scene only to tell him that there was nothing they could do. His tenant, Josef knew, could never have afforded to hire a lawyer. And there was nothing Leitner could do except move out.

* * *

By the end of 1993, buoyed by his success in integrating Lisa into the world above without attracting the merest hint of suspicion from anyone, Josef had entered into a period of joyful building activity. He did so equipped with a renewed sense of his own invulnerability. He had got away with it. And now he would push his experiments underground to even more reckless extremes.

The birth of his children had, in Josef's mind, called for an expansion of the cellar. Elisabeth was now living in a single room together with two growing children – Kerstin was 5, Stefan was 3 – and there was no doubt in Josef's mind that other children would be born in the cellar in the future. His plan was to add to the original layout two rooms, rooms that he had in fact discovered years earlier but which he had never connected to his daughter's cell. And he set about preparing the three extra rooms, reclaiming for himself the cellar of number 40, which, through some error in the original plans of 40 Ybbsstrasse, did not officially exist, but which Josef had by chance unearthed during his subterranean wanderings. Now he knocked down its walls and dredged its interior, fashioning from its damp and low-ceilinged chambers what he considered to be an 'apartment'.

He had in mind a total refurbishment. A project to get his teeth into. The kind of exercise he lived for but which he often had difficulty completing in the house above. He had never finished the second swimming pool on the terrace and it would remain there, empty and useless, for as long as Josef lived in the house. Likewise, his initial spell of frenzied building activity on two of the flats in the apartment block had done little more than turn the ground floor into a building site. For years it would remain an uninhabitable space with holes in the walls and piles of bricks strewn across the floor.

Upstairs he was always enthusiastically throwing himself into some project or other and then losing interest. But in the cellar he behaved very differently. Nothing was left to founder. In the cellar Josef always started as he meant to go on and the things that he set in motion there would always reach their logical conclusion.

Work on the cellar had begun when Elisabeth found herself pregnant with Lisa. But Josef had intensified his labours some months after the birth.

Now all sorts of things went into the cellar: tiles, wood laminate, a shower unit, flat-pack cupboards, two wooden bed frames, two mattresses, and a bathroom cabinet. If she was at home at the time it must have been difficult for Rosemarie not to have noticed her husband lugging these various heavy and unwieldy objects into the cellar. Envisioning a total 'modernization' of the cellar, Josef also bought many new electrical items which he hooked up to the mains and which, unknown to Leitner, would account for the sudden rise in his electricity bill in the same period: a refrigerator, an oven, an extractor fan, pipes that he would use to better ventilate the cellar. Things were endlessly disappearing into the cellar but never coming out.

The rooms had been there since he had excavated them in the late seventies and early eighties, behind one of the walls of the original cellar. They were accessible through a corridor next to the boiler room, which he now used as a 'goods entrance' and sealed off with a concrete door. But he had never told Elisabeth of their existence, and she remained under the impression that he was building the rooms from scratch. She and the children could hear him working on the other side of the wall, imagining that he was tunnelling into the earth when, in fact, all he was doing was furnishing and equipping the rooms with various electrical appliances, and disposing of any rubble in the space behind what was to become a shower room. Finally he punched a hole in the wall of the room that divided the new rooms from Elisabeth and her children. But he had put iron bars on the hole and they had been forced to wait until, with some ceremony, on 17 December 1993, he removed the bars and allowed his family for the first time to explore their new home.

By the standards of how they had been used to living, this was an unhoped-for improvement. Josef had converted Elisabeth's old room into a twin room with two single beds. From there a narrow corridor, 60 centimetres in width, ran into the new combined kitchen and washing area, where there was hot running water for the first time, serving a shower as well as a sink, cooking facilities, a table, and some chairs. Along another narrow corridor was the second, 'parental' bedroom, in which stood a double bed and the television. In order to give the place a more 'homely' feel, Josef had fixed Alpine-style varnished pine planks to the ceilings and installed wall lights. He had bought a toilet seat in what he considered to be a cheerful lime green and lined one of the tables in the cellar with brightly coloured adhesive plastic sheeting in a swirling, red and orange pattern, probably left over

from the redecoration of some part of the house above.
He had covered the walls and floor with stone-effect
vinyl laminate and tiles. He had given the children some
permanent marker pens with which to draw pictures on
the walls.

But nothing he could do managed to convert this
dank, windowless space into a normal household. No
matter how hard he tried to dress up the cellar with toys
or new furniture, within days these objects would start to
show evidence of decay. 'The stink of the cellar,' the
Governor of Amstetten County would some day say, 'a
smell that I could never forget': a fertile, fetid odour that
would attach itself to your clothes and permeate them
even after they were washed. In the cellar the mould
would burrow deep into the mattresses and wooden
furniture and play havoc with the television and the
lights, which continued also to be subject to the occasional
failure of the mains electricity, when the cellar would be
unexpectedly plunged into darkness for days. In its new,
expanded form the cellar had an area of about 55 square
metres (592 square feet). The ceiling height, which was
just 1.7 metres in the 'old cellar', increased slightly to
almost 1.8 metres, but Josef and Elisabeth, and later
Stefan and Kerstin, would still have had to move about
all the rooms in a perpetual stoop.

Nevertheless, the mood in the cellar had been buoyant,
if you believe Josef. Elisabeth and Kerstin were later said
by their father to have been 'thrilled' at the thought of
these new rooms, the luxury of all that extra space: warm
running water for the first time. Elisabeth was thrilled at
the idea of taking a normal shower. Only Stefan was left

untouched by the sudden feeling of general optimism. Stefan was frightened. At first there was nothing anybody could do to persuade Stefan to enter the new rooms. He wouldn't budge. He was terrified by all this new space and activity. It was overwhelming for a 4-year-old whose entire world until then had been contained within four walls.

Elisabeth would note the heights and weights of the children as they grew older, as well as all their health problems. They were constantly ill. One or other always had flu or toothache or a cold, suffered from symptoms resembling mild epilepsy. One of the reasons that Elisabeth had felt relieved when Lisa and Monika had been taken upstairs was because of the persistent health problems of the two girls. Almost immediately after she had been released from the cellar, Lisa was diagnosed with a heart condition and underwent surgery. Elisabeth was still very afraid for her little girl. She knew she would fight; she had proved capable of it when she was born. She wished she could be by her side and help her. She missed her terribly and thanked God they noticed the condition right away. She was going almost mad at the thought that something could go wrong ... She prayed and thought only of Lisa.

Lisa had recovered, but life continued to be frightening and precarious for Kerstin and Stefan. When they were ill Josef would bring down aspirin and cough medicine – that was as much of a concession as he was prepared to make. On special occasions, 'to cheer everybody up', he would do Elisabeth the 'favour' of bringing Lisa downstairs. This was until Lisa started speaking. So from then on it was only Monika who would, every now and again, be carried down into the cellar by her father, to be babysat by Elisabeth if he was busy with work. But in time even these much-anticipated visits were terminated. It was too upsetting for Kerstin and Stefan to be confronted by this evidence of the other life. And it had been Elisabeth who had eventually asked Josef not to bring the babies any more. It was too painful for the older children to watch their siblings disappear upstairs where they had never been and would never be permitted to go there.

For the first ten years the cellar had been chaos, but its expansion in late 1993 and early 1994 – as well as the furniture and labour-saving electrical devices that were now installed – had in some ways ushered in a new era in the life of Elisabeth and her children. It was still mouldy, the air was foul, and it was a full-time job just cleaning the place. But gone were the utter confusion and uncertainty of previous years: in their place some semblance of order and routine.

And there was television. Perpetual day in the perpetual night of the cellar. The television in the cellar was often constantly on – when it was working – which is why it would be wrong to assume that, living in the cellar as they did, Elisabeth and her children were living in ignorance of the things that were going on above their heads: the everyday things, as well as the momentous events and innovations of the age. They watched them all on television, of course. Every day in the cellar there would be the things that happened in the cellar and then there would be the things that happened on TV: besides Josef, their only real source of information. They were often glued to the set. Nature documentaries were their favourites: so the children knew what grass and sunshine and rain looked like, though wouldn't, for many years, know what they felt like or how it smelled or tasted like. The television gave them a rich participatory life. A very painful reminder, every day, of how things might have been. In fact Elisabeth and her children would have been acutely aware of how things were in the life above. They needed the information. Sometimes Josef would join them down in the cellar to watch the evening news and, Elisabeth would later tell the prosecution team, whenever a story of drug abuse came on, Josef would turn to her and say, 'Look, that could have been you.'

Two years now passed in relative tranquillity. The day would begin with the sound of the alarm clock at 6 a.m: breakfast, then a wash, then lessons, as taught to Kerstin and Stefan by their mother with the help of books and newspapers that Josef could occasionally be persuaded to buy for them. Around the kitchen table the children learned reading, writing, and the rudiments of arithmetic. They would take regular exams. Much of the rest of the time would be spent either watching television – films were their favourites – or at meals, with Josef joining them at table as often as he was able: a regular participant, he liked to think, in 'family life'.

The Mercur supermarket was barely ten minutes' walk from Ybbsstrasse, but Josef, in his continued efforts to avoid detection, preferred to buy his groceries in the relative anonymity of the Metro supermarket in Linz, an hour and a half's drive away. A receipt later discovered by the police would show that the provisions with which he would furnish the cellar included frozen fish fillets, bottles of Fanta, bread dumplings, sausages, tins of various preserved foods, potatoes, rice, beans, spaghetti, and ice cream. From these basic ingredients Elisabeth would, three times a day, attempt to conjure up a meal. And there was usually sufficient flour, butter, and sugar for her to bake a cake for the children's birthdays. Although the atmosphere of the cellar did not naturally lend itself to festive occasions, Elisabeth would attempt to provide them with 'parties' of sorts, decorating the rooms with paper chains and sewing together patches of different materials to make 'dressing up' costumes for them; parties that would delight Kerstin and Stefan except on those occasions when their father was present. Josef liked to join in the celebrations by appearing in the cellar wearing a mask, always the same mask: it depicted the face of Krampus, a horned creature from Germanic fairy-tales which, according to tradition, would beat unruly children. He would creep up on his children in the mask 'as a joke'. But Josef was a frightening man at the best of times. And, more often than not, the day would end with one or other of the children in tears.

There were 'good times', although the highlights of these monotonous days could be counted on one hand: the time Josef brought the gift of a shovelful of snow to the cellar; the time he presented his family with their first mirror, the only one Elisabeth had seen in over eight years and an object of wonderment and fascination for two children who had so far only glimpsed their reflections on the back of spoons and kitchen knives: four years into Elisabeth's incarceration he had replaced the plastic cutlery with metal. When Kerstin turned 5 and her father, in a fit of uncharacteristic generosity, had brought down to the cellar a yoghurt, a strawberry cake, a bottle of Fanta, a packet of crisps, and two Kinder Surprise eggs. And the time, in June 1993, Elisabeth had switched on the television and recognized an old friend from her days training in Waldegg, who had become a prominent psychotherapist. She was so happy to see him. But these episodes were always short-lived and sooner or later her father's unpredictable and violent behaviour would return. By far the happiest times in the cellar were the times when he wasn't there at all.

Life carried on as it had always done. The assaults continued, with the difference that, now that his daughter had apparently given up any attempt at resistance, Josef had convinced himself that the two of them were engaged in 'a proper relationship'. He would take her into one of the bedrooms while the children stayed in another room. He later said that his feelings towards his daughter had become mutual. If you believe Josef, Elisabeth would kiss him when he came down to the cellar, as a wife might kiss her husband when he comes home from work. Just like any other couple.

April 1996: Elisabeth's twelfth year underground. Above ground it was the year that Josef finally sold the Seestern, the family's holiday home and B&B at Mondsee, and began to invest his money in properties closer to home.

By the end of 1995 Elisabeth knew she was pregnant again. And both the movements in her womb and the size of her belly suggested that she was carrying twins. The delivery of twins, even by the best obstetricians, is considered a complicated undertaking and for months Elisabeth had been preparing herself for the birth in a state of unusually profound anxiety. But around 6.50 p.m. on 28 April 1996 she succeeded in giving birth to two identical twin boys. Three days later one of them would be dead.

Having accustomed himself to dropping in on his 'downstairs family' with increasing frequency, Josef was in the cellar when the birth pangs began. 6 p.m. found him with Kerstin and Stefan in the kitchen, where together they ate supper while next door, on the floor beside the double bed, Elisabeth struggled with the agony of labour. Her father was beside her when the first twin, Michael, was born. Josef had taken the baby, whose umbilical cord he noticed to be conspicuously pale, and laid him on the bed. Then came Alexander, a more diffi-cult birth. A situation that, in a hospital, usually requires the intervention of a doctor.

The babies seemed fine until, a few hours later, Michael began to experience difficulty breathing. He was wheezing, refusing to feed, and his legs were becoming rigid. The next day he was still alive but his condition had deteriorated. Observing this, his father, who had come down into the cellar with a new cot for the twins, merely shrugged and said to Elisabeth, 'What will be will be,' at which point Elisabeth panicked and pleaded with him to fetch help. But Josef, hoping that the situation would resolve itself, simply disappeared upstairs for another couple of hours.

Michael Fritzl died shortly after midday on 1 May 1996. At the time of his death his mother, in her desperation, tried everything to save him, but it hadn't worked and she saw how his body had turned quite rigid and blue in her arms. For twenty-four hours his tiny corpse, which Elisabeth wrapped in a blanket, remained in the cellar. On 2 May Josef returned to the cellar, picked up the body, carried it through to the furnace room, and burned it. In a characteristically sentimental – and false – recollection of the events Josef would later claim that he and Elisabeth had first baptized their dead son and together resolved to cremate him because 'we didn't want to bury him and let the worms eat him'. Josef, he claimed, then gathered up Michael's ashes and scattered them in the garden. Josef would later say to her, 'Perhaps he would have been disabled. Who knows, maybe this was a good thing.'

Another year passed. On 3 August 1997 a third child was found on the doorstep of number 40: Alexander, a little blond boy of fifteen months who would grow up, despite the glasses he would need for near-sightedness, looking 'the spit of Josef', according to Paul Höra. The first Paul had heard of the discovery was in an 'angry phone call' from Josef on 5 August. 'Pauli, they've dumped another kid in front of the house,' Josef's irate voice had barked down the line. To which Paul, calling Josef by the familiar form of his name and only half-joking, had replied, 'Sepp, this has got to stop. Your house is turning into a kindergarten.' Again the case was reported by the Fritzls to social workers, who noted: 'Lisa and Monika are jealous of the boy and are asking when the boy will be picked up again.' The Fritzls 'try hard to give Lisa and Monika the necessary attention so that they would not feel neglected'. Even though the arrival of a third child required an 'adjustment' by the Fritzls, they were deemed 'capable' of coping. 'Herr and Frau Fritzl treat the children with love and they obviously feel and the children obviously feel happy in the family.' Also noted by social workers was a complaint by the Fritzls, who felt they were 'limited in their ability to plan holidays' because Alexander had not yet received Austrian citizenship and were now 'hoping' for the direct intervention of the Governor of Lower Austria, Erwin Pröll, who, they expected, might be able to fast-track the procedure.

Amstetten's social services had been happy enough for the Fritzls to become Alexander's legal foster parents. But, as was the case with Monika, Josef hadn't applied to adopt the boy because, as a foster parent, he stood to be paid more by the state: around 400 euros per month per child. For a third time he escaped detection. It appears that no attempt was made to find Elisabeth, nor to examine the note she had left behind with her son. And, despite the displeasure Josef had initially shown at the discovery of the child, he soon seemed to accept Alexander into the family 'as one of his own'. Indeed, he felt confident enough of Rosemarie's ability to take care of the children that later that year he took off on a safari holiday in Kenya, leaving both his 'families' for over two weeks. In Kenya he had written a postcard to Paul Höra and his new girlfriend, Andrea Schmidt. He chose 'one of the funny ones', with a photograph of two mating rhinoceroses on the front:

> Dear friends,
> By the time you get this postcard, I will already be at home.
> The weather's lovely and I'm as brown as a coconut and
> already on the rhinoceros. Food's good, lots of entertainment
> and action, three bars in the hotel across the road, two discos.
> Impossible to be bored here.
> Looking forward to seeing you again, Sepp.

As an afterthought Josef had added, in English, the words 'bush baby', a slang term for a woman's pubic hair, suggesting that his interest in travelling all the way to Kenya extended beyond his wish to familiarize himself with the local wildlife. Because he hadn't got round to finding a stamp in Africa, the card had arrived at Paul's house in Bavaria several weeks later bearing an Austrian postmark.

Elisabeth's children had given her reason to live. And she would later say that the only way she had been able to cope throughout the terrible twenty-four years of her captivity was to survive for their sakes. Elisabeth's role as a mother was seriously compromised, not only by the physical restrictions of the cellar but by the dangers that living there entailed. While Josef had been away in Kenya, her health had begun to deteriorate in ways that sometimes made it difficult for her to function. She was just 31, but she began to exhibit the health problems of a woman many years older. At times like these she missed her family even more ... she wished she was not feeling so sick all the time. She also had the problem of explaining to her children the reality of their situation. Josef would often come down to the cellar with news of the things Lisa, Monika, and the rest of the family were doing in the outside world. At Elisabeth's request he also started bringing down photographs of the family: holiday snaps and happy scenes that made it plain to the children he was forcing to live in the cellar that theirs was not a normal family life, whatever their father chose to tell them or wanted to believe. And over time they too would evolve their own double lives: the life they led when their father was there, and the other life which existed only when he was not. Playing along with his fantasy, humouring him, sitting with him silently at dinner, which was always an ordeal as he would lose his temper at the slightest thing: if one of the children didn't, in his opinion, hold a spoon properly or wasn't sitting straight enough, he would retaliate so violently it was hard for the children not to cry. Behind her father's back Elisabeth would always remind her children of the true facts of their incarceration. She insisted on that, because it was important for her that they understood reality and realized that what was going on down there was not normal – that there was another world, not only the horrible, bad one.

* * *

Sixty-one when he sold the house at Mondsee, Josef was approaching an age when many men begin to look forward to retirement. But he showed no signs of slowing down. He was still an unusually energetic man who, it was often said, could have passed for someone twenty years younger and he had set about looking for new ways to occupy himself. In the late nineties he established a clothing company selling women's underwear but after that venture proved unprofitable there was a lull in his business activities, which he would not resume with any real vigour until 2002.

In between there were fishing trips, several new, never-to-be-completed additions to the house, and another holiday. In 1998 he again travelled with Paul Höra to Pattaya, this time with Andrea accompanying them. Paul, who had by then bought himself a video camera, doesn't just remember his friend's relaxed and jocular composure throughout the trip, he has the footage to prove it: Josef, tanned and laughing uproariously at some private joke, his belly bulging over a tiny pair of swimming briefs; Josef lying on Pattaya beach, being massaged by a local man; and Josef tearing into an enormous loin of pork in a German-style restaurant. The three of them were gone for four weeks, and Paul still can't believe how his best friend could have managed to idle away his time in such apparent high spirits knowing what he did about what was going on at home. 'Look at him laughing. He's laughing,' Paul will still say incredulously when he watches the holiday tape. 'What was he thinking? What was going on inside his head?' In one shot Andrea, who was filming at the time, takes in the interior of a clothes shop. The lens lingers over a table full of T-shirts, then zooms in inquisitively on the far corner of the shop, where Josef can be seen asking a member of staff to show him one of the pretty red party dresses on display. A few seconds later the film ends. Josef, having suddenly become aware of being watched, had shouted at Andrea to switch off the camera. Paul recalls that: 'He was really quite angry, saying, "Nobody needs to see that," and I was saying "We're only filming the goods here, Sepp. Relax, I can cut it out. What are you buying that for anyway?" It was obvious that the dress was far too small for Rosemarie, it would never have fitted her and that's when Sepp said that it wasn't for Rosemarie but for his "girlfriend". Well, we weren't about to argue. What business is it of ours if he has a girlfriend? That sort of thing happens in plenty of families.' Paul, knowing what he does today, adds that: 'It's as if he had convinced himself that Elisabeth really was in that cult and that the woman in the cellar was his girlfriend. That's who the dress must have been for: Elisabeth.'

Living under Rosemarie's guardianship as they did, Lisa, Monika, and Alexander were progressing well at the local school. They were healthy and, although they were never the best students, they were to become proficient, especially in music, with Monika and Alexander taking up the trumpet, Lisa the flute. Alexander, particularly, would grow to be an outgoing and cheeky little boy, the 'class clown', a Gameboy and Nintendo 'addict' like many of his classmates. Michaela Bernhard, the mother of Alexander's best friend from school, was among the mothers who would sometimes leave their children in Rosemarie's care at the house in Ybbsstrasse, where they would splash around in the outdoor pool of a summer afternoon. Frau Bernhard would remember that most of the other mothers felt both pity for and solidarity with Rosemarie, who was judged to have been very badly treated by her daughter who had landed these three children on her. She remembers: 'Rosemarie was always very engaged with the children, always organizing parties, working with the voluntary fire brigade who would put together events for the kids, cooking at school or preparing confetti and that kind of thing.' Rosemarie, she says, was also viewed in the community as a perfect example of 'a good Catholic woman', 'family-orientated', and 'devoted' to her foster children, and on good terms with both her local priest and the school's religious education teacher. A keen volunteer, she belonged to the group of '*Tisch-Mütter*', mothers who would entertain groups of children preparing for their first communion at their houses, where together they would bake bread, make candles, and get to grips with the basics of the Catholic faith. It remains Frau Bernhard's view that Rosemarie couldn't have possibly known about her husband's abduction of Elisabeth, primarily because she seemed to be 'a very naive woman' but also because 'it would have taken nerves of steel to have all those parents coming in and out of the house, if you knew what was going on in the cellar right underneath them'. Although the Fritzls came from an era when domestic violence was all too commonly accepted as the lot of a married woman, Frau Bernhard never detected in Rosemarie the signs of an abused spouse. Indeed, like many other parents, she had been impressed at Josef's engagement with the children. Not that he helped much around the house – a husband's non-participation in the rearing of children was nothing unusual even in the marriages of Frau Bernhard's generation – but Josef was often to be seen driving Lisa, Monika, and Alexander to school in his beaten-up old black Mercedes, and on his arrival at the school gates in Allersdorf he would meet the approving glances of the teachers: bringing up these three foster children, he would explain, called for particular vigilance from their grandparents: 'I have to be careful in case those people from the cult come to get them.'

Although there was no denying that Rosemarie made an excellent foster mother, for Josef one of the unforeseen drawbacks of having his wife raise the children he had conceived with Elisabeth was the attachment they would later develop to their grandmother. He would later say that he had never felt sufficiently loved by the children he had with his wife and that his 'downstairs children' had always been much more forthcoming in their affections. But this state of affairs always seemed to change once the children were allowed up into the house and permitted the same degree of freedom as other boys and girls, with the result that, after a year or two, they too seemed to 'desert' Josef. Alexander, for example, who had long been Josef's favourite child, now became, in his father's view, an 'Oma-Burli', a 'Granny's boy', clinging to Rosemarie's apron strings and ceasing to lavish on his 'grandfather' what he considered to be the right degree of affection. And so when, a week and a half before Christmas Day 2002, Elisabeth gave birth for a seventh, and final, time in the cellar of Ybbsstrasse, and the resulting child turned out to be a boy, Josef was overjoyed.

For a few years Josef had done little in the way of investing the capital that had been freed up by the sale of the house at Mondsee, but with the birth of Felix he once again threw himself into frenetic activity. Starting with the purchase in 2002 of a 'villa' in Waidhoffnerstrasse, in one of the smarter areas of Amstetten, he now bought four properties in quick succession: in December 2004 he purchased a block of flats in St Pölten, the capital of Lower Austria. Two years after that, on 6 February, he would acquire another apartment block, in Waidhofen an der Ybbs, the so-called 'town of spires'. And in 2007 he became the owner of another nondescript three-storey apartment block in the neighbouring town of Kematen an der Ybbs. Like the house in Ybbsstrasse, all these properties were conspicuously plain buildings on main roads which Josef would do up with his son Josef and rent to tenants. It is some measure of his persuasiveness that he had, within just five years, persuaded the banks to lend him close to 3.5 million euros.

And it was no coincidence that his dreams of building a property empire finally began to be realized in the year of Felix's birth. Sixty-seven by the time the boy was born, Josef would increasingly turn his thoughts to the future. He now began to ponder the fate of his family in the cellar, not, he later admitted, through any late-emerging altruism, but rather because, for the first time in his life, he began to perceive the cellar as a threat. Kerstin was 14, Stefan 12. Soon they would be adults. And Josef would later tell a psychiatrist that he began to feel 'frightened' of the 'three against one' scenario that he could see developing in the cellar. He worried that sooner or later his children would rise up against him. And the thought that the cellar might one day claim even Josef Fritzl among its victims was at least part of the reason that a plan for his 'underground family's' eventual evacuation now began to form in his mind.

Part of his solution was to secure for all his children an economically viable future: hence the property-buying spree. Later he would often refer to what he had achieved in the cellar as his 'realm', 'kingdom', or 'domain', and it is more than likely that he had similarly acquisitive ambitions in the outside world. Knowing that work, in any normal sense of the word, would be beyond both Kerstin and Stefan, should he ever hope to integrate them in the world above – permanently traumatized, perhaps: they were poorly educated, unused to open spaces, and unlikely to take well to socializing with other people – he assigned them small roles in the house above. While Elisabeth, Josef envisaged, would be his 'secretary', Kerstin could 'cook' and Stefan, who had shown himself to have inherited some of his father's talent for engineering – he was always playing around with his father's tools – would help with the building work in much the same way that Josef junior had been doing. Felix, however, Josef judged still young and impressionable enough to be 'saved'. And there hatched in his mind the idea that his youngest son would now be groomed as his 'heir and successor'.

It was a hugely ambitious if not unachievable plan, although Josef never regarded it as such. He would often sit around the kitchen table with Elisabeth discussing the various options. And she, on numerous occasions, saw him walking about in the cellar talking out loud to himself in a deeply involved way that suggested to her that he had now become completely obsessed with the problem of reuniting the two families. It was agreed between the two of them that at some point in the future, once he had smashed together the rooms of the ground floor in Ybbsstrasse and built from them an apartment for his 'downstairs family', his long-lost daughter and her children would 'come back from the cult' to live together with his wife and the three 'upstairs' children. Having, from early youth, been instilled with a terror and distrust of authority, Elisabeth went along with it. Late one evening in 1983, during their escape to Vienna, she had shared with Brigitte her reasons for never having reported her father to the police: 'I knew this wasn't the kind of thing that was supposed to be happening in a family. And they'll never believe me. If it's a fight between me and him, he'll always win.' If anything, Elisabeth had become more helplessly subordinated to her father since then. It had never crossed his mind that his 'downstairs family' would attempt to expose the lie of the 'cult story'. Had it not been for the exceptional circumstances of her 'escape', Elisabeth may well have gone along unquestioningly with her father's plan, at least until the first chance of escape had presented itself.

* * *

Old age made Josef sentimental. In 2006 he and Rosemarie would celebrate their golden wedding anniversary
in their new Amstetten 'villa', and Michaela Bernhard
would remember thinking 'how sweet' when she came
across a photograph of the Fritzls in the local paper
where they were seen being congratulated by the town's
deputy mayor. Josef also became a regular fixture at the
Kirchenstrasse school reunions, joining his old friends
Karl Dunkl and Friedrich Leimlehner on excursions to
historic sites or nature reserves around Austria. By 2005
these 'field trips, organized by Karl, had become so popular among the school's former pupils that their spouses
had been invited along. And in the same year a group of
perhaps thirty Amstetten pensioners, including Josef and
Rosemarie Fritzl, would hire a bus to make a day trip to
the Wachau, a popular tourist destination, equidistant
between the towns of Melk and Krems, where Maria
Nenning, towards the end of her life, had been sent to
live in a nursing home. On their arrival the old teacher,
Josef Freihammer, delivered to his former pupils a
specially prepared lecture on the history of the many
fortresses of the region and some little-known facts about
the excellent Rieslings that are produced in the local vine-
yards. The group visited the Greinburg Castle, which
stands on a small hill above the town of Grein and over-
looks the River Danube, where they hired a local tour
guide, and take in the castle's magnificent Knights' Hall,
its chapel with its baroque altarpiece, and the *Diamant-
gewölbe*, or Diamond Vault, whose arched ceiling is
pierced with dozens of tiny glass windows. After a light
supper at one of the local guesthouses, the group

returned, contented, to Amstetten towards late evening. The Fritzls, however, turned down the offer of one last beer at a local pub because their foster children were waiting for them at home and it did not do to leave them alone so long. Still, his friends would later remember Josef as one of the most enthusiastic participants of the reunions. He hadn't missed a single one of the get-togethers and seemed to genuinely enjoy the company of his old schoolfriends.

Josef Fritzl: looking nostalgically back over the past, and enthusiastically forward to the future, the desire in him to fuse the two different worlds growing very strong in him now. By 2003 he was down in the cellar almost constantly: in time for the 7 o'clock news, then dinner, more television, and sometimes he would stay the night. They would spend some of Christmas together, a ritual that had begun in the nineties when Josef had brought down a plastic tree – made in China – and sometimes he brought with him other gifts: teddy bears, a model train for Felix, a toolbox for Stefan, a goldfish, a budgerigar even. He would often talk to Elisabeth about the day he would take them to live upstairs, merging the two 'families'. By the autumn of 2007 he had written to tenants of two of the downstairs flats telling them that he would need them to move out by the end of the year. He told them he needed their apartments for his daughter, who was coming back to live in Amstetten. She 'was getting divorced' and bringing her three children to live at number 40. As soon as his tenants had gone he smashed the two flats together with a view to creating an apartment large enough for the imminent arrival of his 'downstairs family'.

At around the same time he extracted from Elisabeth another letter. He sent it to himself at 40 Ybbsstrasse from Kematen, a town not 20 miles away where he had two properties, and when, a few days later, it arrived in the post he opened it and read it out in front of Rosemarie and other people. Elisabeth, the letter said, was intending to return home with her children.

It had been his intention to stage a spectacular 'reunion' of the two 'families' towards the end of 2008. But when, around the middle of March 2008, 19-year-old Kerstin had, for the first time in her life, become life-threateningly ill, he saw an opportunity to orchestrate Elisabeth's 'miraculous return from the cult'.

It had begun with Felix. His health had suddenly severely deteriorated. And not long afterwards Kerstin too became ill. And while Felix gradually recovered, his sister's health began to seriously falter. She was coughing a lot, feverish, and dropping in and out of consciousness. When, by the beginning of April, she began to suffer fits which seemed to resemble epilepsy, it became clear that hers was not an affliction that could be remedied in the cellar with aspirin. Elisabeth was telling her father that now was the time.

Josef had successfully carried out the masquerade of 'finding' a child abandoned on his doorstep three times. Now he prepared to 'discover' a fourth.

PART THREE

CHAPTER TEN

INTO THE LIGHT

It came as a profound shock to Hubert Schrankmaier when, one sunny morning in late April 2008, his favourite classical music programme was interrupted by the news that a man from Amstetten, Lower Austria, had been arrested for having 'fathered seven children with the daughter he kept in a cellar for twenty-four years'. Schrankmaier had been driving through the Mostviertel at the time with the radio on and had at first failed to make the connection between the 'Herr F' in the breaking news story and the man he had, only three days previously, spoken to at some length about the risk of flooding posed to a house in Amstetten's Waidhoffnerstrasse by a stream towards the back of its garden.

A tall, likeable, well-spoken man in his early fifties, Schrankmaier had been doing business with Josef Fritzl since 2004. They had first been introduced through a colleague of Schrankmaier's and had subsequently become business partners, working closely together on

the acquisition of a handful of properties in Lower
Austria with a view to either developing them or letting
them to tenants. Schrankmaier, a surveyor by training,
had been involved in the development of the Waidhoffnerstrasse 'villa' project, the two-storey, detached house
whose large garden made it an ideal candidate for
converting and expanding into flats, penthouses, and
offices. Although the proposed expansion had caused an
outcry among the neighbours – fearing that their peace-
ful residential street would thus be horribly commercial-
ized, they had sought to block the project by sending a
petition to the council – it was more or less a foregone
conclusion that, what with Fritzl's connections, there
would be no problem obtaining planning permission. By
the time Schrankmaier came to know him, Fritzl was on
friendly terms with almost everyone there was to know
in the region – certainly all the 'important' people – and
once, Schrankmaier had been impressed to observe,
Fritzl had even been greeted warmly in one of the smart
restaurants they would meet in by the district governor,
Hans-Heinz Lenze.

Fritzl, it had become Schrankmaier's opinion over the
course of their acquaintance, was a 'solid, totally depend-
able' person. He was also 'one of the most dynamic people
I've ever met: a great negotiator and fascinated by new
technology, anything that was new on the market, he'd
know about. And he had a very quick mind. I mean, he
could take one look at a plan of a house and immediately
grasp its potential. That was his strength: these terrific
ideas combined with that rare ability to actually carry them
out. In Austria you'd say he has a good "handshake qual-

ity": he always stuck to his word. He was so reliable that he wouldn't borrow a pen without making sure to return it the next day. Just the other day the 73-year old Fritzl had said to Schrankmaier, 'One thing I can't imagine is retiring and spending all day on the sofa watching television with a beer in my hand. I'm going to live to be 120.'

The two men had rapidly become friends of sorts, with Schrankmaier introducing his business partner to the haute cuisine and fine wines of Austria – about which Fritzl had been embarrassed to admit he knew virtually nothing – and Fritzl, in return, sharing his vast knowledge 'about just about everything else'. One of the many things that Schrankmaier particularly admired about Fritzl was his capacity for soaking up new information at an age when many people have begun to decline. Often the two of them would set off in the car first thing in the morning to drive around to have a look at some property or other. But no matter how early they met, Fritzl would always have been up since at least 5 a.m., scanning the internet for news and committing to memory the exchange rates: 'how the yen was doing against the Swiss franc, or he'd have checked the share prices of all the local companies. He was always totally clued up.' It was Schrankmaier's role, as Fritzl's adviser in such matters, to survey any properties in which his business partner showed an interest, assess them for future profitability, and help raise the money to buy them. 'We'd always go to two or three banks for loans. It was never a problem to get credit. Herr Fritzl had a good reputation and he would always pay back his loans on time. He would mainly do up the properties himself – with his son, Josef.

And I respected him for that. You could tell he was proud of what he had achieved in his life but he never got lazy. He was a total professional and very ambitious.'

The first thought that occurred to Schrankmaier as he listened to the revelations about 'Herr F' on his car radio was that the newsreader's normally mellifluous voice had taken on a 'starchy and abrupt' tone, as if even she had been shocked by what she was now reading out over the airwaves. And it was only when she went on to report that 'the man had previously claimed to police and social services that his daughter had joined a cult' that Schrankmaier's memory of a conversation he had had with Josef Fritzl on their very first meeting suddenly came into sharp focus. 'I remembered him mentioning something about his daughter having gone missing and something to do with a commune. And, to be honest, I sympathized. To me Herr Fritzl always came across as a relaxed, though firm, grandfather. I saw how he was with the children: he had his boundaries but he was always laughing or amusing them with jokes or wordplay. In a funny way I sort of looked up to him as a role model. I remember thinking: that's how I want to be when my turn comes around. So to hear this. Well, it was just … beyond comprehension.'

So appalling were the charges that were now being relayed on every radio station in Austria at fifteen-minute intervals that Schrankmaier actually began to feel unwell and was forced to pull into a lay-by. There was now no doubt in his mind that 'Herr F', as the majority of Austrian media would continue to refer to him for reasons of confidentiality, and Josef Fritzl were one and the same. 'I simply couldn't believe it,' he says. 'It didn't make sense. They were two completely different people: this grotesque person I was hearing about on the radio and the decent, incredibly industrious man I had worked with for four years.' Nevertheless, Schrankmaier couldn't help but question the veracity of the story. 'I was completely convinced that someone had made a mistake or that Herr Fritzl had been, I don't know, set up in some way – you know, that kind of thing has been known to happen in Austria. Our police service hasn't the best reputation. And there's the issue of loyalty. You don't just drop your friends because of an allegation. You stick by them. I thought, well, they must have made some kind of mistake. By tomorrow it will have all blown over.' Schrankmaier continued the rest of his car journey with the car radio turned off.

Both the Austrian authorities and the majority of the Fritzls' tenants and neighbours had spent the past twenty-four years accepting as fact anything Josef Fritzl had chosen to tell them about the story of his missing daughter. And when, on the morning of Saturday, 19 April, a week before Schrankmaier had been forced in disgust to turn off his car radio, the 'grandfatherly' 73-year-old Josef Fritzl had reported the discovery of a fourth 'grandchild' – the 19-year-old Kerstin – on his doorstep, suspicions once again immediately turned in the direction of Fritzl's missing daughter, Elisabeth. Indeed, had it not been for Dr Albert Reiter's disquiet about the story, and later the common sense of an employee of St Pölten Catholic

Diocese who was an expert on religious fringe groups, it is more than likely that Fritzl's version of events would have simply been accepted as the truth, along with all the other lies that had, over the years, come to define his occupancy of number 40. Given the reluctance of those who knew the Fritzls to question any of the extraordinary and often very public goings-on at the house in Ybbsstrasse, it is not inconceivable that his secret might not have come to light at all.

Rosemarie Fritzl was holidaying with a friend near Lake Maggiore in Italy when, shortly before dawn on Saturday, 19 April, Josef had finally been persuaded to evacuate his now seriously ill daughter, Kerstin, from the cellar. Josef and Elisabeth had carried Kerstin up from the cellar, into the house, which was empty of any other adults: only the three 'grandchildren' – Lisa, Monika, and Alexander – were at home and still fast asleep in their beds. They continued up the stairs and into the corridor that connected the old house and the new extension, then through this to the apartment block and into Josef's first-floor flat, where, at the end of another corridor, Elisabeth and her father now entered his sparsely furnished bedroom and laid Kerstin in his single bed. It was the first time that Elisabeth had been out of the cellar in almost twenty-four years. But, mindful of the effect that her absence would have on Felix and Stefan, she remained in the house for only a few minutes. Having extracted from her father a promise to take Kerstin to a hospital, she was back in the cellar by about 6 a.m.

An hour and a half passed. Josef then made the call to the emergency services, which was relayed to an ambulance team of three paramedics at exactly 7.56 a.m. They arrived outside number 40, together with a doctor, less than ten minutes later. Josef answered the door and led them through the house and into his apartment on the first floor of the extension, where Kerstin was now lying pale, injured, and unconscious, in white trousers, a torn or lacerated orange pyjama top, and a pair of red socks. Although the emergency doctor was not able to diagnose her condition, it was clear from their preliminary examination that, even with medical intervention, Kerstin might not survive. While the paramedics lifted Kerstin onto a stretcher, Josef repeated what he had earlier told the operator over the phone, namely that 'I found her on the doorstep. I've never seen her before.' One of the paramedics, Dr Reiter's son, would later that day share with his father the 'strange feeling' he had about the practically furnitureless room where Kerstin had lain.

Although it was suggested to Josef that he travel in the ambulance to the hospital, he declined and suggested that it would make more sense for him to follow in his car. And the reason why it would take him twenty minutes longer than it did the paramedics to reach the Intensive Care unit of Amstetten Hospital was that Josef had taken the opportunity to descend to the cellar again, where he had quickly made Elisabeth write one final letter, a brief note in which she described her daughter's symptoms over the previous forty-eight hours. She also alluded in the letter to the existence of Stefan and Felix and the fact that they were still in her care. It ended with the words:

'Kerstin, please hold on until we see each other again! We'll be there soon!'

Armed with the letter, and leaving Stefan, Felix, and Elisabeth underground, Josef set off in his old black Mercedes, through the still sleepy streets of Amstetten, south towards the hospital.

Throughout the long years of their imprisonment Josef had come to employ, as one of the most effective methods of manipulating Elisabeth, death threats against their children. He had shown no compunction about using the children as weapons against her – indeed, he had made it clear that he would rather 'kill you all' than risk exposing his secret – and this had the effect that, by the time of Kerstin's illness, Elisabeth and her children had become unquestioningly submissive to their father. Even she would later admit that she had returned to the cellar voluntarily. And, as far as Josef was concerned, there was no danger that either Elisabeth or Kerstin, should she recover, would divulge to anyone the real reason behind their long absence from Amstetten. He was also confident enough in his own ability to convince the authorities of just about anything he chose to tell them that it never crossed his mind that the hospitalization of Kerstin would prove be the first step in a dramatic, almost farcical, unravelling of his double life.

So it was a noticeably calm Josef Fritzl who walked into Amstetten Hospital's reception area at around 8.20 that Saturday morning, and who was summoned upstairs into Intensive Care to have a 'private chat' in the office of

Dr Reiter about the exact circumstances surrounding Kerstin's sudden appearance. Kerstin's condition, Dr Reiter would take pains to emphasize to her 'grandfather' a few minutes later when he first walked Fritzl over to his department where Kerstin now lay in an artificially induced coma hooked up to a life-support machine, was 'hanging in the balance'. The smallest scrap of information 'could save her life'. Once the two men had seated themselves in Reiter's office, it seems that Josef saw in the doctor's concern for Kerstin an opportunity to manipulate the situation for his own ends. He had lied his way out of potentially dangerous situations often enough. If earlier that day he had been worried about the possible consequences of taking his daughter out of the cellar for the first time in almost a quarter of a century, these doubts were now rapidly fading. In their place was the old confidence he had employed many times over the years when dealing with the unsuspecting Amstetten authorities. Josef judged the moment was right to produce Elisabeth's handwritten note which he now told the doctor he had found on Kerstin's body.

Focused as he was on trying to gather together any clues that might save Kerstin's life, Reiter would only later remember becoming vaguely aware of another feeling creeping up inside of him as he sat alone with Josef Fritzl around the small coffee table in his office. Reiter had instinctively felt 'puzzled' by the notion that any mother of a perhaps terminally ill girl would abandon her daughter on her father's doorstep. It seemed a counter-intuitive thing for a parent to do, something he'd never witnessed before in all his thirty-odd years as a doctor. But such 'gut feelings' remained, for now, second-ary considerations. And, fully taken in by Fritzl's 'grand-fatherly concern', Reiter proceeded in their ten-minute talk to extract from Kerstin's 'grandfather' any informa-tion that could possibly lead to either a treatment or a diagnosis. It would take another three days before the gnawing feeling in Reiter's gut would compel him to question with any seriousness the validity of the story of the cult.

A hundred miles away, in the former military barracks in Vienna's Rennweg that now functioned as the head-quarters of Lower Austria's Criminal Police, two middle-ranking detectives attached to the Homicide Department, had been keeping an eye on the case ever since the local police in Amstetten had informed them of what doctors now suspected to be a poisoning case. Convinced that their only hope of either rescuing Kerstin or uncovering the mysterious circumstances in which she had been found, Reiter had agreed with the inspectors, and with Christiane Burkheiser, the State Prosecutor, who happened to be on duty at the time, that an appeal for Elisabeth's return to Amstetten would be made through the media. By mid-afternoon on Monday, 21 April, three days after Kerstin had been rushed to hospital, a public appeal for Elisabeth's return was made on local radio. On the same day the police issued a warrant for her arrest under Code 21. She was suspected of grievous bodily harm through neglect, abusing or neglecting a minor or defenceless person, and abandoning an injured person.

One of the thousands of people who heard the appeal was Otto Stangl, a television reporter living in St Pölten who worked for the national television channel, ORF. Once he had confirmed the story with Dr Reiter by telephone, it was decided that Stangl would put together a news story on the events of the morning which would include a piece to camera from the doctor. Stangl, hoping to interview other members of Kerstin's family for his report, now rang Amstetten police station for any contact numbers. He got through to Josef Fritzl on his mobile phone at exactly 11.54 a.m. the same day and asked her 'grandfather' whether he would be prepared to make a public statement. 'I was in the studio and asked him if he would give us an interview so we could help find his daughter,' says Stangl. 'He wasn't at all confused or withdrawn as, with hindsight, one might have expected. It never occurred to me that he might have been hiding something. He was completely normal, but very articulate. Nothing about what he said seemed remotely suspicious.'

Fritzl seemed forthcoming enough at the beginning of their conversation, and Stangl still has the notebook in which he wrote down fragments of what Fritzl told him:

'Herr Stangl, how do you think we feel? We've tried everything. I've looked all over the country for her. You wouldn't believe what we've been through.'

'There's a rumour that she was living in Upper Austria.'

'... I don't know what to do because I'm not sure it should be made so public ... I mean, we have seven children.'

'She left her babies with us and from time to time a letter would appear. I'm already 73 years old. We're completely desperate. Nobody understands this situation. We're immensely grateful for any leads.'

But when Stangl asked him whether he would be prepared to appear on television, Fritzl began to hesitate. 'He then said he didn't want to go on camera, and I told him he could think about it and that I would call him again once we'd arrived in Amstetten. Before he rang off he said, and, knowing what I know now, I find this particularly cynical, "Please make an appeal for Elisabeth. For me."' Stangl and his cameraman then headed for Amstetten Hospital in the car.

In another car, another man was driving to the same hospital, equally baffled by the events of the past three days. He was on his way there to pick up from Dr Reiter the letter that Josef Fritzl had discovered on Kerstin's body, and he spent the half-mile journey pondering the clues laid before him. At least one other of the letters that the Fritzls had received from their daughter over the years had already been verified by a graphologist as having been written by Elisabeth. Amstetten social services had copies of some of these letters and one of the detectives had been able to cast an eye over them himself after Hans-Heinz Lenze, the district governor, who also functioned as the head of Amstetten's social services, had passed on to the police the caseworker's file. Meanwhile a further conversation between Josef Fritzl and the police had revealed that, as recently as February, Elisabeth had written a letter to her parents in which she had conveyed her desire to return to Amstetten. That letter had borne a Kematen postmark, a fact that had confused the detective who had seen it: Kematen was a town just eight miles

down the road from Amstetten and, although he wasn't
to make the connection until long after the case was
'solved', it was where Josef Fritzl had spent the best part
of the past five months doing up the block of flats that he
had bought there in November 2007.

Having picked up from Dr Reiter the note that Josef
Fritzl had found on Kerstin's body, the two police detectives from the Homicide Department now determined to
put all the letters under the nose of a different kind of
expert. By mid-afternoon they were on the phone to Dr
Manfred Wohlfahrt, the Catholic Church's local diocese's
expert on cults and fringe religious groups.

Wohlfahrt, a veteran in all matters concerning sects
and communes, had occupied his position in St Pölten
Diocese since 1980, four years before Elisabeth Fritzl had
disappeared. But he had never been consulted about the
Fritzl case before Kerstin's hospitalization even though
he was a resident of Amstetten and actually lived close to
both the Fritzls' house and the police station. Late on
Monday afternoon he too arrived in Amstetten. In front
of the detectives he examined the evidence. 'The handwriting was plain and her style was very simple, though
grammatically correct,' he remembers. 'I can't remember
noticing any grammar or spelling mistakes. But there was
nothing in the content or the style of this letter that indicated any connection with a cult. The "cult" wasn't even
mentioned, and so I immediately assumed that the whole
idea that Elisabeth had joined a cult must have derived
from what her father had already told the authorities.
There wasn't a single reference to this woman's life or
whereabouts and everything about it was very vague.

Normally people who live in cults make numerous references to their religious beliefs, for example, or their way of life – anything that's important to them. And the writing was far too plain, formal even, too colourless, and I said that it didn't appear remotely authentic, and that it resembled something that had been dictated. I told the officers that they should really start turning their attention to Elisabeth's family, to the environment she grew up in. And that they should try and talk with the father about the reasons she ran away. Of course, I never suspected the real truth about her father's involvement. But, in the majority of cases where a young person leaves home to join a religious group, the first question that needs to be asked is: why did they run away in the first place? More often than not it's because of whatever has been going on in the family.'

Wohlfart then began to cast further doubt on the 'cult' story. He pointed out that there were only a handful of cults in existence at the time of Elisabeth's disappearance: Otto Mühl's commune, the Moon Cult, Jehovah's Witnesses, Mormons, Adventists, Scientologists, Hari Krishna, and the Children of God plus various evangelical fringe groups. 'However, none of them have been known to actually make people disappear. And it would be very untypical for any of these groups to send away children born in their community. On the contrary, they would be more inclined to keep and raise the children according to their religious beliefs or doctrine.' As the detectives from the Homicide Department listened, their suspicions began to shift for the first time from Elisabeth to her respectable-seeming and elderly father. Another telephone call to Reiter elicited the doctor's 'gut feeling' about Josef Fritzl's 'abandoned grandchildren' story, as well as his paramedic son's thoughts on the 'strange' room at number 40 in which Kerstin had been found unconscious.

While the police and the doctors endeavoured to untangle the clues laid before them, outside on the streets of Amstetten, Otto Stangl and his cameraman were busy interviewing some of the neighbours of the Fritzls to bulk up their news story. Over and over they heard the story of the cult and the missing Elisabeth and the strain that the three foundlings had put on their grandparents. By 5 p.m. they had gathered enough material and were editing it down in time to be broadcast that evening. Stangl had been unable to persuade Fritzl to be interviewed. But Stangl had managed to interview Dr Reiter and about a minute of this interview was included into the report. Looking straight into the camera with an expression of unmistakable seriousness, Dr Reiter says: 'I would like the mother to contact us. We will treat any contact with discretion and we will probably get a step further with our diagnosis and treatment.' The report was screened on ORF that evening between 7 and 8 p.m.

Monday evening: Elisabeth Fritzl and her sons Stefan and Felix had now spent three days in the cellar without Kerstin, unaware of what was going on above their heads, frantic with worry about the fate of Kerstin and the non-appearance of their father in the cellar. Because of the increased police presence in the house – inspectors were now making regular calls at number 40 – Josef had been hard-pressed to find the time to go down there. In addition, Rosemarie had by this stage rushed back from Italy and she was at home most of the day, save for a couple of hours when she visited Kerstin in hospital. And other family members had started arriving at number 40, among them Elisabeth's eldest sister, Ulrike. Beneath them, Elisabeth, Stefan, and Felix waited.

As had become normal in the cellar, the television was on almost constantly. By chance Elisabeth and her children had been watching ORF when Stangl's news story was aired. Now they watched in terror as a doctor they had never seen before appealed in the strongest terms for the return of Kerstin's mother.

Nobody who knew or came across Josef Fritzl during those few days, or the week that followed, would remark on anything remotely out of the ordinary about his behaviour. Only Rosemarie seemed in any way traumatized by the sudden appearance and hospitalization of Kerstin. Shortly after 9 a.m. on Tuesday, 22 April paramedics were once again dispatched to 40 Ybbsstrasse. Rosemarie had called the emergency services – all that had been audible to the operator was the sounds of a woman apparently moaning, and it was thought that she had collapsed – and a request was put through to the Amstetten police that they send an officer to the house in case Rosemarie had fallen unconscious and the paramedics needed to force the door. It is unclear what happened in the interim but it seems that the situation had resolved itself within the ten minutes or so that it took either the police or the ambulance to arrive there. The call-out was later logged as a 'false alarm'.

Rosemarie's husband, though, carried on with his building work as calmly and industriously as he ever had done. He was often on the phone to Schrankmaier, who, two weeks earlier, had taken him to see a property in Hölzöster, a lakeside town in the area, which Fritzl was now considering buying. The rest of the time he seemed to be spending driving, with his son Josef, to and fro between Amstetten and Kematen, where father and son continued to renovate the block of flats that he had bought there the previous November. Wednesday passed without any notable occurrences. On Thursday, however, Fritzl received a telephone call from a police detective in which he was asked to come down to the station to undergo DNA testing. The police had concluded that a woman with 'as many children as Elisabeth' might have conceived them with multiple partners, or even – they had heard that such situations were common in communes – raised another woman's child as her own. In Elisabeth's absence they had decided to request DNA samples from both her parents, hoping thereby to firmly establish that Kerstin was in fact her daughter. Although Josef agreed to the DNA test, he apologized for the fact that, as he would be working all day on the property in Kematen, he wouldn't be able to find the time to come to the police station. He was simply 'too busy with work'. He was equally 'busy' the next day, Friday, although he did find time to ring Governor Hans-Heinz Lenze to thank him 'for all your good work in trying to find Elisabeth'. Lenze reassured him, 'Somehow we'll find her, Herr Fritzl.'

Late on the evening of Friday, 25 April, Josef returned home to Ybbsstrasse. Unbeknown to his family, the authorities, or indeed anybody else in Amstetten, he had been visiting the cellar at regular intervals during the week with news of Kerstin's still worsening condition. It had long since been his intention to somehow, that year, reintegrate Elisabeth and her children into the house above: he had often discussed the plan with Elisabeth and it had been with a view to enabling her to make a more convincing show of her eventual 'return' to Amstetten that he had, back in February, made her write the letter that he had sent to himself and Rosemarie from Kematen. Elisabeth, mindful of the fact that her father was, as she would later say, incapable of tolerating a situation that did not go exactly according to his plan, seems to have persuaded him that now would be a credible moment for her to 'reappear' from the cult.

She knew that he would do almost anything to save Kerstin, if only because it had been part of his plan that she should be integrated into his life upstairs as some sort of maid. Fritzl was always complaining that doing the shopping was a burden. It would have been far more convenient for him if the downstairs family were brought upstairs – he'd have more people under his control.

Among other things, Josef had spent the week taking legal advice. He had explained to Elisabeth that there was no point in her resurfacing until he had arranged for a lawyer to sit with her during her questioning by the police. His plan was to convince a lawyer of the story of the cult and how he had managed to 'buy off' the leaders of the cult his daughter had supposedly disappeared to and have him protect her from any legal consequences of having abandoned her, in one case possibly terminally ill, children. He intended to brief the lawyer not to allow Elisabeth to be questioned by police on her own, in order that she would not be pressured by investigators into revealing the true story of her long absence. Elisabeth was to say nothing if she didn't want to endanger the children. Fritzl had threatened to kill all the family before and he constantly reminded Elisabeth of the horror the media would put them through if it all came out in the open.

Just before midnight on the same Friday Josef returned to the cellar with a change of clothing for Elisabeth, Stefan, and Felix: A pair of Levi's jeans, slightly scuffed at the left knee, a grey T-shirt, and a black sweater for Elisabeth; a pair of pleated dark-blue trousers and a T-shirt bearing the Austrian flag for Stefan; and a light-blue T-shirt, matching jumper, and grey tracksuit trousers with an orange stripe for Felix.

It is not difficult to see how the story of Kerstin's sudden reappearance, her life-threatening illness, and the desperate attempt to track down her mother had fired the imagination of the media. And it is a measure of how very far most people were from guessing the true facts of the case, not to mention how susceptible even reporters were to the story of the 'cult', that, while Fritzl moved between the upper floors of the house and the cellar, ORF's sister channel ORF2 had, a few hours before Josef had gone down to the cellar with the fresh laundry, circulated a press release to newspapers about a documentary that was scheduled to be screened on Monday in which it was hypothesized that Elisabeth had been living in a 'sect' in which 'only female children are tolerated'.

Nor is it difficult to understand that, with Kerstin's condition so grave, the adult children of the Fritzls now began to rally around their parents. They were in and out of the house and making regular visits to the hospital.

What is, however, almost impossible to imagine is how, late on the same Friday evening, once Elisabeth and the children had changed into the clean clothes that Josef had brought down to the cellar, they had followed him, first through the two electronically secured doors of the 'dungeon', then through the hole in the wall that he had hidden behind a shelf unit in his workshop, through many doors, up the staircase that led into the little courtyard at the centre of the house, and eventually into number 40 itself, where they would, the next day, be either reunited with, or meet for the first time, the children who had grown up in number 40. They were taken to a room upstairs at about midnight. The next day they were introduced to the other kids and the rest of the family. It was all strangely normal and then they went off to the hospital. All the while, unaware of this significant breakthrough in the case, the police

continued to chase up clues to their possible whereabouts.

It was only the next day at 4 p.m., exactly a week after
paramedics had rushed Kerstin Fritzl to hospital, that
Josef Fritzl finally called Dr Reiter on his mobile with the
news that his daughter had 'returned'. And the two
detectives from the Homicide Department, having been
alerted by Reiter, finally made an arrest. Fritzl and Reiter
agreed that they would meet that evening in Intensive
Care at 8 p.m. and that Fritzl would be accompanied by
Elisabeth. Having driven the four hours back from a
conference in Carinthia, Dr Reiter was waiting for them
upstairs in the unit and, from the window in Kerstin's
room that looked out onto the hospital's car park, he saw
Fritzl's black Mercedes turn in from the main road and a
woman he correctly assumed to be Elisabeth get out of
the passenger seat as her father emerged from the other
side of the car. Everyone who caught sight of Elisabeth
saw a 'distressed', 'troubled' woman who resembled the
picture they had in their heads of a person who had spent
a lifetime in a commune. Josef Fritzl looked as calm,
concerned, and neatly dressed as ever. He and Elisabeth
spent several minutes in Kerstin's room, but doctors were
disappointed when neither of them was able to shed any
further light on the cause of Kerstin's condition. Towards
9 p.m. father and daughter finally made their way downstairs towards the hospital's exit. But they never got as far
as the car park. Tipped off by the doctors, the two detectives were waiting for them in the lobby. Some time
between 8.30 and 9 p.m. Elisabeth Fritzl was apprehended.

* * *

The interrogation rooms of Amstetten police station are a simply furnished, pared-down affair. In a town of just 20,000 predominantly law-abiding citizens, they can stand empty for days and, when occupied, are used for the questioning of petty criminals. It was now left to the two detectives to interrogate their two suspects by themselves, a job that, with their very limited experience in the field of abduction and incest, they might well have not managed to do. To all intents and purposes this was a missing-person case and, with the return of Elisabeth, it seemed to have been more or less solved.

The details of the police interviews are sketchy. Having first made the decision to separate father and daughter, the detectives set about interrogating Elisabeth. The interview began between 9 and 10 p.m. and for three hours she repeated the oft-rehearsed story of the cult and how, overwhelmed by the demands of motherhood, she had left it to her parents to raise her children. But either because her explanations proved to be too vague to satisfy, or because the inspectors felt that Elisabeth could not have acted as she did without the help of other 'cult members', they began to needle her. Did she realize that she was facing some very serious charges? That her daughter could now die as a result of her negligence; and that, if this should occur, Elisabeth could be charged with manslaughter? When this didn't seem to move the suspect, the detectives now decided to risk bluffing her into a confession. Picking up the phone in front of her, he now started dialling a number. 'Well, if you're not going to tell us anything,' he said, 'we're going to be forced to call social services. Because your children are going to be put into care.'

It was to be a decisive point in the case. At around midnight Elisabeth, fearing that her children would be taken away from her, requested her right to make a phone call. She wasn't sure what to do. She was terrified of saying anything, but the threat of losing her children seemed to have made her reconsider. A few minutes later, she finally agreed to talk, but only on the condition her children would stay with her and that they would never have to face her father again. Ulrike, speaking to her sister for the first time in twenty-four years, could not believe what she was hearing. After their brief conversation Elisabeth then turned to the detectives and agreed to talk. She finally told her interrogators the full facts of the case, and spoke for almost an hour uninterrupted.

At 11.15 p.m. Josef Fritzl, who was waiting in a neighbouring room, was arrested. A junior officer was dispatched to notify Dr Reiter and Chief Inspector Leopold Etz was telephoned at his house in the Austrian countryside with news of the breakthrough. Etz would only arrive at Amstetten police station midway through Josef Fritzl's interrogation. He would later describe Fritzl as 'a polite and eloquent man, definitely an educated one. He was calm and composed and admitted to what had happened but tried to present the events very subjectively, in a positive light.' It would be Etz who arrived at 40 Ybbsstrasse that evening and discovered Stefan and Felix in two of the bedrooms. Having been wrapped in blankets, they were taken to the Mauer hospital, in a white Volkswagen police van.

The next day, a Sunday, the police finally got their DNA sample.

CHAPTER ELEVEN

'MOSTLY RESOLVED'

The first reporters began to arrive early on Sunday morning. By midday Ybbsstrasse – never the prettiest road in Amstetten – was beginning to resemble a trailer park, except that the vans camped around number 40 had huge satellite dishes on their roofs and, standing in front of them, were reporters barking urgent communications into their cameras. One after another the journalists first rang the doorbell, then, satisfied that the house was indeed empty of any Fritzls, went around to the back in what would prove to be frustrated attempts to get into the garden, which was now under the close guard of a team of uniformed police. Behind them, coming in and out of the garage, were more men, white-suited forensic experts, carrying objects unidentifiable to the media out of the house and into yet more vans.

Although the Amstetten authorities had prepared themselves, in a meeting convened at dawn that included, among others, the head of the police and of the social services, for something of a 'media storm', they hadn't quite envisaged the enduring fascination the breaking news story would hold for the public, not just in Austria, but all over the world. Nor had they anticipated the lengths to which the press, especially some of the foreign publications, would be prepared to go to get their story. Already one of the German tabloids had chartered a helicopter which now intermittently buzzed overhead, as the photographer inside it craned his neck to get aerial shots of the house. His colleagues on the ground, meanwhile, were busy persuading neighbours of the Fritzls whose houses afforded a view onto number 40 to allow them access to their homes. Others raced to be the first to track down and sign up for exclusive newspaper interviews the Fritzls' current and former lodgers, many of whom would now claim that they had seen Josef Fritzl carrying bags of groceries into the cellar and had heard 'strange sounds' or 'knocking' emanating from the lower regions of the house but which their landlord had explained away as 'the noise of the downstairs boiler'.

Already the tabloid hacks had raided the Fritzls' letterbox, extracting from it, among other items of interest – phone bills, credit-card statements – a postcard which Rosemarie had sent home on the last day of her holiday in Italy, a few hours before her husband had summoned her back to Amstetten. Proof, the *Daily Mail* later claimed when the postcard found its way onto the pages of the UK newspaper, that 'the dungeon fiend Fritzl' had sneaked his daughter out of the cellar without his wife's knowledge: 'Dear Family,' Rosemarie had written, 'I am having a lovely holiday. Although I'm on my feet all the time, I fall into bed dead tired. I'll soon be home. Your Mama.'

Today there was no trace of Rosemarie at the house. She had long since fled and was being looked after – along with Elisabeth and her children – in the Amstetten-Mauer Clinic, a psychiatric and medical facility, not five miles away, also now fenced off from the public by a large police presence. And, frustrated by the absence of any photographs of the suspected perpetrator, his wife, or any of his alleged victims, some reporters were, as a substitute, filing to their newsrooms their thoughts on 'what Elisabeth would look like now': the resulting photofit would show a woman of indeterminate age with no teeth and a shock of white hair. By early the press were almost unanimously referring in their reports to number 40 as 'the House of Horrors', the same phrase that had, in previous years, been employed with the same hysterical zeal to describe almost every other house in which there had been uncovered a grizzly secret of some kind: 4 Cromwell Street, Gloucester, the home of Fred and Rose West; 924 North 25th Street, Milwaukee, the apartment of the serial killer Jeffrey Dahmer; and 23 Cranley Gardens, north London, where Dennis Nilsen had dismembered his victims. Most people agreed, however, that the prolonged cruelty of Josef Fritzl's incarceration of his daughter in the cellar somehow seemed to over-shadow even these horrific crimes.

At the centre of this tumult the old house stood 'tomb-like', according to a newspaper, its curtains drawn. The only thing that could be seen from outside were children's drawings displayed in the upper windows: innocent pictures of stars and rainbows which would be eerily echoed the next day, when police released the first photographs of the cellar, by the cartoons that Kerstin, Stefan, and Felix had drawn on the walls of their squalid underground 'bathroom'.

If the police were initially tight-lipped about the case, this was because, to some extent, they still weren't exactly sure what they were dealing with. It was only when, some time towards noon the same day Josef Fritzl had given investigators the electronic passwords to the two remote-control doors at the entrance to the 'dungeon', that the terrible reality of the case began to make itself felt.

The forensic team entered the cellar on Sunday afternoon, together with Chief Inspector Leopold Etz, and other investigating officers. Already, at the entrance to the courtyard, they had seized a plastic bag containing four mismatching socks, two pairs of tights, a flannel, two women's smocks, a T-shirt, and a sanitary napkin. Once down in Fritzl's workshop they would discover a rifle and six packs of ammunition, an expired passport in the name of Josef Fritzl, and two remote-control devices with their delivery receipt and instructions for use.

Then it was through the small hole, 83 centimetres high, in the workshop wall that Josef Fritzl had obscured behind a shelf unit. On the floor was a plastic drinking straw. The space was so narrow that the investigating team were forced to crawl in, one after another, to the first heavy door, through to the padded corridor, where a pair of children's trousers were lying crumpled on the floor next to a cardboard box. Next they came to the second door and, using the code and instructions that Fritzl had finally reluctantly given them, they now entered the 'dungeon' proper, where the walls were wet with condensation and the air so foul that it was immediately decided that they would work in three-hour shifts.

The following items were confiscated from the scene:

From a shelf in the 'laundry room': fifteen annotated diaries, a yellow folder covered in stickers, and another folder containing letters and newspaper clippings.

From the floor next to the washing machine: a packet of ten Rohypnol tablets, the 'date rape drug'.

From the children's bedroom: four blankets, a journal in which had been written various birthdays, a receipt from the Metro supermarket in Linz that inspectors had found pinned to the wall, and two video tapes, one of which was marked 'Private!'.

It was the contents of the yellow folder and the innocuous-looking cardboard box that were to prove the most disturbing. Among the items in the folder was a Christmas card bearing Felix's handprints and footprints; a photograph of an unknown child; a handwritten description of Felix's symptoms during an illness in September 1997; a debit card bearing the name Elisabeth Fritzl; a copy of the note sent from Amstetten Council confirming the fostering of Alexander Fritzl; a letter, dating from 1995 and sent to the Fritzls by the producer working at the German television station RTL, which outlined a planned documentary about Elisabeth's disappearance; a clear-plastic folder containing one of Elisabeth's own end-of-term reports, dating from the eighties;

two newspaper articles: one that outlined the risks of heart operations on young children; a handwritten note discussing the notions of 'Good and Evil'; an astrological profile of Elisabeth Fritzl; and a red paper heart in the centre of which was a passport picture of Alexander Fritzl.

The contents of the cardboard box were even more sinister. It held two pairs of handcuffs, a leather whip, two colour photographs of an unknown girl sitting naked in one of the bathtubs of the apartment block, five black and white photographs of naked women on a beach, a Billyboy condom, a sex toy, a typewritten story entitled 'The St Bernard' which described a young widow's sexual relations with a dog, a ten-page sado-masochistic questionnaire headed 'Imaginary Conversation Between a Whore and a Slave', and the photocopied contents of a diary of a young woman who, it would later be established, had been a tenant at Ybbsstrasse between 1989 and 1991: Josef Fritzl must have secretly entered her flat to obtain the diary, photocopied it, then replaced it without anyone having noticed, she later told detectives.

The things that the police found in the cellar on the morning of Sunday, 27 April were to make up just a small sample of the horrific and abundantly incriminating physical evidence that would, over the coming weeks, be discovered at number 40. But when Josef Fritzl was later questioned about the meaning of these objects by the State Prosecutor, Christiane Burkheiser, he would continue to appear calm, even jaunty, for a man at the centre of such serious allegations, taking every opportunity to wave away or minimize their significance. Asked about the purpose of the handcuffs, he would say, 'I bought the handcuffs some time ago in a flea market. I can no longer remember why exactly. I never used handcuffs with Elisabeth.' He added that he and his daughter had never played what he referred to as 'tying-up games'. Josef Fritzl was a man who would always gloss over even his cruellest behaviour. Far from rendering him more convincing, however, the transparency of the lies he would, over the coming weeks, repeatedly tell the police and State Prosecutor about the evidence collected in Ybbsstrasse made it difficult for his interlocutors to understand why anybody had ever believed a word he'd said.

Towards late afternoon on Sunday, Colonel Franz Polzer, the head of Lower Austria's Criminal Police, Etz's superior by several ranks, held an impromptu press conference outside the house in Ybbsstrasse. A youthful-looking man in his fifties, Polzer had made a name for himself when he led an investigation into the so-called 'wine scandal' of 1985 in which hundreds of gallons of Austrian wine were found to have been adulterated with antifreeze. Now he outlined the bare facts of the Fritzl case for the benefit of the huddle of expectant journalists: 'Josef F' had kept his daughter in his cellar for twenty-four years and she had borne him several children; 'Herr F' had ruled his family with 'an iron fist'; and the cellar had been 'off-limits' for the rest of the family.

The next day, Monday, Fritzl made a partial confession, and Polzer was able to speak about the accused in more explicit terms. Another press conference was held, this time in a room at Amstetten's Hotel Excel. Flanking Polzer on a long, rectangular table were Gerhard Sedlacek, the St Pölten prosecutor's office spokesman, Hans-Heinz Lenze, the district governor, Dr Franz Prucher, the Security Director of Lower Austria Franz Prucher and Dr Albert Reiter. A photograph of Josef Fritzl was now distributed to the press for the first time: it showed an exhausted-looking elderly man with a greying moustache, dressed entirely in black: a rumpled shirt tucked into trousers from the bottom of which peeped workman's boots with both laces undone. His thin lips were clamped tightly shut – no more than a line on his strikingly unsymmetrical face – and his hair was dishevelled into something that almost resembled a bouffant. Although he stood in an almost apologetic posture, with his hands clasped in front of him, his gaze was unflinching, pragmatic, and, it was said, 'cold'. Also disseminated for the first time were two photographs of the dungeon.

Colonel Polzer declared the case 'mostly resolved'. He bridled, however, when a reporter asked him why the police seemed to be excluding the possibility that Rosemarie Fritzl knew about the cellar. 'Would any wife accept such a thing if she knew about it?' Polzer had replied. To the further dismay of some of those present, he also described the accused as 'extraordinarily sexually potent'. Fritzl, Polzer continued, was 'extremely fit and in excellent physical condition', a man who was known to be a 'tyrant' at home, appeared to be unrepentant about what he had done, and had something of a 'stately air' about him. A British journalist asked Polzer: 'Do the Austrian authorities accept any responsibility for having allowed this crime to go unnoticed for almost a quarter of a century?' But, as was to happen every time the same question was brought up in the future, the authorities either misunderstood or deliberately misinterpreted it. 'The result of the investigation so far shows that the accused must be seen as a person who acted alone,' Polzer replied. In broken English the district governor, Lenze, later attempted to respond to accusations that the social services had failed in their duty to protect Elisabeth: 'I don't know which fault I have made. I'm really shocked.' In an almost farcical scene that he would subsequently describe to reporters, Lenze had visited Josef Fritzl in Amstetten jail, unaware that this was 'the same Fritzl' whom he had greeted on the street over the years and who had called him in his office on the Friday to thank him for his efforts to find Elisabeth. 'Mr Fritzl, it's you! I'm appalled,' Lenze had cried out, to which Fritzl had replied, 'I'm very, very sorry for my family but it cannot be undone.' 'Well, you should have thought about that earlier,' Lenze had shot back.

Another day passed. The press had unearthed a newspaper report of Josef Fritzl's conviction for rape, dating from 1967, of which the police had made no mention and the veracity of which they now refused to confirm or deny. The same day Fritzl's DNA test came in. It showed that he was indeed the father of Kerstin, Stefan, Lisa, Monika, Alexander, and Felix. Polzer gave another statement in which he reiterated the police's belief that Rosemarie

Fritzl could not have been involved in her husband's crime, this despite the fact that she had only been interviewed once, and only informally. 'It defies logical thought to believe that a woman who had seven children with her husband would make it possible for him to have another relationship and father a further seven children with her daughter,' he said. Because Rosemarie was in a fragile condition, the police decided against questioning her in any more depth. By the summer of 2008 Rosemarie Fritzl had still not been questioned again. And records available don't suggest she ever was.

On the evening of Tuesday, 29 April the people of Amstetten held a candlelit vigil for the victims of the cellar. Although Kerstin's condition remained precarious, the 'two families' now being looked after in the Amstetten-Mauer Clinic were said by doctors to be bonding 'remarkably quickly'. It was also announced that the children had received an aquarium and some of their favourite stuffed toys from the cellar.

There remained the matter of appointing for Elisabeth and her children a legal representative. This was a decision that lay in the hands of Erwin Pröll, the Governor of Lower Austria, whose name would be mentioned, some months later, in an article in the German magazine *Spiegel*, which revealed that Fritzl had hoped that the Governor would help him fast-track Alexander's Austrian citizenship because the family wanted to go on a holiday abroad. It's not clear whether Pröll ever intervened on the matter. But he now made the controversial decision to appoint Dr Christoph Herbst, a corporate lawyer with no significant experience in criminal law, as

Elisabeth Fritzl's legal representative. Herbst and Pröll were said to be close and Pröll had personally asked his friend to take on the case. When Herbst declined, Pröll had insisted. But the only public condemnation in Austria of Herbst's appointment came from a women's group who argued that, as a corporate lawyer, Herbst was not a suitable candidate to represent the alleged victim of abduction, multiple rape, and incest. To appease public opinion, a second lawyer, Eva Platz, was assigned to the case. Platz had spent her career deeply involved in cases of abuse of women. Herbst, however, remained in charge of the day-to-day running of the case and he would show no inclination to investigate the role of the authorities in his client's ordeal. Despite demands, mainly from the foreign press, for a public enquiry, there was no backing from Herbst, although there might have been very good grounds to argue that, for example, the social services department had exhibited naivety or even negligence in its handling of the Fritzls' many fosterings. Austria's oft-quoted stringent privacy laws and its press's reluctance to do any digging of their own ensured the case files on the fosterings and adoption would appear only much later, published not in Austria, but Germany. The revelations caused not a ripple of outrage in Austria.

Meanwhile Josef Fritzl had chosen as his lawyer a certain Rudolf Mayer, a veteran presence at Austria's most obscure criminal cases, on the walls of whose ramshackle Vienna office he liked to plaster press cuttings of his past career triumphs: his successful defence of a neo-Nazi charged with sending letter-bombs, as well as a man suspected of having been involved in the murder of a Georgian mafia boss. But many of Mayer's most prominent clients, such as the 'Black Widow', Elfriede Blauensteiner, a serial poisoner, had received lengthy sentences.

Mayer wasted no time in announcing to the media that his client had heard about him 'from TV' and that Fritzl was a 'shattered and emotionally broken man' who had spent the past twenty-four years torn apart by feelings of guilt. Mayer advised Fritzl to say nothing when, on 29 April, he was questioned by a remand judge, Claudia Matzka-Löschenberger. Fritzl did as his lawyer told him, opening his mouth only to admit that, forty years earlier, he had been convicted for rape. Later that day he would be transferred to a cell in the Lower Austrian capital, St Pölten, where the police confiscated from his person one key, a notepad, a mobile phone, and a wallet containing three bank cards, a Metro supermarket 'loyalty card' and a family-discount rail pass.

The picture that investigators were beginning to assemble of Josef Fritzl showed him to be very far from the guilt-ridden personality described by Mayer. Having searched the cellars of all Fritzl's other properties and found nothing of significance, they had experienced better luck in the upper storeys of the house in Ybbsstrasse, notably in Fritzl's office on the first floor of the extension. There they had seized a second gun – a 22-millimetre Bernardelli pistol – a firearms licence, a small bag containing five bullets, a voice recorder – possibly the one used years before to play a recorded message down the telephone to Rosemarie – two desktop computers, Josef Fritzl's current passport, a contract for an 'erection enhancing product' from an online company specializing in sex aids; and another cardboard box, this one green.

The police were used to watching detective series in which stalkers, murderers, or sex offenders would keep files of press cuttings on their victims, but it was very rare to come across a criminal doing so in real life. Nevertheless, it was about to become clear that, true to his meticulous nature, Josef Fritzl had, for years, kept in his possession such a file. Or rather two files: the green cardboard box discovered in his office, and a red plastic bag the police would later retrieve from the cellar. Together these formed a sort of chronicle of the whole of Elisabeth's life: tens of documents spanning the unhappy years of her childhood, her thwarted attempts to escape her father in her teens, and the twenty-four years that she had been forced to spend in the cellar as an adult. It was a conclusive and very disturbing collection of evidence against Fritzl. The police knew they had a cast-iron case.

In the green box was a neatly-ordered red ring-binder. It contained:

- four copies of the letter that Josef had 'discovered on the body of Kerstin'.
- two copies of the letter which Elisabeth Fritzl had written earlier that year about her intention of returning home and which Josef had posted at the end of January from Kematen.
- the original letter that Elisabeth had written when Monika was 'abandoned on the Fritzl's doorstep' in 1994.

- a list of Lisa's school things
- a memo from Amstetten Council regarding the deeds of a property
- documents pertaining to the fostering of Alexander, Monika, and Lisa by the Fritzls
- the original letter written by Elisabeth that had been found, alongside Lisa, when she was 'discovered on the doorstep' in a cardboard box.
- the graphological analysis of Elisabeth's handwriting that had proved, in the year that Monika was 'found', that the letters had been written by her.

Also in the box were:

- a newspaper article of 24 April 2008 which reported an interview given by Natascha Kampusch (a Viennese teenager who, in 2006, was released after being held captive in a cellar for eight years) about Elisabeth's experience
- handwritten documentation on the 'appearance' of Kerstin
- several copies of letters that Elisabeth had written to her family, including one that Josef had sent from the town of Grieskirchen on 13 April 2007
- a three-page receipt from the electronics store Conrad
- a photograph of an unknown woman
- the blueprints of a house in the Hölzöster 'holiday village' which he had looked at with Hubert Schrankmaier a few weeks before his arrest
- a hand-drawn plan of a door
- Two pornographic video tapes; an erotic video entitled *Through the Keyhole: Girls Who Work Their Way Up*; and a fourth tape, a recording of a celebrity news programme, *Klass*.

The red plastic bag, meanwhile, was full of letters. Twenty-one letters: letters that had been written to Elisabeth in her teens but which she had never received. Letters that she had intended to post but which had never arrived at their destinations. All of them dated from the early eighties. Most were love letters: simple, innocent scribblings written on paper that was now yellowing with age. Letters that Josef had intercepted, confiscated, hoarded, pored over countless times and used as justifications for raping and locking up his daughter, the basis of his groundless assertion that as a teenager Elisabeth had been 'consorting with people of questionable repute'. Mixed in with the love letters was the note that Harald had sent to Elisabeth when they were still teenagers – ten sides long – in which he had attempted to comfort his sister about the situation at home and advised her how to deal with her father. She had never read it. But Josef had and promptly filed it away. Another letter, from Elisabeth's sister Gabriele, tells of how Gabby has just started a new job in Linz. The letter was sent on 6 August 1984, just over a month before Elisabeth was due to move there, just over two weeks before Elisabeth disappeared. She had never received Gabby's letter either. In among the letters was a notepad of squared paper in which police found a description of Elisabeth in English and a rough diagram of her classroom at her secondary school, complete with a seating plan and the names of the other students. Who sat where, what their names were: there was hardly anything that Elisabeth had been able to keep secret from her father. He had always been watching her.

* * *

Josef Fritzl was cross-examined for the first time by State Prosecutor Christiane Burkheiser on 7 May 2008. Earlier in the week the Austrian magazine *News* had carried on its front page an exclusive interview with Rudolf Mayer in which Fritzl's lawyer had conveyed his client's disappointment with 'the completely one-sided' press coverage of the case. 'I'm no monster,' Fritzl had said. Through Mayer, Fritzl had released a statement in which he was quoted as saying: 'Kerstin would not be alive today if it wasn't for me. I made sure that she got to a hospital. I could have killed all of them, and nothing would have ever been known about it. No one would have ever found about it.' This self-justifying, occasionally self-pitying tone would characterize all the other 'exclusives' that Mayer would leak to *News* over the coming months. Fritzl was in prison on remand but he still had a voice, and this voice would dominate and manipulate public opinion from behind the scenes. All the way up to the trial. 'I am not the monster the media depicts me as,' Mayer quotes him as saying. 'When I was in the bunker I bought flowers for my daughter and books and toys for the children, and I watched adventure videos with them while Elisabeth was cooking our favourite dish. And then we all sat around the table and ate together.' It was speculated that Mayer was going for an insanity plea.

Josef Fritzl's account of what had happened in the cellar over the past 24 years would contain a striking element of fantasy to it. In his first cross-examination by Christiane Burkheiser, Josef Fritzl said that he had originally taken

Elisabeth down to the cellar for 'a talk'. It had never been his intention to lock her up. It was a Wednesday morning. At 7 a.m. he had gone into her room and found her lying fully clothed on her bed. She had looked as if she had 'fallen over' and he had immediately suspected that she had been 'sniffing paint stripper'. He had therefore decided that this would be a good time for a conversation: about her 'drug problem', her absenteeism from work, her inability to hold down any job whatsoever. Ever since she'd got back from Vienna she'd been difficult: answering back, locking herself in her room, telling him she didn't 'give a stuff' about what he thought. So he'd decided to sit her down and have a proper conversation. And the best place to do this seemed to be the cellar.

He claimed she had accompanied him down to the office in the cellar, where he had then shown her a letter he'd found, addressed to Elisabeth from a married man. It was a love letter, and she was obviously having an 'affair', and he hadn't liked the sound of it at all. Not under his roof. Of course, Elisabeth had reacted typically defensively and had threatened to leave the family home. He could tell that she was high on paint stripper, 'because she was giving strange answers'. And he had become angry, threatened to lock her up. The next thing he knew, he had 'grabbed her by the hand and pushed her … into the corridor and locked her in the store room … I picked her up, because she was under the influence of the paint stripper. But then she went on her own. I took her by her upper arm but didn't grab her. She could have defended herself at any time and she could have run away because I had accidentally activated the remote control and left the garage door open.' She 'never protested or said anything'.

He claimed that he had never used handcuffs, as his daughter had claimed, nor had he tied a chain around her waist and attached it to a metal post that he had screwed to the floor for this purpose. That was nonsense. 'I've no idea why she would come up with that. For a start, I'd have had to have had a padlock with me and, secondly, she wouldn't have been able to get out anyway.' Possibly he'd threatened to chain her up but he had never actually done so. And he certainly had never starved her. Indeed, he brought 'a plastic bottle of lemonade, bread, and cheese' to the cellar the very same day. Elisabeth's memory of the day of her incarceration was bound to be hazy considering her 'solvent abuse'. And there had never been a gun on the shelf in the workshop: this was another false memory of hers. 'I only have one pistol but it was never in the downstairs office, I kept it in my bedroom.' Elisabeth must have got confused. 'I'd bought a gun to protect myself.'

He claimed that he had never in any way prepared the cellar in advance for Elisabeth's arrival. Everything had been completely spontaneous. Despite what she had since claimed to the police, he hadn't yet installed the toilet or brought down the bed, or the video recorder, or the television. As the day had worn on he had taken down cushions forming a mattress to make her more comfortable. A few days later he had attempted to broach the issue of the 'drug problem' and told her that he might let her go if she was prepared to find a job in Amstetten. He suggested that they could pretend that she had run away again but that she hadn't wanted to listen or discuss it or even engage with anything he said. She had only wanted to move to Linz and live there independently of her family, which would have been fine had it not been for the drugs. But there had to be some boundaries. 'A framework'. He had had no choice but to intervene. He had been a fairly relaxed father until she had disappeared to Vienna. 'It was only when Elisabeth came back from running away that my wife and I decided to monitor her, so that she had no more contact with people from the drug scene.'

He claimed that he had never in his life sexually abused his daughter as a child. He'd been travelling so much with his job that he would never have had the time. And she was always around other children so there would never have been an opportunity anyway. She must have got him mixed up with 'uncle Franz' or made it up. Or perhaps confused him with one of her other adventures. He claimed he had caught her once with one of the builders. She'd certainly never had occasion to fend him off with her hands and feet, as she had said in her statement to the police. It was 'a total mystery' why she'd told the police that he had made death threats against her when she was only 12 or 13 because she had refused to comply with his sexual advances.

No hint of remorse or self-doubt, not the remotest trace of regret: needing to cast everything in a positive light, to shift the blame, to make things less bad than they were and, if the truth was too terrible, as was often the case, to tell elaborate lies. Outrageous lies that he would elaborate on further during his second cross-examination by Christiane Burkheiser, two months later, on 10 July. Between them the two hearings would form the bulk of his defence.

According to Josef Fritzl, he had never actually raped his daughter. There had been no sexual contact between them until 'after four or five months [in the cellar]. I was trying to comfort her because I realized she wasn't happy being locked up. She was crying and was very unhappy and pale.' He had tried to work something out: a solution that would suit both of them. He had 'personally' been afraid of the legal consequences of 'what had happened'. And his thoughts had also turned to Rosemarie and his other children, 'who might have had problems with the situation. It would have brought scandal on the family.'

According to Josef, Elisabeth had, with time, become quieter and more pliant, once she realized that 'I wanted to lock her up for longer'. One day she had intimated to him that 'she wanted to live her life differently in the future'. And he had taken her in his arms 'and stroked her ... It was a father–daughter relationship.' At the same time, 'I now realized for the first time that my daughter was a desirable woman. She didn't fight against it ... She never said that she didn't want it ... If she'd said no, I would have accepted it.' The whole thing had taken place without any violence at all, no force, no threats. He had treated her 'tenderly'. And although he conceded that Elisabeth wasn't happy about things as they were, 'she gave in to her fate. What I mean by that is that Elisabeth probably put up with my sexual demands so that she'd have a chance of one day escaping.' He never heard her scream for help or bang on the walls, his explanation being, 'The ceilings are relatively thick.' When Burkheiser asked him the purpose of the many sex toys that the police had found in the cellar, Josef replied that he had bought them only for Elisabeth's own personal use, 'when I wasn't there. But she told me she didn't use them either.'

According to Josef, it wasn't true that he had hardly talked to her for the first few years when she was down in the cellar. With Elisabeth 'things tend to go in one ear and out the other'. That was his explanation. But things had improved: he had become 'open' to the idea of children with Elisabeth, an inevitable part of their future together because Elisabeth, he said, had never wanted to use condoms anyway: 'she would have felt less'.

It is a measure of Josef Fritzl's total inability to either find fault with himself or empathize with his victims that he also told the State Prosecutor that what he was having with Elisabeth in the cellar was a 'relationship'. 'After Kerstin was born there developed between us a marriage-like relationship which became more intense with the birth of the other children.' Elisabeth's allegation that he hit the children was untrue: 'No, I wasn't violent towards either Elisabeth or the children. It wasn't at all necessary because Elisabeth would always acquiesce and would never pit herself against me. If Elisabeth says that I hit her in the first years, then the only explanation is that [she did so] because it will make her charges sound more believable. If it says in Elisabeth's testimony that I hit Stefan, then that's not true. I only playfully tussled and boxed with him and Kerstin. With Stefan I did it for practice because he was so slow. As a "reaction test" I would wave my hand in his face and tell him he should be faster.' On second thoughts, maybe he had smacked Stefan on the bottom once or twice. But nothing more. He denied that he had ever threatened to chain up any of his children from the iron rings that he'd bored into the walls. The iron rings were there to hang a swing. When asked whether he had ever had thoughts about having sexual relations with Kerstin he replied, 'No, I never had that thought. One woman is enough for me.'

When the Prosecutor asked Josef about what had happened to his son, Michael, Josef said that he had been born dead: 'One day I came into the dungeon and Kerstin and Stefan told me that Elisabeth had had a baby. When I went into the bedroom, Elisabeth was lying in bed and crying. She told me that she had given birth to twins and that one of them was dead … I never saw Michael alive … [he was] already dead when I came into the dungeon and wrapped in a piece of cloth. I'd never seen Elisabeth so downcast.' He had then spent 'at least three hours' talking to his daughter about 'what we should do with the dead child and we came to the joint conclusion that we should burn the corpse. I told Elisabeth that I would come and take the child the next day.' He had then turned up the boiler and put Michael's corpse inside it. 'The body burned without a trace.' He had scattered his ashes in the garden.

It defied logic, Josef Fritzl claimed, that he would have let Michael die: 'I had already rescued two children by that point. If I'm asked why Elisabeth would say such a thing I'd have to admit that she wants to dump me in it as much as possible. I can only speak about the facts.'

Among other lies and embellishments that Josef made about Elisabeth's twenty-four-year incarceration, he told Burkheiser that several times he had taken Elisabeth upstairs through the house to look at the view from the roof terrace. They had gone onto the terrace when Rose-marie was out and he showed her the garden and the swimming pool. He hadn't taken her into the garden, though, because that would have been too risky. One of the tenants might have seen her. He couldn't remember how many time he had allowed her upstairs in this way but the main point was that she had never attempted to flee.

The Prosecutor wanted to know about the time-delay switch that he had told police he had installed on both the remote-control doors to the 'dungeon'. Josef replied that he had made sure, right from the start, to ensure that his 'second family' would never be trapped underground. Should anything have ever happened to him, the doors would have opened eventually of their own accord. Because the time-delay switch made a 'buzzing noise' every time he opened one of the doors, he knew it was fully operational.

Almost sentimentally he would try to explain why he had kept his daughter in the cellar for so many years: 'I had always wanted someone there for me with whom I could exchange intimacies, a person who wouldn't be influenced by other people. What was also important for me was that Elisabeth was at my disposal for all my needs all the time. I mean, for conversations as much as sexual contact.' When asked whether it was true that he had repeatedly told Elisabeth that it was all 'her fault', he conceded that 'it is true. I always told her that she had been locked up because she had taken drugs. I told her that she wouldn't have been locked up had she not taken any drugs and that it was her fault.'

Many of his lies would be read back to Elisabeth when she underwent her own cross-examination by a judge. Almost every word of his account of what had happened in the cellar was false. To spare her the ordeal of facing her father in court, her testimony would be pre-recorded and played back to the jury on a screen. But investigators had enough evidence for themselves to suggest that almost everything her father said would be a lie.

The intense media interest and speculation that the case had generated all over the world continued to intensify over the summer and autumn of 2008. Despite the virtual blackout on news regarding Elisabeth Fritzl and her children, their father would be in and out of the papers almost constantly for the remainder of the year, thanks in part to a steady stream of revelations regarding his past published in the pages of *News* and, later, other Austrian publications. The only other member of the family speaking to the media was Fritzl's sister-in-law, Christine Renner, who would regularly share her thoughts on his treatment of her sister. Journalists working for some of the British tabloids, frustrated by the lack of photographs of Elisabeth or the 'cellar children', were meanwhile in hot pursuit of any illicitly taken picture and were disappointed when a man who had been convalescing in the

Amstetten-Mauer clinic after a failed suicide attempt had been banned from selling the hundreds of photographs he had secretly made of the family in hospital. All sorts of alleged former victims of Josef Fritzl now suddenly recollected their somewhat vague and unsubstantiated maltreatment at the hands of 'evil Fritzl'. A woman who was marketing herself as 'Fritzl's lover' was offering, for 8,900 euros, the story of how she had been 'sexually attacked' by him in Thailand shortly before Elisabeth disappeared. Starved of enough new material about the Fritzl family to satisfy their editors, some journalists now began to fabricate stories. Fritzl 'was a regular at a brothel where he ordered terrified prostitutes to pretend to be dead' and he had 'humiliated his dowdy wife Rosemarie at a swingers' club by forcing her to watch him romp with another woman'. These reports began to circle the globe, indistinguishable to the public from the equally bizarre, often unimaginable, but true facts of the case.

Sections of the conservative Austrian press were appalled. 'The greed for news and pictures needs to end once and for all,' thundered one, while another columnist's thought on the matter was: 'The press pack is hungry for prey, it needs feeding.'

When the story had broken, many foreign journalists had assumed that it would provoke a period of deep self-analysis in Austria. Just two years earlier, in a strikingly similar case, 18-year-old Natascha Kampusch had finally escaped her own cellar in the outskirts of Vienna, where Wolfgang Priklopil, a technician, had imprisoned ever since abducting her when she was 10. Over in Linz in Upper Austria a respected female lawyer had, in the same year, been found to have kept her three daughters in the house in squalor and total darkness for almost seven years. A journalist at the BBC had, in April 2008, predicted that the clear similarities in the Fritzl case were bound to provoke 'a period of soul searching' in Austria. 'Austrians can't understand how this could have happened and they want answers,' he had asserted. But the truth was quite the opposite. In April the first remark the then Austrian Chancellor had made about the case was: 'We won't allow the whole country to be held hostage by one man. Austria is not the perpetrator. This is an unfathomable criminal case but also an isolated case.' He had immediately set about boosting the country's tourism industry. Except for an admission by the Minister of Justice, Maria Berger, that the Austrian authorities might have been guilty of 'a certain gullibility' in their dealings with Josef Fritzl, there was little appetite within government or the press for any thorough investigation of the case.

And now, as tabloids from other countries, particularly Britain, became increasingly intrusive and aggressive in their 'investigations' – at one point they would publish Elisabeth Fritzl's new home address as well as paparazzi pictures of her and her daughter – many Austrian papers retaliated by attacking the foreign press in print. What they failed to notice, or perhaps merely to point out, was that the main generator of stories surrounding the case was *News* and the tabloid newspaper *Österreich* which now printed extracts from the confidential psychiatric assessment that had been prepared on Josef Fritzl for his trial. Although printing such prejudicial material before the trial was highly controversial, the magazine was neither fined nor prevented from doing it again with various other documents that should not have at this stage found their way into the public domain.

The psychiatric report on Fritzl was not the only expert witness that the State Prosecutor would be relying on to win her case when it came to trial, as it was now decided, on 16 March 2009. Behind closed doors the results of a neonatologist's assessment of Michael Fritzl's death had concluded that his father could have saved his life and was therefore liable to a charge of either manslaughter or murder. Another specially commissioned report, from an electrical engineer, had also found that the time-delay switch that Josef Fritzl had made so much of during his cross-examination had never existed. But the conclusions of a third report into how well soundproofed the cellar had been were less satisfactory. And they would never be heard in court or discussed in public. Peter Kopecky, an engineer and expert witness had tested the cellar's acoustics from the ground floor, where the lodgers lived, and delivered his findings to the prosecution on a single sheet of paper in June. His findings were very clear.

Fist on rafters – very audible
Broom handle on ceiling wall – very audible
TV – just about audible
Radio – just about audible
CD player – just about audible
Chairs moving – very audible
Cries for help – audible

Fists on the wall of the corridor – very audible
Knocking and cries for help – very audible
Knocks on the ceiling – very audible
Knocking on entrance – very audible

Although it had been assumed by almost everyone who had come across the story of Josef Fritzl that his underground 'dungeon' must have been soundproofed, the results of Kopecky's research revealed a very different picture. It revealed a scenario almost too terrible to contemplate: one in which Elisabeth Fritzl had not only spent her entire adult life thus far living in the most wretched circumstances conceivable, but that, all the while, the people who lived above her had been able to hear, but had never been able to identify as anything out of the ordinary, the noises that occasionally came from the cellar. The noises that the tenants 'thought' they had heard coming from the cellar beneath them had been real: the thumping, the moaning, the strange clanking noises emanating from deep underground. But nobody had thought to investigate.

And this is where the myth that Josef Fritzl was in the possession of a 'brilliant criminal mind', espoused by both the police and the press, began to fall apart. In fact his life was a catalogue of violent, strange, and suspicious behaviour, much of which had attracted the attention of the police: he was known by a number of his friends to be a physically abusive husband and father; he had a conviction for violent rape, had twice more been arrested for sexual offences, and had been suspected of arson. He had a daughter who had issues with her weight, a history of self-harming, and ran away from home when she was 16. When she disappeared again two years later she had joined a cult that was happy enough for her to give up three of her children, who had appeared on the doorstep of their 'grandparents' under increasingly murky circumstances. He had spent long periods of time in his cellar: his tenants and neighbours had seen him going down there late at night with a torch and bags of groceries. Over the years he and his wife had received dozens of letters from their daughter but no attempt had been made to find her, and this despite the fact that many of these letters bore the postmarks of towns not five miles from Amstetten and where her father was known to spend much of his time.

Everything pointed to the fact that Josef Fritzl was not in fact the brilliant operator that the authorities and the media had painted him. He was clumsy. He was a bad liar. He had left clues all over the place. But he had an unshakeable belief in his own fantasies, and he had been lucky. Even when everything had pointed to the fact that something very wrong was happening in the house in Ybbsstrasse, nobody had looked. But when, a few days before Josef Fritzl was tried, in the second week of March 2009, Austria's Minister of Justice was interviewed again, she was adamant: 'You can never really prevent these kinds of cases.'

CHAPTER TWELVE

THE TRIAL

Two months after Elisabeth, her children, and Rose-marie had first become inpatients at the Amstetten-Mauer Clinic, Rosemarie was asked to leave. The eight of them had been sharing a ward in the neuro-psychiatric unit ever since the night of Josef Fritzl's arrest, on 29 April 2008, the same night that Chief Inspector Leopold Etz had arrived at number 40 and picked up Rosemarie and the children in a police van. And although the doctors at the clinic who were treating them had initially been 'astonished' at how well the 'two families' were getting along, relations between Rosemarie and Elisabeth had become strained.

The cause of the tensions between mother and daughter seems to have centred on 12-year-old Alexander. Having grown up upstairs in number 40, he was used to referring to his grandmother as 'Mama' and when he continued to do so in front of Elisabeth, she had asked her mother to go. By the summer of 2008, while prosecutors were cross-examining her husband in a prison cell in St Pölten, Rosemarie was living under an assumed name in the outskirts of Linz. She lived alone in a council flat, surviving on a monthly pension of 700 euros, of which 400 went towards her rent. Because number 40 was still being treated as a crime scene the police had allowed her to salvage from the house only a washing machine and dryer.

It had been her sister, Christine Renner, who had drawn the public's attention to Rosemarie's impoverished new circumstances. She had done so, in the Austrian tabloid *Österreich*. And it would be Christine who, in various other interviews with journalists, would subsequently come to her sister's defence when the decision by the police not to interview her began to raise questions in the minds of the public. They wondered whether or not Polzer and his team hadn't been a little naive to assume that the wife of a man who had kept his daughter enslaved in the cellar beneath the family home for twenty-four years hadn't known a thing about it. Rosemarie herself kept her own counsel on the matter. She wouldn't speak to the press at all despite the seven-figure sums she was being offered for her story.

But Christine was a constant source of information about the 'shadow children', as she called them, and she never held back either, from airing her views on Rosemarie's plight. The Fritzl family was 'at war', she had told the journalist from *Österreich*, 'torn apart'. Rosemarie had practically been 'thrown out' of the Amstetten-Mauer Clinic, said Christine: 'Let's put it this way. It was made clear to [Rosemarie] that she had to leave. But she didn't know where to go. Rosemarie has no contact with the children from downstairs. But Alexander is attached to her. Elisabeth didn't want him to see Rosi any more. But the boy didn't like it. He said, "If you don't let me see her then I'll stop going to school." ... She was very angry that Alex was saying "Mama" to Rosi rather than "Granny".' Another sister of Rosemarie's had been the one to fix her up with the flat in Linz: for whatever reason the 68-year-old mother had decided not to stay in the home of any of her six other children.

Rosemarie was 'in a really bad way', Christine let it be known. 'She's lonely. She hardly has any money. And she keeps having to hear about how she must have known something about the long years in the cellar.' Christine took particular issue with the fact that Rosie was being 'treated as the wife of a perpetrator rather than a victim. ... I'm 1,000 per cent sure she didn't know. You can't compare Rosie's marriage to other relationships. Josef was a tyrant and treated her like a dog. The two of them had been living separately for years ... and the cellar was completely taboo because he apparently kept important work documents down there.'

Worse that this, Rosemarie was on the brink of destitution, according to her sister. 'Just changing her name cost 350 euros.' And when certain sections of the press had expressed surprise, even disbelief, when it emerged that Rosemarie was not seeking to divorce her husband, it had been Christine who had explained that her sister's restricted financial circumstances had left her no choice. By the time of his arrest Josef Fritzl had accumulated a property empire of sorts: he owned six houses, all of them profitable properties. But now his wife of over fifty years hardly had the means to support herself. She was a pensioner. The only paid work she had ever done in her life had been the stint in the bakery in the very early days of her marriage. But as long as she remained married to Josef, Christine said, 'She'll get 60 per cent of his income if he kills himself in prison or something happens to him.'

And, if Christine was to believed, Elisabeth was exhibiting very few signs of concern about her mother's rapid descent into penury. There had been an unpleasant episode after social services had accidentally transferred to Rosemarie's account 3,000 euros in benefits that should have been paid to Elisabeth: it was intended to go towards the care of Kerstin, Stefan, and Felix. Although Rosemarie had immediately telephoned Elisabeth to tell her about the mistake, she had – according to Christine – secretly hoped that Elisabeth might turn a blind eye and let her mother keep the money. Instead Rosemarie had received a terse letter from her daughter's lawyer, Christoph Herbst, requesting the return of the sum to Elisabeth within a period not exceeding fourteen days. It was Christine's opinion that Elisabeth could have easily afforded to behave a little more generously towards her mother given that she had recently received a lump sum of 60,000 euros in income support, not to mention a 25,000-euro donation that Natascha Kampusch had recently made towards the welfare of Elisabeth and her children. It wasn't fair. 'Rosemarie is as much of a victim of this as the rest of the family.'

Other details from other sources were now beginning to surface about how the Fritzls were coming to terms with their new lives. Kerstin had finally awoken from her coma in May. But it was only on 9 June that doctors had felt confident enough in her 'miraculous recovery' to share details of this momentous turn of events with the public. Dr Reiter had held a press conference in which he had described 'the intensely dramatic moment' when, at 9 a.m. on 15 May, Kerstin had opened her eyes for the first time since she had been 'discovered on the doorstep' of number 40 by her father and rushed by ambulance to Amstetten Hospital, where doctors had put her into an artificial coma. For ten days she had remained dangerously ill, but by the second week of May she had started to show sufficient 'positive improvements' for doctors to have been able to start reducing the levels of anaesthetic they were giving her.

Dr Reiter was there when Kerstin opened her eyes: it had been the first time she had ever seen daylight. 'She slowly started showing signs of emotional reaction,' Reiter said. 'We smiled at her and she smiled back. Later I said "Hi" to her and she replied with a "Hello". Even immediately after she woke up and still had the tracheotomy tube in to help her breathe, she was listening to Robbie Williams until 3 a.m. I then had to put my foot down and ask her to turn down the music and get some rest.' Within a few days Kerstin was even managing to go for short walks around the Intensive Care unit. She could read, write, and communicate easily. Among the many hundred of things she wanted to do once she was discharged was to go on a boat trip and attend a Robbie Williams concert. Kerstin's first words had reportedly been: 'Hello, a new life.'

While Kerstin made a slow but encouraging recovery in Amstetten Hospital, down the road in the Amstetten-

Mauer Clinic her brothers and sisters were being kept under the close supervision of Dr Berthold Kepplinger, the head of the hospital's neuro-psychiatric department. It had been Dr Kepplinger's controversial decision to treat Elisabeth, all her children, and Rosemarie in the same ward. And it was he who assembled the multi-disciplinary team of fourteen doctors, therapists, and nurses who would now work towards rehabilitating Elisabeth and her children, mentally as well as physically. It was a gigantic task, unprecedented in medical history, and significantly complicated by the presence of the hundreds of journalists who had now become a permanent, and occasionally yobbish, presence in and around the hospital's grounds. Britain's *Sun* newspaper alone had sent more than a dozen reporters to cover the story, as had Germany's *Bild*. And in their desperation to catch the first glimpse of what many of them now referred to in their reports as 'the incest family', some journalists had resorted to force: a scuffle with a reporter on one of the balconies of the clinic had sent a security guard flying over the edge of the balustrade. And when, not long after, a Belgian television crew almost succeeded in storming the reception area, the already considerable police presence at the clinic was beefed up with a team of guards from a private security firm as well as over thirty members of Amstetten's fire brigade. But this tightening of security around the hospital only served to encourage the less scrupulous members of the press, especially the paparazzi – the first photographs of the 'cellar children' were now estimated to be worth in the region of 300,000 euros – to resort to increasingly imaginative tactics to get their picture. Hospital staff had already apprehended two photographers who had, separately, attempted to enter the building in disguise – one had been dressed as a policeman, the other as a cleaner. A third photographer was later discovered by a police sniffer dog in a hole he had dug overnight in the grounds of the hospital. He had camouflaged himself beneath a birdwatcher's hide.

And it was partly because of the overwhelming media interest that Dr Kepplinger and his team kept the details of the family's treatment at the Amstetten-Mauer Clinic deliberately vague. In a series of press statements it was revealed that Elisabeth and her children were receiving physiotherapy as well as psychiatric care and were said by Kepplinger to be 'in surprisingly good shape, considering the circumstances'. The aim of the treatment, he said, was 'to give all members of the family support for the future and a good start in their new lives. Because of this it is important that they should be introduced to reality very gently and gradually.' Elisabeth, Stefan, and Felix were making 'good progress where light sensitivity and diffi-culties adapting to open space are concerned', and that, as time had progressed relatively slowly in the cellar, it was important not to rush the family's rehabilitation. Kepplinger reported that Felix and Stefan had shown a remarkable proficiency in computer gaming; that the children spent much of their days in a loose routine of taking lessons from a private tutor, reading children's books and playing table football; and that much of their psychological treatment took the form of games and play. Their ward had also been furnished with many stuffed toys and an aquarium. The only thing they lacked was the freedom to go outside: not only because, for the first few days, the sunlight would have been too harsh on their eyes and skin, but because of the risk of being photographed or even mobbed by journalists. Kepplinger's concluding thoughts in one of his press releases read: 'Owing to an earlier incident between a member of staff and a photographer, I would like to again make an urgent appeal to these people: this madness must end!'

The first drops of rain, the first car journey, the first time the children had ever seen sunlight: these were instances at which other members of the various teams that had been involved in the Fritzl children's hospitalization and rehabilitation had been present and which some of them could not, however, hold themselves back from sharing with the public. Leopold Etz had been particularly touched by 5-year-old Felix's reaction when he had driven Felix and his brother Stefan to hospital on the night his father was arrested: 'We had to drive very slowly because every bit of light made the children flinch,' he told a journalist from *Bild*. 'They'd never in their lives seen street lights, traffic lights, cars, or even other people. It was as if we were suddenly on the moon.' When Felix had seen the moon for the first time that night, he had turned to Etz and asked, 'Is that where God lives?' It was a touching detail that was quickly seized upon by the international press and embellished. The popular press in particular had shown a gift for reporting as fact its own imaginings about how a lifetime's imprisonment in a cellar might have affected the family's appearance and behaviour. In the continued absence of any photographs of Elisabeth, Stefan, Kerstin, or Felix, *Bild* held that the 'incest children' spoke in their own 'animal tongue ... a mixture of growling and cooing'. Meanwhile a journalist on Britain's *Daily Telegraph* reported that Elisabeth Fritzl 'has aged so much she looks more like a sister to her mother Rosemarie'. Felix, the *Sun* conjectured, 'sometimes crawls on all fours ... the little lad walks like a monkey'. Elisabeth, it was also wrongly speculated in the same newspaper, 'never told [her children] the truth about their terrible plight. Instead she invented a fantasy world for them with wondrous stories of princes and princesses.' The British media had been especially thrilled when Josef Fritzl's lawyer, Rudolf Mayer, had released to the public his client's alleged assertion that his 'need to control' stemmed from his country's Nazi past. And the tabloids had devoted many of their pages to articles with headlines such as 'Hitler Made Me Do It' and 'Dungeon Dad and the Nazis'.

In many ways the prosecution had a straightforward case on its hands. The very existence of the cellar, let alone the physical evidence that had been collected by the forensics team in number 40, would incriminate Josef Fritzl beyond reasonable doubt. And Rudolf Mayer seemed to be out of his depth. After there were leaks to the press of sections of Fritzl's confidential assessment by a forensic psychiatrist in which the accused described in self-pitying detail the events of his deprived childhood and his difficult relationship with his mother, Mayer seemed to have changed tack. Fritzl the victim of difficult circumstances suddenly became Fritzl the caring father who, according to his lawyer, would have simply killed his family had he really been 'a monster'. Mayer's public musings on the matter were often glib, off-hand, not to say inappropriate. In one interview he claimed that Fritzl's 'perversion is to be found in the fact that he dealt with [his children] so affectionately. It reminds me of the film *Misery*: a woman smashes up a man's feet so he can't run away. It's just that if someone is in love, there is always the danger that you'll be disappointed. Fritzl thinks that without power you can't hold anyone. It actually shows his inner powerlessness.' They were inconsistent arguments unlikely to convince a jury.

But the prosecution still faced the problem of how to ensure a life sentence was passed on Josef Fritzl: anything else would have been unacceptable, not only to Elisabeth Fritzl and her family, but in the eyes of the public and the media. By Austrian law the crime of incest was punishable by a mere one-year sentence. And although a person charged with rape can expect to serve a fifteen-year term if found guilty in an Austrian court, the prosecution was hamstrung by the fact that Austrian law does not allow for cumulative sentencing. Even if he was convicted of multiple rapes, Fritzl would serve only the longest of the sentences handed down to him. As it stood, of all the offences that the prosecution hoped to pin on Fritzl, the one that carried the longest sentence was slavery, an offence that derived from the country's penal code of the nineteenth century, when slavery in its traditional form still existed in Europe and some of its colonies. But even a slavery conviction carried a maximum sentence of only twenty years and would not serve to reflect the severity of

Fritzl's crimes. And it was more than likely, considering his vitality and determination, that he would outlive even this term. The notion that Fritzl would not end up spending the rest of his days behind bars was not a possibility that the prosecution, or the Austrian state, was prepared to consider.

In the end it was the results of the neonatologist's report commissioned by the State Prosecutor, Christiane Burkheiser that had finally given the prosecution the ammunition it needed. Professor Gerhard Trittenwein, the neonatologist, concluded in his assessment of the case that Fritzl could indeed be held responsible for the death of his infant son, Michael, whose rasping breath and stiff little limbs his father had, 13 years earlier, chosen to ignore. Had Michael been taken to hospital in those first three crucial days of his life, he would have survived, said Trittenwein. Which meant that – Christiane Burkheiser could now argue in court – Fritzl was guilty of murder: a crime which carried a life sentence. On Monday, 12 November 2007 the prosecution team completed its charges: Josef Fritzl was to be tried for the crimes of murder, slavery, rape, deprivation of liberty, coercion, and incest. The trial, which was to be held in St Pölten, was scheduled for December but was moved to January because of the Christmas break, and then moved again to March because – a court spokesperson said – of a timetable clash with the holiday plans of one of the judges who would be involved in the court case. Because of the sensitivity of the case and Elisabeth Fritzl's express wish never to see her father again, it was to be a closed hearing. Elisabeth would testify in a pre-recorded set of interviews which would be shown *in camera* to a jury of four men and four women, and only the opening statements of the prosecution and the defence, as well as the results of the four forensic reports commissioned by Burkheiser, would be held in public. The seriousness of the charges called for a jury trial: Josef Fritzl's future lay in the hands of four male and four female jurors.

When it came, the trial opened amid an almost carniva-lesque atmosphere. While in Amstetten the residents of Ybbsstrasse had prepared for yet another media invasion by erecting barbed wire on their windows to prevent photographers from climbing on to them to get better shots of number 40, many of the citizens of St Pölten saw the impending influx of hundreds of journalists from around the world as an opportunity to promote their hitherto little-known town. By the time members of the press started arriving on Friday, 14 March, the trees and hedges around the courthouse in St Pölten's main square had been trimmed and a large marquee resembling a beer tent had been erected for the convenience of those who required internet access, refreshments, or informa-tion about the town's rich culinary and cultural life: inside, for the benefit of journalists, were stacked hundreds of brochures listing its best restaurants and most fashionable nightclubs. Across the street from the courthouse a restaurant had been banned by the council from serving what it had taken to referring on its menu as 'the Fritzl Schnitzl', but a nearby patisserie had managed to display in its window something called a

Gittertorte, or 'prison bar cake'. Around the corner, Isabella Suppanz, the artistic director of St Poelthen's main theatre, claimed that it was 'sheer coincidence' that an adaptation of Franz Nabel's novel *The Living Grave*, which concerns the fate of a boy who is locked in the cellar of his home, was being staged.

Along with the journalists came various fringe groups. They were there in front of the courthouse by 7 a.m. on the first day of the trial: a far-Right group and a group of artists lead by the Austrian actor Hubsi Kramar, who had achieved a modicum of fame abroad many years earlier when he had played an SS guard in the film *Schindler's List*. Earlier that year Kramer had written and performed a play, *Pension Fritzl*, which, owing to its controversial subject matter, he had been forced to rename *Pension F*. Now he and several other actors stood in front of the courthouse smeared in blood in a street performance that he claimed aimed to condemn Austria's patriarchal mentality. Beside them, the country's most media-friendly psychiatrist, Reinhard Haller, was on stand-by to answer any questions journalists might have on the nature of Fritzl's psychological make-up: he was well acquainted with the case from media reports.

Already the mob of over 700 reporters, camera operators, sound technicians, reporters, photographers, protesters, and hangers-on knew a certain amount about what was going to happen over the next few days. It had been decided some months before that only 98 representatives of the press, the majority of them German-speaking, would be allowed into the courtroom. They also knew that the trial would be compressed into no more than a week, a fact that even some Austrian commentators took to be evidence of a cover-up: 'This is a secret trial,' the respected columnist Ricardo Payerl wrote in the *Kurier*, 'and talking of protecting the victims is really just an excuse for keeping everyone in the dark.' Because investigations into the case had been carried out with such secrecy, what nobody could know was that neither Rosemarie Fritzl nor any of Elisabeth Fritzl's siblings, except for her brother Harald, would be testifying against the defendant. Instead the prosecution had gathered the majority of its evidence from the Fritzls' tenants, friends of both the accused and the chief witness, DNA tests, reconstructions of the offences, and the material that had been collected by the police from the cellar.

At 9.30 a.m. on Monday, 16 March 2009, the first day of the trial, a black Volkswagen police car drew up outside the entrance to St Pölten's courthouse. Flanked by six guards and obscuring his face with a blue ring-binder, Josef Fritzl was led from his seat in the back of the car and up the stairs of the courthouse into room 119, a baroque, oak-panelled chamber, where he took his place on a bench to the right of where Judge Humer and other adjudicating judges, all dressed in black robes, were already seated behind a large oak table. In front of the judges on the table stood a large crucifix and two cream-coloured candles in brass candlesticks. To their left, and in Josef Fritzl's direct line of vision, sat the eight members of the jury. And at the back of the gallery were assembled the 98 members of the international press whose attempts to describe the expression on Josef Fritzl's face were only made possible with the departure of the photographers, at which point Fritzl had finally set down the blue ring-binder. A year in prison had clearly taken its toll: his face, drained of its ruddy complexion, looked almost grey. He wore a mismatched grey suit, dark shirt, and striped tie.

Despite the grave nature of many aspects of the case, the subject that had most preoccupied the Austrian authorities and media in the run-up to the trial had been the reputation of their country abroad. And it was the first subject that Judge Humer now chose to address in her opening statement to the court.

She reminded the packed gallery and the jury that Fritzl 'acted alone' and that 'we are not prosecuting a town or a whole country'. It then fell to Christiane Burkheiser to put her case to the court. In a well-rehearsed, some said 'operatic', speech, delivered in what the *Guardian* would later describe as 'schoolmarmish' tones, the State Prosecutor first directed her attention to the jury. 'Have you ever thought about what actually happened down there in the cellar dungeon,? ' she began. "I have. And I honestly have to say, it's unimaginable. What should we make of it? A Chinese metaphor holds that everything has three sides: the side that you see, the side that I see, and the side that we all see. And so it is with the truth. We are obliged to see many variations of the truth. And that's why, ladies and gentlemen of the jury, you should forget everything that you've heard and seen in the media.'

Gesturing towards the dock, Burkheiser now asked members of the jury to 'take a close look' at the accused.

Josef, who would continue to stare in a detached way at the space in front of him throughout most of the Prosecutor's speech, refused to meet the eyes of the jury. 'He has a neat appearance, a polite air about him, a co-operative manner,' she observed. 'A nice old man from next door. Do you want to know what puzzled me? That he had given no indication of regret nor of remorse.'

Burkheiser then reviewed in chronological detail the more harrowing facts of the case, beginning from the moment on 29 August 1984 when 'Josef lured his daughter [into the cellar] with the excuse that she had to help him carry a door'. She continued: 'On the second day he bound her with a chain with a padlock. This was also the day he raped his daughter for the first time. What did the cellar look like? The area you're sitting in,' she said, gesturing towards the box where the jury were sitting, 'measures 11 square metres. In these 11 square metres Elisabeth Fritzl lived in the first year of her imprisonment. It had no warm water, no shower, and no heating, but the worst thing about it was that there was no daylight.' Burkheiser had been in the dungeon herself twice. 'A morbid atmosphere reigns down there,' she said. 'It begins when you have to crawl on your hands and knees through the 83-centimetre entrance door. It is damp, it is mouldy, there is mildew everywhere.'

Having described in some detail the rapes, the pregnancies, and the conditions to which Josef Fritzl had subjected his children, Burkheiser turned to the reasons why he had done it: 'Josef Fritzl treated his daughter like his property. He made her completely dependent on him. He treated her as if she was a toy ... Do you know what the worst thing is?' she asked the jury in a whisper. 'The not knowing. The uncertainty can break a person.'

What was later referred to as the 'most dramatic' moment of Burkheiser's speech came when she pulled back the lid of a brown cardboard box and invited the members of the jury to take a sniff at what was inside. This was an opportunity, Burkeiser said, for the jury to experience for themselves the foul stink of the cellar where the accused had kept his daughter and their children for twenty-four years. Nobody in the public gallery could see what was inside the box – children's toys, books, clothing perhaps – but the crumpled expressions on the jurors' faces left little to the imagination. 'Smell, smell those twenty-four years,' she said.

Throughout her thirty-minute speech Josef Fritzl would glance up only once, when, addressing him directly about the events surrounding his son Michael's death, she said: 'Herr Fritzl, to your own flesh and blood, you really went too far that time.' But it was difficult for anyone to read from his expression whether this constituted a mark of his regret or indifference.

Next it was Rudolf Mayer's turn to address the court. He did so from his place to the right of where Fritzl was sitting in the dock, separated by about 20 feet from the jurors, never moving from his position except to stand up. Even more astonishing to everyone in the court that day was Mayer's decision to begin his opening statement by reading out the contents of a personal email: one of many death threats that Mayer had received from members of the public ever since he had taken on Fritzl's case. Mayer had even gone so far as to make copies of the email, which were later distributed among members of the press. 'I can no longer understand why I have been threatened in this way,' Mayer began in a calm, slightly nasal voice before warning the court that Austria risked becoming 'like Italy', where lawyers representing notorious criminals had been known to come to grief. A few minutes into his rambling and at times seemingly irrelevant speech, Mayer eventually came round to the matter in hand. 'What is so spectacular about this case?' he asked. 'The unusual thing about it is that here is somebody who has a second family.'

According to Mayer, Fritzl was not a 'monster'. A 'monster', he said, would have left his family to perish in the cellar. But Fritzl, said his lawyer, not only saved the life of his desperately ill daughter by 'bringing her to hospital', but he had done so in the knowledge that he was thereby sabotaging his own reputation. 'Do you know what the monster would have done? The monster would have killed them all. The end, finished.' 'A monster', said Mayer, would have ended his days in Amstetten with his reputation intact. Then, speaking as if he were Fritzl, he continued: 'I go on with my life as a good citizen of Amstetten. It says on my grave stone that I was a model citizen of the town who never did anything bad to anyone.'

Mayer, who had on behalf of his client only 'partially' accepted the charges of rape (Fritzl had denied murder and slavery but was pleading guilty to incest and deprivation of liberty, and partly guilty to coercion), then closed his brief and unconvincing speech by implying that Elisabeth Fritzl had not technically been raped throughout the entirety of her imprisonment because: 'of course, a sense of resignation will have set in. There would have been an attempt [by Elisabeth Fritzl] after a while to go along with him.'

Before the hearing went into private session, Judge Humer put two questions to Fritzl himself. She asked him to explain his purpose in building the cellar, to which Fritzl had replied: 'It was partly conceived of as an office, and partly as a place to store spare parts.' When Humer further asked Fritzl to describe his relationship with his late mother, the defendant said that it had been 'normal': 'We didn't have any difficulties with each other.'

That evening Mathias Stadler, the mayor of St Pölten, invited the journalists covering the trial to a lavish reception in the handsome old baroque town hall in the main square. Addressing the group of journalists who had come to the town for the sole purpose of reporting on the sentencing of one of the world's most reviled criminals, Herr Stadler talked of how he hoped the occasion might be used to promote St Pölten as a tourist destination and cultural centre in the future.

On his desk lay a book, *A Hundred Proposals for a Better Austria*. And on the walls of his office hung oil portraits of past mayors of the town, going back to the eighteenth century. Conspicuously absent from this parade of dignitaries, the journalists noticed, were Franz Hörhann and Emmo Langer, both well-known Nazis.

On the second day of the trial it snowed and most of what happened in court proceeded behind closed doors: Elisabeth's pre-recorded testimony and the cross-examination of her father by the prosecution. Josef Fritzl had appeared that morning from the black Volkswagen in much the same manner as on the previous day, again obscuring his face with the blue ring-binder. On closer inspection, some journalists later noted in their articles, the ring-binder was found to have been 'made by the office supply manufacturer Esselte'. It contained, a photographer with a zoom lens had managed to ascertain, what appeared to be a breakdown of the costs – 63,672 euros – for Monika Fritzl's hospital treatment. Outside the courtroom Reinhard Haller was still debriefing journalists, and now explained the deep meaning of the ring-binder: 'The disguise is deeply symbolic,' he said. 'The folder is like a wall, similar to those involved in the crime.' It was further noted in some newspapers the following day that Fritzl had breakfasted on 350 grams of bread, the daily ration, a miniature portion of jam and butter, lunched on soya loaves, and dined on frankfurters with mustard.

The first sign that something momentous was about to happen in court the next day, Wednesday, was the fact that Fritzl was no longer hiding his face behind the ring-binder. Rumours had already circulated that Elisabeth Fritzl had paid a surprise visit to the court the previous day, and her father's new demeanour seemed to confirm it. At 9 a.m. the session began. Humer briefly surmised the planned itinerary, then turned to Fritzl:

'Do you have anything to say to me?', asked Humer, to which, to the great astonishment of even the judge, Josef Fritzl replied: 'I recognize that I am guilty. I regret it.'

'Why are you saying this now?'

'Because of the video tape testimony of my daughter.'

The judge then asked the defendant why he had done nothing to save his son Michael: 'Did you not realize he was gravely ill?' In a barely audible whisper, Fritzl replied: 'I just overlooked it. I should have done something. I thought the little one was going to survive. It was only yesterday that I realized for the first time how cruel I was to Elisabeth. I had never realized it before.'

A few minutes of silence passed while the implications of what the defendant had just confessed to sank in.

Two more assessments were due to be heard that day, but owing to the astonishing turnaround in the day's events, it was decided that only the report of the forensic psychiatrist Dr Adelheid Kastner would be heard. Dr Kastner had prepared a 130-page psychiatric assessment of Fritzl after having interviewed him six times. Because most of of what she now said had already been published in the pages of *News* and other publications, Kastner's assertion that his mother's failure to love him as a child was central to his understanding did not provoke the consternation that it otherwise might have done among those present, although some journalists noticed that Fritzl began 'twisting his fingers' as Kastner described his relationship with his mother. The rest of the time he listened passively with his hands crossed on his lap, alternatively sitting with his legs crossed or jiggling his left leg and wiping his nose with a tissue. Kastner told the court that it was her belief that his sexual behaviour and his need to dominate women was his way of 'compensating for the defencelessness and humiliation he felt as a child': Fritzl had described himself to her a 'volcano' who felt 'torn' and had come to the conclusion that he possessed a 'mean streak' and a 'flood of destructive lava that was barely controllable'. It was Kastner's judgement that Fritzl could be deemed 'responsible for his actions' but that he suffered from 'a severe combined personality disorder'. She believed that the defendant had a 'thin grasp of the gravity of his crime', having expressed to Kastner the belief that he would spend his final days with his wife and pleading for a short prison sentence so that he could continue to run his property business and so provide for his family. It would take the jury four hours – including the time it took them to eat lunch – to make their decision. The next day, Thursday, 19 March, Josef Fritzl was declared guilty on all counts. For a week he stayed in his cell in St Pölten, after which he was transferred to a Mittersteig Prison in Vienna to be psychiatrically assessed at 2.30 p.m. From there he would eventually be moved to a psychiatric unit in Garsten Prison, one of the best-equipped prisons in Austria, to undergo counselling and therapy, and where he would have, it was emphasized in the press, access to 'a startling array of leisure facilities': tennis courts and football fields, a generous library, a large gym superior to those of many hotels, and an art studio. Garsten had recently been described by one of its wardens as 'full board without your wife'. Surrounded by woodland, Garsten sits in the foothills of the Alps; in a car it is possible to get to Ybbsstrasse in approximately twenty minutes.

CHAPTER THIRTEEN

A KIND OF CLOSURE

With the sentencing of Josef Fritzl to life imprison-ment, the Austrian authorities finally put behind them one of the most unpleasant episodes in the country's recent history. The verdict had satisfied not only the Fritzl family, but also the general public and the media, who had expressed both relief at the outcome of the trial and satis-faction with the fact that, so late in his life, Josef Fritzl had come to understand and regret the gravity of his actions.

His lawyer, Rudolf Mayer, would later claim that Fritzl had been reduced to tears when, behind closed doors, he had watched his daughter's testimony on the second day of the trial. Her unexpected appearance in court that day had convinced her father that he should change his plea. 'Fritzl cried as she watched the tape and then he turned around and saw his daughter sitting in the public gallery,' Mayer said. 'At that point it was all over. It was obviously the effect the court hoped to induce. He was shattered and broken inside.' And, for several weeks in the build-up to the trial, there had been concerns for Josef Fritzl's well-being. His cell-mate in St Pölten Prison had been asked to keep a close eye on him and to sound the alarm if he noticed any marked changes in his behaviour. Fritzl was then put under suicide watch: a psychiatrist and expert in the suicidal behaviour of especially sex offenders, Patrick Frottier, had been engaged to observe him closely throughout the trial. According to his lawyer, Fritzl had been particularly upset when, on video tape, his daughter said that she had 'screamed many times during all those years but nobody ever heard me'. Afterwards Fritzl had apparently turned to Mayer and said, 'What I saw there was truly devastating.' According to his lawyer, Fritzl had not pleaded guilty from the start, because 'that would have meant he didn't have any power'.

But although Fritzl's 'epiphany' was accepted as genuine by almost everyone who had attended the proceedings, there would be very little evidence in his behaviour before the trial to suggest that Fritzl had meant it at all. Even while in prison on remand, Fritzl had spent his time scanning the business pages of the newspapers and communicating regularly with business acquaintances. At the time of his arrest Fritzl owed several banks a total of around 3 million euros in loans. When he was subsequently declared insolvent, the state had engaged a lawyer to liquidate the properties and to pay off his creditors: in the process, the lawyer in question had taken the unusual step of offering to the media for a fee an interview with Fritzl in prison as well as a tour of the dungeon in Ybbsstrasse. The money would go towards Fritzl's family. Fritzl had also let it be known, through Mayer, that: 'I would like to be examined by as many profilers, psychologists, psychiatrists as possible, preferably the most renowned in the world.'

It was completely out of character for a man who had shown no compunction about subjecting his family to a lifetime of horrific abuse to find himself suddenly plunged into the depths of remorse. And it is well worth bearing in mind what Christiane Burkheiser had warned the jury in her address: 'As always, never believe a word he says.'

Fritzl's character reveals a meticulous, controlling, emotionally cut-off man who behaved throughout his entire life with a profound lack of concern for the well-being of others. He was callous, often sadistic, and, except for that one day in the courtroom in St Pölten, never exhibited the remotest trace of remorse. An extremely dangerous man whose sexual preoccupations were always somehow in the foreground, and served to maintain his fantasies of power and control: It was Elisabeth's firm conviction that he would not change, because for him it was a reason for living ... if he didn't have that, he didn't feel like a man, and he needed it for his self-confidence. Although her father had claimed in court that he had never realized that his infant son Michael was ill, Elisabeth had interpreted his behaviour differently. She believed that he hadn't saved Michael's life because he could not deal with such emotional things. Life in the cellar meant always having to be careful not to make him feel guilty, because otherwise he would take it out on them in some way. He had threatened Elisabeth often, especially in the early years of her imprisonment: She was afraid and often the children would be at a loss as to how to behave, because they were afraid of him all of the time. All he needed to do was raise his voice or look at them and they would know what was going on, and that was worse than being beaten, because there was a constant state of fear and a feeling that they were at his mercy.

It was Elisabeth's wish that neither she nor her family would ever see their father again, that he would spend the rest of his life behind bars where he stood no chance of terrorising his family which, his daughter felt, he would continue to do if given any opportunity.

Elisabeth and her children now live in a small town in the Austrian countryside. Shortly before the trial a British newspaper revealed the name of her new home town. And it was another British newspaper that published the first photograph of Elisabeth and her daughter Kerstin in their new life. The picture shows two inconspicuous-looking women – one blonde, the other brunette – walking down the street. They are dressed modestly in casual shirts and jeans and have nothing in common with how many sections of the press had imagined them to look like.

For a few days in the aftermath of the trial there were some rumours, denied by the court, that a deal had been struck whereby Josef Fritzl had been persuaded to plead guilty in return for a comfortable cell in which to serve out his sentence. Even before he was tried he had been granted the right to a computer – although no internet – and by the time of the verdict the components were being assembled for his use. Those who have visited Fritzl in prison describe a remarkably upbeat man who is now in the process of writing his memoirs. And a formal complaint made to the authorities by his adult children revealed that their father telephones them constantly, although there is talk of banning him from doing so. Except for his hoarse-voiced confession in court, there is nothing about him to indicate that he is plagued by guilt or in any way on the brink of despair.

The Austrian authorities, in their zeal to find a neat resolution for an episode that has caused the country such embarrassment, have shown little inclination to examine in any detail many aspects of the case. And although the law has been changed so that sex offences will now be kept on police files indefinitely, the Austrian government has never launched an investigation into the role, over the years, of either Amstetten's police force or its social services department. Instead, even the prosecution relied solely on the assurances of the district governor, Hans-Heinz Lenze, that the circumstances surrounding Elisabeth's disappearance had been looked into. Lenze, who had managed to review the conduct of Amstetten's social services throughout Elisabeth's twenty-four-year disappearance within days of the story breaking, had pronounced himself satisfied that the authorities shouldered no blame for the incident. Within 24 hours of the news of the crime breaking, Lenze declared that the authorities could 'not be accused of any wrongdoing'. Social workers had observed no 'noticeable problems' with the three children that the Fritzls either adopted or fostered in such quick succession in the nineties: the children were 'very good in school and had been "well accepted" by their schoolmates'. And although there had been some 'suspicious moments' when Elisabeth Fritzl had initially disappeared, nothing 'inappropriate' had arisen. The mother of the three foundlings was never searched for, according to a press release that had been prepared by the Lower Austrian police, because, in all three cases, the children were without birth certificates and therefore treated as 'parentless'. Although in each case a letter had been found from the biological mother, 'no court would have accepted [it] as proof of motherhood'. Elisabeth Fritzl was never looked for because 'officially the mother was unknown'. Social workers had paid many visits to the Fritzl household and been particularly moved by the way the children's 'grandmother' had looked after the children, who 'were educated to a good standard, were integrated in school, and learned musical instruments'.

The journalists have gone. And life in Amstetten has resumed its sedate, provincial pace. Its mayor is keen to rebuild its reputation and has let it be known in one of his newsletters that, as a 'mark of respect for the local population and this beautiful town', the *Fall Fritzl* (the Fritzl Case) will be referred to only as *Fall F*.

The journalists have gone. But the house is still there. For a while lawyers acting on behalf of Elisabeth Fritzl attempted to persuade the regional authorities to have the cellar destroyed. But all sorts of red tape and paperwork got in the way: laws and building restrictions, as well as the bailiff's instructions to sell the house to the highest bidder so that the banks could in some way recoup their loans. The house is still there, and so is the cellar. Demolishing the cellar, even as a symbolic gesture, is not something the citizens of Amstetten see it as their business to undertake.

ACKNOWLEDGEMENTS

We would like to thank the following for their invaluable knowledge and support during our writing of this book: Mary de Young, Professor Judith Herman, Karl and Elisabeth Dunkl, Friedrich Leimlehner, Jessica Hynes, Dr Adelheid Kastner, Richard Dawes, Claire Paterson, Nicoletta Avanzi, Jackie Craissati, Malcolm Rushton, James Lever, Professor Oliver Rathkolb.

Also of considerable help were the following books:

50 Jahre Stradt Amstetten, 1948
100 Jahre Amstetten: Werden, Wachsen, Wandel, 1998
Amstetten 1938–1945, Gerhard Zeilinger
The Austrian Mind, William M. Johnston
Character Styles, Stephen M. Johnson
Cool Memories, Jean Baudrillard
Discipline and Punish: The Birth of the Prison, Michel Foucault

The Elementary Structures of Kinship, Claude Lévi-
    Strauss
Father–Daughter Incest, Judith Herman
The Guilty Victims: Austria from the Holocaust to Haider,
    Hella Pick
Hiob, Josef Roth
Incest and the Medieval Imagination, Elizabeth Archibald
The Incest Theme in Literature and Legend, Otto Rank
Rethinking Architecture, Neil Leach
Sex and Character, Otto Weininger
*Trauma and Recovery: From Domestic Abuse to Political
    Terror*, Judith Herman